Language Arts 100
Teacher's Guide Part 2

CONTENTS

Revision Editor: Alan Christopherson, M.S.

Alpha Omega Publications®

804 N. 2nd Ave. E., Rock Rapids, IA 51246-1759

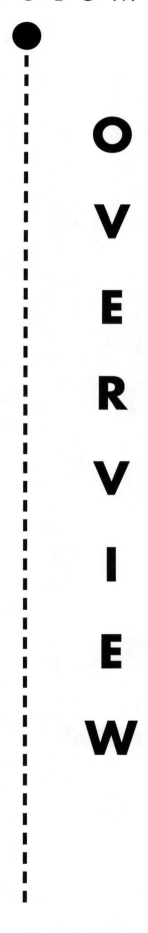

OVERVIEW

LANGUAGE ARTS

◼━━━━━━━━━━━━━━━━━◼

Curriculum Overview
Grades K–12

Language Arts Lessons

1-40	41-80	81-120	121-160
Alphabet-say the alphabet **Colors-**recognize colors **Directions-**left to right **Following directions-**given once **Grammar-**form simple sentences **Listening skills** **Personal recognition-**read and write first name -know age and address -recognize names of family members **Phonics-**short *a, e, i* vowels -initial: *b, t, m, r, s, n, d, p, l* -form and read simple words -form rhyming words **Shapes-**circle, square, triangle, and rectangle -recognize shapes in objects **Stories and Poems-**create simple stories and poems **Writing-**form circle and lines -*Aa, Bb, Dd, Ee, Ii, Ll, Mm, Nn, Pp, Rr, Ss, and Tt*	**Grammar-**sentences begin with capital, end with period **Patterns-**simple shape, color patterns **Personal recognition-**read and write first and last name **Phonics-**short *a, e, i, o, and u* vowels -initial: *k, c, ck, f, h, g, j, v, w, y, z, qu, and x* -read simple sentences **Position/direction concepts-**in/out, in front of/behind, up/down, on/off, open/closed, over/under **Sequencing-**alphabetical order -simple story **Shapes-**oval **Size concepts-**big/little, large/small **Writing-***Kk, Cc, Ff, Hh, Oo, Gg, Jj, Vv, Ww, Uu, Yy, Zz, Qq, and Xx*	**Phonics-**recognize the short vowel sounds -recognize all initial consonant sounds -recognize long *a, e, i, o,* and *u* sounds -silent *e* -initial consonant digraphs: *sh, ch,* both soft and hard *th* -final consonant sounds: *_b, _ck, _k, _l* **Word recognition-**color words, number words & shape words **Writing-**name -complete alphabet, capital and small letters -all color words -number words: *one, two, three, four, five, six* -shape words: *circle, square, triangle*	**Phonics-**recognize the long vowel sounds -initial consonant diagraphs: *wh*; review *ch, sh, th* -recognize all final consonant sounds: **Stories and poems-**create, tell, and recite stories and poems **Word recognition-**position/direction words: *up/down, high/low, in, inside, out, outside, top/bottom* -number words: *seven, eight, nine, ten* -shape words: *rectangle, oval, star* **Writing-**number words: *seven, eight, nine, ten* -shape words: *rectangle, oval, star* -position/direction words: *up/down, high/low, in, inside, out, outside, top/bottom*

5

	Grade 1	Grade 2	Grade 3
LIFEPAC 1	**FUN WITH PHONICS** • Short vowel sounds • Consonants • Main ideas • Rhyming words	**KNOW YOUR NOUNS** • Review vowels & consonants • Beginning, middle, ending sounds • Singular & plural nouns • Common & proper nouns	**OLD AND NEW SKILLS** • Vowels • Consonants • Sentence phrases • Capital letters • Reading skills
LIFEPAC 2	**FUN WITH PHONICS** • Kinds of sentences • Cardinal • Ordinal numbers • Suffixes • Plurals • Classifying	**ACTION VERBS** • Vowel digraphs • Action words – verbs • Following directions • The dictionary • ABC order	**BUILDING WORDS SENTENCES** • Vowels - long, short • Questions • ABC order • Capital letters
LIFEPAC 3	**FUN WITH PHONICS** • Consonant digraphs • Compounds • Syllables • Possessives • Contractions • Soft c and g	**SIMPLE SENTENCES** • r-controlled vowels • Consonant blends • Using capital letters • Subjects & verbs in sentences	**WORDS • GETTING TO THE ROOTS** • Root words • Dictionary guide words • Synonyms • Antonyms • Capital letters
LIFEPAC 4	**FUN WITH PHONICS** • Paragraphs • Silent letters • Sequencing • Subject-verb agreement	**TYPES OF SENTENCES** • Consonant digraphs • Statement, question, exclamation sentences • Using capital letters • The library	**WORDS • HOW TO USE THEM** • Noun • Verb • Adjective •Adverb • Irregular vowels • Composition
LIFEPAC 5	**FUN WITH PHONICS** • Long vowels • Homonyms • Poetry • Syllables • Possessives • Contractions • Plurals • Suffixes	**USING PUNCTUATION** • Diphthongs • Punctuation review • Using a comma • Rules for making words plural • Writing a biography • Contractions	**SENTENCE • START TO FINISH** • Main idea • Capital letters and punctuation • Paragraphs • Making words plural
LIFEPAC 6	**FUN WITH PHONICS** • R-controlled vowels • Writing stories • Pronouns • Following directions	**ADJECTIVES** • Rhyming words • Biblical poetry • Adjectives in sentences • Synonyms, antonyms • Thesaurus • Comparative, superlative adjectives	**ALL ABOUT BOOKS** • Main idea • Books • Stories • Poems • Critical thinking
LIFEPAC 7	**FUN WITH PHONICS** • Vowel digraphs • Letters - business, friendly, invitations • Syllables	**POSSESSIVE NOUNS** • Introduction to letter writing • Pronunciation key • Possessive nouns • Silent consonants • Homonyms	**READING AND WRITING** • For directions • Friendly letters • Pronouns • Fact • Fiction
LIFEPAC 8	**FUN WITH PHONICS** • Vowel digraphs • Subject-verb agreement • Compounds • Contractions • Possessives •Pronouns	**PRONOUNS** • Author's intent & use of titles • Predicting content • Suffixes • Character, setting, & plot • Analogies • Writing in cursive	**READING SKILLS** • For sequence • For detail • Verbs - being, compound • Drama
LIFEPAC 9	**FUN WITH PHONICS** • Vowel digraphs • Titles • Main ideas • Sentences • Paragraphs • Proper nouns	**VERB TYPES AND TENSES** • Review action verbs • Dividing words into syllables • State of being verbs • Past & present verb tenses	**MORE READING & WRITING** • For information • Thank you letters • Book reports • Reference books
LIFEPAC 10	**LOOKING BACK** • Letters and sounds • Contractions • Plurals • Possessives • Sentences • Stories	**LOOKING BACK** • Nouns & verbs • Word division • Consonant blends, digraphs • Prefixes, suffixes, root words • Possessives • Pronouns, adjectives	**LOOKING BACK** • Reading for comprehension • Sentence punctuation • Writing letters • Parts of Speech

Grade 4	Grade 5	Grade 6	
WRITTEN COMMUNICATION • Word derivations • Story sequence • Writing an outline • Writing a report	**STORY MESSAGES** • Main idea • Plot • Character • Setting • Dialogue • Diphthong • Digraph	**READING FOR A PURPOSE** • Critical thinking • Research data • Parables • Synonyms	LIFEPAC 1
SOUNDS TO WORDS • Hard and soft – c and g • Parts of dictionary • Accented syllables • Haiku Poetry	**MAIN IDEAS** • Poetry • Story • Synonyms • Compounds • Topic sentence • Adjectives • Nouns	**FORMING NEW WORDS** • Prefixes • Suffixes • Synonyms • Antonyms • Adjectives • Adverbs • Critical thinking	LIFEPAC 2
WORDS • HOW TO USE THEM • Prefixes • Suffixes • Homonyms • Antonyms • Poetry • Stories • Writing an outline	**WORDS TO STORIES** • Subject • Predicate • Adverbs • Idioms • Critical thinking • Writing a short story	**BETTER READING** • Story elements • Author's purpose • Information sources • Outline	LIFEPAC 3
MORE WORDS • HOW TO USE THEM • Parts of speech • Possession • Written directions • Verb tenses	**WRITTEN REPORT** • Outline • Four types of sentences • Metaphor • Simile • Writing the report	**SENTENCES** • Capitals • Punctuation • Four types of sentences • Author's purpose • Propaganda	LIFEPAC 4
WRITING FOR CLARITY • Figures of speech • Capital letters • Punctuation marks • Writing stories	**STORY ELEMENTS** • Legend • Implied meaning • Dialogue • Quotations • Word order • Usage • Story elements	**READING SKILLS** • Following directions • Literary forms • Phrases • Nouns • Verbs • Paragraph structure	LIFEPAC 5
FUN WITH FICTION • Book reports • Fiction • Nonfiction • Parables • Fables • Poetry	**POETRY** • Rhythm • Stanza • Symbolism • Personification • Irregular plurals	**POETRY** • Similes • Metaphors • Alliteration • Homonyms • Palindromes • Acronyms • Figures of speech	LIFEPAC 6
FACT AND FICTION • Nouns • Verbs • Contractions • Biography • Fables • Tall Tales	**WORD USAGE** • Nouns - common, plural, possessive • Fact • Opinion • Story • Main idea	**STORIES** • Story elements • Nouns • Pronouns • Vowel digraphs • Business letter	LIFEPAC 7
GRAMMAR AND WRITING • Adjectives to compare • Adverbs • Figurative language • Paragraphs	**ALL ABOUT VERBS** • Tense • Action • Participles • Of being • Regular • Irregular • Singular • Plural	**NEWSPAPERS** • Propaganda • News stories • Verbs – auxiliary, tenses • Adverbs	LIFEPAC 8
THE WRITTEN REPORT • Planning a report • Finding information • Outline • Writing a report	**READING FLUENCY** • Speed reading • Graphic aids • Study skills • Literary forms	**READING THE BIBLE** • Parables • Proverbs • Hebrew - poetry, prophecy • Bible history • Old Testament law	LIFEPAC 9
LOOKING BACK • Reading skills • Nouns • Adverbs • Written communication • Literary forms	**LOOKING BACK** • Literary forms • Parts of speech • Writing skills • Study skills	**LOOKING BACK** • Literary forms • Writing letters • Parts of speech • Punctuation	LIFEPAC 10

7

	Grade 7	Grade 8	Grade 9
LIFEPAC 1	**WORD USAGE** • Nouns – proper, common • Pronouns • Prefixes • Suffixes • Synonyms • Antonyms	**IMPROVE COMMUNICATION** • Roots • Inflections • Affixes • Interjections • Directions – oral, written • Non-verbal communication	**STRUCTURE OF LANGUAGE** • Nouns • Adjectives • Verbs • Prepositions • Adverbs • Conjunctions • Sentence parts

LIFEPAC 2	**MORE WORD USAGE**
	• Speech – stress, pitch
	• Verbs – tenses
	• Principle parts
	• Story telling
		ALL ABOUT ENGLISH
		• Origin of language
		• Classification–
		   nouns, pronouns, verbs,
		   adjectives, adverbs
			NATURE OF LANGUAGE
			• Origin of language
			• Use – oral and written
			• Dictionary
			• Writing a paper

LIFEPAC 3	**BIOGRAPHIES** • Biography as a form • Flashback technique • Deductive reasoning • Words – base, root	**PUNCTUATION AND WRITING** • Connecting and interrupting • The Essay • Thesis Statement	**PRACTICAL ENGLISH** • Dictionary use • Mnemonics • Writing a paper • Five minute speech
LIFEPAC 4	**LANGUAGE STRUCTURE** • Verbs – tenses • Principle parts • Sentence creativity • Speech – pitch, accent	**WORDS • HOW TO USE THEM** • Dictionary • Thesaurus • Accent • Diacritical mark • Standard • Nonstandard	**SHORT STORY FUNDAMENTALS** • Plot • Setting • Characterization • Conflict • Symbolism
LIFEPAC 5	**NATURE OF ENGLISH** • Formal • Informal • Redundant expressions • Verb tenses • Subject–verb agreement	**CORRECT LANGUAGE** • Using good form • Synonyms • Antonyms • Homonyms • Good speaking qualities	**LANGUAGE IN LITERATURE** • Collective Nouns • Verbs • Use of comparisons • Gerunds • Participles • Literary genres

LIFEPAC 6	**MECHANICS OF ENGLISH**
	• Punctuation
	• Complements • Modifiers
	• Clauses – subordinate,
	   coordinate
		LANGUAGE AND LITERATURE
		• History of English
		• Coordination and
		   subordination
		• Autobiography
			STRUCTURE & MEANING IN LITERATURE
			• Reading for purpose
			• Reading for meaning
			• Reading for persuasion
			• Understanding poetry

LIFEPAC 7	**THE NOVEL**
	• The Hiding Place
	• Sequence of events
	• Author's purpose
	• Character sketch
		CRITICAL THINKING
		• Word evaluation
		• The Paragraph –
		   structure, coherence,
		   introductory, concluding
			COMMUNICATION
			• Planning a speech
			• Listening comprehension
			• Letters – business,
			   informal, social

LIFEPAC 8	**LITERATURE** • Nonfiction • Listening skills • Commas • Semicolons • Nonverbal communications	**WRITE • LISTEN • READ** • Business letters • Personal letters • Four steps to listen • Nonfiction	**LIBRARY AND DRAMA** • Library resources • Drama – history, elements, reading • The Miracle Worker
LIFEPAC 9	**COMPOSITIONS** • Sentence types • Quality of paragraph • Pronunciation • Nonsense literature	**SPEAK AND WRITE** • Etymology • Modifiers • Person • Number • Tense • Oral report	**STUDIES IN THE NOVEL** • History • Define • Write • Critical essay • Twenty Thousand Leagues Under the Sea
LIFEPAC 10	**LOOKING BACK** • Parts of speech • Sentence structure • Punctuation • How to communicate	**LOOKING BACK** • Composition structure • Parts of speech • Critical thinking • Literary forms	**LOOKING BACK** • Communication – writing speaking, listening • Using resources • Literature review

Grade 10	Grade 11	Grade 12	
EVOLUTION OF ENGLISH • Historical development • Varieties of English • Substandard & standard • Changes in English	STANDARD ENGLISH • Need for standard English • Guardians of the standard • Dictionaries • Types of standard English texts	THE WORTH OF WORDS • Word categories • Expository writing • Sentence structure • Diction	LIFEPAC 1
LISTENING AND SPEAKING • Noun plurals • Suffixes • Creating a speech • Nature of listening	EFFECTIVE SENTENCES • Subordinate – clauses, conjunctions • Relative pronouns • Verbals • Appositives	STRUCTURE OF LANGUAGE • Parts of speech • Sentence structure • Subordinate phrases • Subordinate clauses	LIFEPAC 2
EFFECTIVE SENTENCES • Participles • Infinitives • Prepositions • Gerunds • Sentences – simple, compound, complex	SENTENCE WORKSHOP • Understanding pronouns • Using pronouns correctly • Using modifiers correctly • Parallel sentence structures	READ, RESEARCH, LISTEN • Reading skills • Resources for research • Taking notes • Drawing conclusions	LIFEPAC 3
POWER OF WORDS • Etymology • Connotations • Poetic devices • Poetry – literal, figurative, symbolic	WHY STUDY READING? • Greek and Latin roots • Diacritical markings • Finding the main idea • Analyzing a textbook	GIFT OF LANGUAGE • Origin–Biblical, • Koine Greek • Purpose of Grammar • Semantics	LIFEPAC 4
ELEMENTS OF COMPOSITION • Paragraphs • Connectives • Transitions • Expository writing – elements, ideas	POETRY • Metrical feet • Sets • Musical effects • Universality • Imagery • Connotation	ENGLISH LITERATURE • Early England • Medieval England • Fourteenth century • Chaucer	LIFEPAC 5

STRUCTURE AND READING
• Subordinate clauses
• Pronouns – gender,
  case, agreement
• Reading for recognition
	NONFICTION
	• Elements
	• Types – essays, diaries,
	  newspaper, biography
	• Composition
		ELIZABETHAN LITERATURE
		• Poetry
		• Prose
		• Drama
		• Essay
			LIFEPAC 6

ORAL READING AND DRAMA • Skills of oral reading • Drama – history, irony elements, allegory • Everyman	AMERICAN DRAMA • Development • History • Structure • Purpose • Our Town	17TH—18TH CENTURY LITERATURE • Historical background • Puritan literature • Common sense – satire • Sensibility	LIFEPAC 7
THE SHORT STORY • Elements • Enjoying • Writing • The Literary Critique	AMERICAN NOVEL • Eighteenth, nineteenth twentieth century • The Old Man and the Sea • The Critical Essay	WRITING • SHORT STORY, POETRY • Fundamentals • Inspiration • Technique and style • Form and process	LIFEPAC 8
THE NOVEL • Elements • In His Steps • The Critical Essay • The Book Review	COMPOSITION • Stating the thesis • Research • Outline • Writing the paper	POETRY • ROMANTIC , VICTORIAN • Wordsworth • Coleridge • Gordon • Byron • Shelley • Keats • Tennyson • Hopkins • Robert and Elizabeth B Browning	LIFEPAC 9

LOOKING BACK
• Writing skills
• Speech skills
• Poetry • Drama
• Short stories • Novel
	LOOKING BACK
	• Analyzing written word
	• Effective sentences
	• Expository prose
	• Genres of American literature
		LOOKING BACK
		• Creative writing
		• English literature –
		  Medieval to
		  Victorian
			LIFEPAC 10

MANAGEMENT

STRUCTURE OF THE LIFEPAC CURRICULUM

The LIFEPAC curriculum is conveniently structured to provide one teacher handbook containing teacher support material with answer keys and ten student worktexts for each subject at grade levels two through twelve. The worktext format of the LIFEPACs allows the student to read the textual information and complete workbook activities all in the same booklet. The easy to follow LIFEPAC numbering system lists the grade as the first number(s) and the last two digits as the number of the series. For example, the Language Arts LIFEPAC at the 6th grade level, 5th book in the series would be LAN0605.

Each LIFEPAC is divided into 3 to 5 sections and begins with an introduction or overview of the booklet as well as a series of specific learning objectives to give a purpose to the study of the LIFEPAC. The introduction and objectives are followed by a vocabulary section which may be found at the beginning of each section at the lower levels, at the beginning of the LIFEPAC in the middle grades, or in the glossary at the high school level. Vocabulary words are used to develop word recognition and should not be confused with the spelling words introduced later in the LIFEPAC. The student should learn all vocabulary words before working the LIFEPAC sections to improve comprehension, retention, and reading skills.

Each activity or written assignment has a number for easy identification, such as 1.1. The first number corresponds to the LIFEPAC section and the number to the right of the decimal is the number of the activity.

Teacher checkpoints, which are essential to maintain quality learning, are found at various locations throughout the LIFEPAC. The teacher should check 1) neatness of work and penmanship, 2) quality of understanding (tested with a short oral quiz), 3) thoroughness of answers (complete sentences and paragraphs, correct spelling, etc.), 4) completion of activities (no blank spaces), and 5) accuracy of answers as compared to the answer key (all answers correct).

The self test questions are also number coded for easy reference. For example, 2.015 means that this is the 15th question in the self test of Section II. The first number corresponds to the LIFEPAC section, the zero indicates that it is a self test question, and the number to the right of the zero the question number.

The LIFEPAC test is packaged at the centerfold of each LIFEPAC. It should be removed and put aside before giving the booklet to the student for study.

Answer and test keys have the same numbering system as the LIFEPACs and appear at the back of this handbook. The student may be given access to the answer keys (not the test keys) under teacher supervision so that he can score his own work.

A thorough study of the Curriculum Overview by the teacher before instruction begins is essential to the success of the student. The teacher should become familiar with expected skill mastery and understand how these grade level skills fit into the overall skill development of the curriculum. The teacher should also preview the objectives that appear at the beginning of each LIFEPAC for additional preparation and planning.

TEST SCORING and GRADING

Answer keys and test keys give examples of correct answers. They convey the idea, but the student may use many ways to express a correct answer. The teacher should check for the essence of the answer, not for the exact wording. Many questions are high level and require thinking and creativity on the part of the student. Each answer should be scored based on whether or not the main idea written by the student matches the model example. "Any Order" or "Either Order" in a key indicates that no particular order is necessary to be correct.

Most self tests and LIFEPAC tests at the lower elementary levels are scored at 1 point per answer; however, the upper levels may have a point system awarding 2 to 5 points for various answers or questions. Further, the total test points will vary; they may not always equal 100 points. They may be 78, 85, 100, 105, etc.

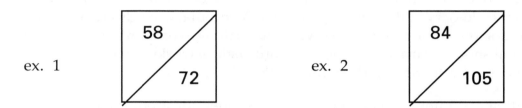

ex. 1   ex. 2

A score box similar to ex.1 above is located at the end of each self test and on the front of the LIFEPAC test. The bottom score, 72, represents the total number of points possible on the test. The upper score, 58, represents the number of points your student will need to receive an 80% or passing grade. If you wish to establish the exact percentage that your student has achieved, find the total points of his correct answers and divide it by the bottom number (in this case 72.) For example, if your student has a point total of 65, divide 65 by 72 for a grade of 90%. Referring to ex. 2, on a test with a total of 105 possible points, the student would have to receive a minimum of 84 correct points for an 80% or passing grade. If your student has received 93 points, simply divide the 93 by 105 for a percentage grade of 89%. Students who receive a score below 80% should review the LIFEPAC and retest using the appropriate Alternate Test found in the Teacher's Guide.

The following is a guideline to assign letter grades for completed LIFEPACs based on a maximum total score of 100 points.

LIFEPAC Test   =   60% of the Total Score (or percent grade)
Self Test   =   25% of the Total Score (average percent of self tests)
Reports   =   10% or 10* points per LIFEPAC
Oral Work   =   5% or 5* points per LIFEPAC
*Determined by the teacher's subjective evaluation of the student's daily work.

Example:

LIFEPAC Test Score	=	92%	92	x	.60	= 55 points
Self Test Average	=	90%	90	x	.25	= 23 points
Reports						= 8 points
Oral Work						= 4 points

TOTAL POINTS   =   90 points

Grade Scale based on point system:

100	–	94	=	A
93	–	86	=	B
85	–	77	=	C
76	–	70	=	D
Below		70	=	F

TEACHER HINTS and STUDYING TECHNIQUES

LIFEPAC Activities are written to check the level of understanding of the preceding text. The student may look back to the text as necessary to complete these activities; however, a student should never attempt to do the activities without reading (studying) the text first. Self tests and LIFEPAC tests are never open book tests.

Language arts activities (skill integration) often appear within other subject curriculum. The purpose is to give the student an opportunity to test his skill mastery outside of the context in which it was presented.

Writing complete answers (paragraphs) to some questions is an integral part of the LIFEPAC Curriculum in all subjects. This builds communication and organization skills, increases understanding and retention of ideas, and helps enforce good penmanship. Complete sentences should be encouraged for this type of activity. Obviously, single words or phrases do not meet the intent of the activity, since multiple lines are given for the response.

Review is essential to student success. Time invested in review where review is suggested will be time saved in correcting errors later. Self tests, unlike the section activities, are closed book. This procedure helps to identify weaknesses before they become too great to overcome. Certain objectives from self tests are cumulative and test previous sections; therefore, good preparation for a self test must include all material studied up to that testing point.

The following procedure checklist has been found to be successful in developing good study habits in the LIFEPAC curriculum.

1. Read the introduction and Table of Contents.
2. Read the objectives.
3. Recite and study the entire vocabulary (glossary) list.
4. Study each section as follows:
    a. Read the introduction and study the section objectives.
    b. Read all the text for the entire section, but answer none of the activities.
    c. Return to the beginning of the section and memorize each vocabulary word and definition.
    d. Reread the section, complete the activities, check the answers with the answer key, correct all errors, and have the teacher check.
    e. Read the self test but do not answer the questions.
    f. Go to the beginning of the first section and reread the text and answers to the activities up to the self test you have not yet done.
    g. Answer the questions to the self test without looking back.
    h. Have the self test checked by the teacher.
    i. Correct the self test and have the teacher check the corrections.
    j. Repeat steps a–i for each section.

5. Use the SQ3R* method to prepare for the LIFEPAC test.
6. Take the LIFEPAC test as a closed book test.
7. LIFEPAC tests are administered and scored under direct teacher supervision. Students who receive scores below 80% should review the LIFEPAC using the SQ3R* study method and take the Alternate Test located in the Teacher Handbook. The final test grade may be the grade on the Alternate Test or an average of the grades from the original LIFEPAC test and the Alternate Test.

  *SQ3R: **S**can the whole LIFEPAC.
  Question yourself on the objectives.
  Read the whole LIFEPAC again.
  Recite through an oral examination.
  Review weak areas.

GOAL SETTING and SCHEDULES

Each school must develop its own schedule, because no single set of procedures will fit every situation. The following is an example of a daily schedule that includes the five LIFEPAC subjects as well as time slotted for special activities.

Possible Daily Schedule

8:15	–	8:25	Pledges, prayer, songs, devotions, etc.
8:25	–	9:10	Bible
9:10	–	9:55	Language Arts
9:55	–	10:15	Recess (juice break)
10:15	–	11:00	Mathematics
11:00	–	11:45	Social Studies
11:45	–	12:30	Lunch, recess, quiet time
12:30	–	1:15	Science
1:15	–		Drill, remedial work, enrichment*

*Enrichment: Computer time, physical education, field trips, fun reading, games and puzzles, family business, hobbies, resource persons, guests, crafts, creative work, electives, music appreciation, projects.

Basically, two factors need to be considered when assigning work to a student in the LIFEPAC curriculum.

The first is time. An average of 45 minutes should be devoted to each subject, each day. Remember, this is only an average. Because of extenuating circumstances a student may spend only 15 minutes on a subject one day and the next day spend 90 minutes on the same subject.

The second factor is the number of pages to be worked in each subject. A single LIFEPAC is designed to take 3 to 4 weeks to complete. Allowing about 3-4 days for LIFEPAC introduction, review, and tests, the student has approximately 15 days to complete the LIFEPAC pages. Simply take the number of pages in the LIFEPAC, divide it by 15 and you will have the number of pages that must be completed on a daily basis to keep the student on schedule. For example, a LIFEPAC containing 45 pages will require 3 completed pages per day. Again, this is only an average. While working a 45 page LIFEPAC, the student may complete only 1 page the first day if the text has a lot of activities or reports, but go on to complete 5 pages the next day.

Long range planning requires some organization. Because the traditional school year originates in the early fall of one year and continues to late spring of the following year, a calendar should be devised that covers this period of time. Approximate beginning and completion dates can be noted on the calendar as well as special occasions such as holidays, vacations and birthdays. Since each LIFEPAC takes 3-4 weeks or eighteen days to complete, it should take about 180 school days to finish a set of ten LIFEPACs. Starting at the beginning school date, mark off eighteen school days on the calendar and that will become the targeted completion date for the first LIFEPAC. Continue marking the calendar until you have established dates for the remaining nine LIFEPACs making adjustments for previously noted holidays and vacations. If all five subjects are being used, the ten established target dates should be the same for the LIFEPACs in each subject.

FORMS

The sample weekly lesson plan and student grading sheet forms are included in this section as teacher support materials and may be duplicated at the convenience of the teacher.

The student grading sheet is provided for those who desire to follow the suggested guidelines for assignment of letter grades found on page 3 of this section. The student's self test scores should be posted as percentage grades. When the LIFEPAC is completed the teacher should average the self test grades, multiply the average by .25 and post the points in the box marked self test points. The LIFEPAC percentage grade should be multiplied by .60 and posted. Next, the teacher should award and post points for written reports and oral work. A report may be any type of written work assigned to the student whether it is a LIFEPAC or additional learning activity. Oral work includes the student's ability to respond orally to questions which may or may not be related to LIFEPAC activities or any type of oral report assigned by the teacher. The points may then be totaled and a final grade entered along with the date that the LIFEPAC was completed.

The Student Record Book which was specifically designed for use with the Alpha Omega curriculum provides space to record weekly progress for one student over a nine week period as well as a place to post self test and LIFEPAC scores. The Student Record Books are available through the current Alpha Omega catalog; however, unlike the enclosed forms these books are not for duplication and should be purchased in sets of four to cover a full academic year.

WEEKLY LESSON PLANNER

Week of:

	Subject	Subject	Subject	Subject
Monday				
	Subject	Subject	Subject	Subject
Tuesday				
	Subject	Subject	Subject	Subject
Wednesday				
	Subject	Subject	Subject	Subject
Thursday				
	Subject	Subject	Subject	Subject
Friday				

21

WEEKLY LESSON PLANNER

Week of:

	Subject	Subject	Subject	Subject
Monday				
	Subject	Subject	Subject	Subject
Tuesday				
	Subject	Subject	Subject	Subject
Wednesday				
	Subject	Subject	Subject	Subject
Thursday				
	Subject	Subject	Subject	Subject
Friday				

Bible

LP #	Self Test Scores by Sections 1	2	3	4	5	Self Test Points	LIFEPAC Test	Oral Points	Report Points	Final Grade	Date
01											
02											
03											
04											
05											
06											
07											
08											
09											
10											

History & Geography

LP #	Self Test Scores by Sections 1	2	3	4	5	Self Test Points	LIFEPAC Test	Oral Points	Report Points	Final Grade	Date
01											
02											
03											
04											
05											
06											
07											
08											
09											
10											

Language Arts

LP #	Self Test Scores by Sections 1	2	3	4	5	Self Test Points	LIFEPAC Test	Oral Points	Report Points	Final Grade	Date
01											
02											
03											
04											
05											
06											
07											
08											
09											
10											

Student Name _____   Year _____

Mathematics

| LP # | Self Test Scores by Sections | | | | | Self Test Points | LIFEPAC Test | Oral Points | Report Points | Final Grade | Date |
	1	2	3	4	5						
01											
02											
03											
04											
05											
06											
07											
08											
09											
10											

Science

| LP # | Self Test Scores by Sections | | | | | Self Test Points | LIFEPAC Test | Oral Points | Report Points | Final Grade | Date |
	1	2	3	4	5						
01											
02											
03											
04											
05											
06											
07											
08											
09											
10											

Spelling/Electives

| LP # | Self Test Scores by Sections | | | | | Self Test Points | LIFEPAC Test | Oral Points | Report Points | Final Grade | Date |
	1	2	3	4	5						
01											
02											
03											
04											
05											
06											
07											
08											
09											
10											

N
O
T
E
S

LANGUAGE ARTS

■——————————————————————————————————————■

Teacher Notes

Concepts

Phonics/Spelling/Syllable Rules

Teaching Pages

INSTRUCTIONS FOR FIRST GRADE LANGUAGE ARTS

The first grade handbooks of the LIFEPAC curriculum are designed to provide a step-by step procedure that will help the teacher prepare for and present each lesson effectively. In the early LIFEPACs the teacher should read the directions and any other sentences to the children. However, as the school year progresses, the student should be encouraged to begin reading and following his own instructional material in preparation for the independent study approach that begins at the second grade level.

Language Arts includes those subjects that develop the student's communication skills. The LIFEPAC approach to combining reading, spelling, penmanship, composition, grammar, speech and literature in a single unit allows the teacher to integrate the study of these various language arts subject areas. The variety and scope of the curriculum may make it difficult for students to complete the required material within the suggested daily scheduled time of forty-five minutes. Spelling, reading and various forms of composition may need to be completed during the afternoon enrichment period.

This section of the teacher handbook includes the following teacher aids: 1) Index of Concepts 2) Phonics/Spelling/Syllable Guidelines 3) Teacher Instruction Pages.

The Index of Concepts is a quick reference guide for the teacher who may be looking for a rule or explanation that applies to a particular concept. It does not identify each use of the concept in the various LIFEPACs. The Phonics/Spelling/Syllable Guidelines are another convenient reference guide.

The Teacher Instruction Pages list the Concept to be taught as well as Student Objectives and Goals for the Teacher. Sight words are words that either are needed before their phonetic presentation or do not follow the standard phonetic rules. The Vocabulary Lists are made up of sight words that are needed by the student for better understanding of the subject content. These words need to be learned through memorization and children should be drilled on them frequently. The Teaching Page contains directions for teaching that page. Worksheet pages contained in some lessons follow this section and may be duplicated for individual student use. The Activities section at the end of each lesson is optional and may be used to reinforce or expand the concepts taught.

Materials needed are usually items such as pencils and crayons which are readily available. Additional items that may be required are Alphabet-Penmanship Charts (purchased through the catalog) and writing tablets or any lined paper, alphabet cards, color and number charts, and flash cards for vocabulary words.

Five Readers are necessary for the first grade Language Arts curriculum. Each Reader gives the student an opportunity to practice concepts that have been taught in the LIFEPAC in which it appears as well as the one that precedes it. For example, Reader 1 is used for both LIFEPACs 101 and 102. "Instant Words" located after the Table of Contents of the Reader, lists words which may need to be introduced to the student as sight words. Readers are an effective tool to develop the student's reading vocabulary and when they are no longer directly associated with a lesson may be used throughout the school year for independent reading purposes.

The Spelling Words are on the self test and LIFEPAC test Teacher Instruction Pages in the Teacher's Guide and may be written by the student on writing tablet pages. Unlike the upper grade levels, there are no spelling lists for the student to study. Instead, the spelling tests, for both self tests and LIFEPAC tests, are designed to test the student's auditory phonics. The teacher should stress the sound of the word when administering the test. A student who spells the word *sat* as *sad* has not learned to discriminate between the phonetic sounds of *t* and *d* and should receive further drill on these sounds. Words such as *road* and *rode* should be presented to the student in sentences. A misspelled word suggests the teacher should review the concepts of vowel digraph *oa*, silent *e* and homonyms with the student.

Concept	LIFEPAC	Section	Concept	LIFEPAC	Section
Abbreviations and Titles	109	3	vowels - short	101	all
			vowel digraphs	105	1
Alphabetical Order	108	1		107	1
				108	1,3
Composition				109	1,2
letters - invitation,			y as long i and e	105	1
business, friendly	107	3			
paragraph definition	108	2	Parts of Speech		
writing a report	109	2	nouns	107	3
writing a story	103	2	pronouns	106	3
			verbs		
Compound words	103	3	forms	102	3
				107	2
Contractions	103	1	definition	107	3
			tense	104	1
Following Directions				108	2
oral and written	102	1	Plurals	102	1
				103	1,3
Homonyms	105	1			
	106	2	Poetry	105	1
	107	3		109	1
Introductions	108	2	Possessives	103	2
Oral Expression			Sentences		
discussion boxes	108	3	definition	108	2
tell a story rules	102	3	quotations	106	1
			types		
Phonics			exclamation	102	3
c - soft	103	2	question	102	2
consonants	101	all	statement	102	1
consonant blends	104	1,2			
	106	2	Suffixes	102	3
	108	2,3		105	3
consonant digraphs	103	1			
consonants - silent	101	2	Syllables	103	3
	104	2			
consonants -			Telephone Use	106	2
special blends	104	2		108	2
g-soft	103	3			
letter groups - gh,ph,igh	104	2			
	105	1			
r-controlled vowels	106	1			
vowels - long	105	1,2			
	107	all			

Reader	LIFEPAC	Page in LP	Reader	LIFEPAC	Page in LP
Reader 1 *Dog in the Tub*			The Pup and the Box	104	7
			Pigs	104	13
A Map	101	2	Fish, Fish, Fish	104	16
The Sun	101	15	Ann and the Fish	104	18
Dog in the Tub	101	29	Little Lamb	104	20
Dad	101	30	Glad Tammy	104	22
Wet	101	31	Cotton Candy	104	23
	102	5	The Last Trick	104	24
			The Lemonade Stand	104	26
Getting Dressed To			I Talk to God	104	29
Go Out in the Rain	102	2	Stuck Again	104	31
Sis	102	6	The Gift	104	33
My Bible	102	7			
What Is In The Pot?	102	8			
My Rag Doll	102	10	**Reader 3** *Oats Are For Goats*		
Tom	102	11			
A Very Big Mess	102	14	Kelly's Daisies	105	2
Our Pet	102	15	Nonsense Poem	105	3
Jesus	102	16	I Don't Know About Snow	105	6
Run	102	17	The Tree Fort	105	7
Little Red Fox	102	18	Mike's Light Bites	105	11
Bzz	102	21	A Tale of a Tail	105	12
Mom	102	22	Adam and Eve	105	14
The Big Fat Hen	102	24	Oats Are For Goats	105	15
Tim Kicks	102	25	Clean Machine	105	16
Ball Fun	102	26	The Ball Game	105	18
Fast Jim	102	27	Just Like Jesus	105	28
Little Black Ants	102	30	Jack's Table	105	29
Bug	102	31	Lion Fun	106	2
			Rose's Rose	106	6
Reader 2 *Cotton Candy*			Working	106	7
			The Cross	106	12
The Red Ball	103	2	Fun with Words	106	13
The Mess	103	4	That Buzzing Sound	106	16
Three Missing Pups	103	7	I Like Stripes	106	17
Clickety Clack	103	9	Big Blue	106	20
The Twins Fix Lunch	103	12	Jesus Prays	106	25
Fun!	103	14	A Sea Horse is a Fish	106	27
The New Little Bug	103	19	My Little Black Pony	106	28
Pets	103	21	A Sea Horse is Not a		
The Cowboy	103	26	Race Horse	106	29
Betty the Bat	103	27			
Black and White Keys	103	31			
A Big Problem	104	2			

Reader	LIFEPAC	Page in LP	Reader	LIFEPAC	Page in LP
Reader 4 *Flying My Kite*			God is our Rock	110	5
			The Old Red Barn	110	6
Sisters	107	2	Joseph's Dream	110	7
Waiting For Grandma	107	2	Cory's Kitten	110	8
Julie's Painting	107	3	The Kitten Gets a Name	110	9
Sheep	107	4	Clouds	110	10
Steven and Taylor	107	5	Dolphin	110	17
What Do You Want To Be?	107	8	My Father and Mother	110	18
Surprise! Surprise!	107	9 & 10	Little Garden	110	21
Casey's First Lesson	107	10	The Wait	110	24
The Pet Show	107	17 & 18	What is Tall?	110	29
Going to Florida	107	18			
Flying My Kite	107	22			
The Lazy Little Train	107	31			
No More Alligator Fear	108	5			
Friends	108	6			
A Little About Alligators	108	7			
Joan's New School	108	14			
The Bee Chase	108	16			
Baby Zebra	108	21			
Playing	108	24			
Busy Bees	108	26			
Leaves	108	28			
The Quilt	108	29			
I Am Always With You	108	30			
Snow	108	32			

This listing is for those instructors who would like to reference the Teaching Page for each one of the stories. For example, the activities for *Ball Fun* are in the Teacher Notes for Page 26 of LIFEPAC 102.

Reader 5 *The Gold Coin*

Reader	LIFEPAC	Page in LP
Bobo, the Clown	109	3 & 4
Snoopers	109	4
My Gift	109	6
Thank You, God	109	7
Building a Town	109	12 & 13
The Gold Coin	109	14
The Pony Show	109	15
Nurse Jane	109	15
Tornado	109	16
Old, Old Goat	109	24
Animals	109	27
Playmates of the Sea	109	28
Building Rockets	109	30

PHONICS for Language Arts 100

The following letter and letter combinations are introduced in Language Arts 100.
They may be put on cards for drilling purposes.

a e i o u

b c d f g h j k l m n p q r s t v w x y z

th wh sh ch, ng nk, ck mb lk gn kn gh

ar er ir or ur, ai ay, au aw, ei ey, ea ee, ie

oa, oo, ew, ou, ow, oi, oy

gh ph, igh

				Teacher Notes
1.	short vowels	-	a (bat) e (bet) i (bit) o (cot) u (but)	101
2.	long vowels	-	a (bait) e (beat) i (bite) o (coat) u (use)	105
3.	consonants	-	b d f h j k l m n p r s t v w x z	101
4.	c and g	-	hard sound before a, o, u	101
		-	soft sound before e, i	103
5.	q (qu)	-	always has the sound of kw	101
6.	y	-	as y (yard)	101
		-	as e (baby)	105
		-	as i (cry)	105
7.	consonant digraphs	-	th, wh, sh, ch	103
8.	special blends	-	ng (sing) nk (sank)	104
9.	silent consonants	-	ck (lock)	101
		-	mb (lamb) lk (talk) gn (sign)	104
		-	kn (know) gh (though) t (often)	104
10.	r-controlled vowels	-	ar (car) or (for)	106
		-	er (her) ir (sir) ur (fur)	106
11.	vowel digraphs	-	ai, ay as long a (pail) (pay)	107
		-	au, aw (Paul) (paw)	107
		-	ei, ey as long a (veil) (they)	105
				107
		-	ea, ee as long e (beat) (feet)	107
		-	ie as long e (piece)	107
			as long i (pie)	107
		-	oa as long o (boat)	108
		-	oo long sound (boot)	108
			short sound (book)	108
		-	ew as long u (few)	108

-		ou as long u (soup)	108
			109
-		as `ow' (cloud)*	109
-		ow as long o (slow)	108
		as `ow' (clown)*	109
-		oi, oy (boil) (boy)*	109
12.	letter groups	-	gh ph as f (laugh) (phone)	104
		-	igh as long i (sigh)	105

12.	letter groups	-	gh ph as f (laugh) (phone)	104
		-	igh as long i (sigh)	105

*sometimes referred to as diphthongs

DIRECTION WORD FLASHCARDS for Language Arts 100

Begin constructing a set of direction words flashcards—Circle, Say, Write, Listen, Cut and Paste, etc.—for key words in the activity instructions. Add to this set of direction words as new ones are encountered in the activities.

SPELLING RULES for Language Arts 100

1. Double the final consonant of a short vowel word before adding -*er*, -*ed* and -*ing*, and drop the final *e* in long vowel words and some short vowel words before adding -*er*, -*ed* and -*ing* (102 p. 32).
2. Even though the sound is the same, some words with the *ch* sound are spelled *tch* (103 p. 6). In *ch* words, if the letter right after the *h* is an *l* or *r*, the *ch* will usually have the sound of *k* as in *Christmas* or *chlorine* (103 p. 6).
3. Words ending in *s, x, sh* or *ch* must have the *es* ending to make them plural (103 p. 30).
4. *Y* is used at the end of short words to make the sound of *i*. *Y* is used at the end of long words (those with two or more syllables) to make the sound of *e*.
5. A word that has a long vowel sound may have a silent *e* at the end of the word (105 p. 10).
6. Because *er, ir, ur* and sometimes *or* all have the same sound, it becomes necessary to remember how the word is spelled (106 p. 9).
7. Words that end in *y*, change the *y* to *i* before adding *es*. Words that end in *f*, change the *f* to *v* before adding *es* (106 p. 18).

THE SYLLABLE RULE for Language Arts 100

There are as many syllables in a word as the number of vowels you can hear.(103 p. 27)

Example:	boat:	One vowel is heard. (*oa* is a vowel digraph)
		This is a one-syllable word.
	basket:	Two vowels are heard - *a* and *e*.
		This is a two-syllable word.
	difference:	Three vowels are heard - *i, e, e*.
		(The final *e* simply makes the *c* a soft sound.)
		This is a three-syllable word.

Page 1: FUN WITH WORDS

CONCEPTS: purpose of the LIFEPAC, children's objectives

TEACHER GOALS: To teach the children
To understand what will be taught in this LIFEPAC, and
To understand what will be expected of them in Language Arts LIFEPAC 106.

TEACHING PAGE 1:

Read the title and sentences at the top of the page with the children. Talk about each one so children will know what they will be learning about in this LIFEPAC.

Ask the children to tell what objectives are. Read the list of objectives with them and talk about each one. The children should understand that these are the things they will be able to do when this LIFEPAC is finished.

Have the children write their names and ages on the lines.

FUN WITH WORDS

You can have fun reading, listening, and writing.

In this LIFEPAC
you will learn about r-controlled vowels.
You will learn to read stories.
You will learn to write good sentences.
You will learn to spell and write rhyming words.
You will learn to write paragraphs and stories.

 Objectives

1. I can choose words with r-controlled vowels.
2. I can read and write good sentences.
3. I can learn about contractions and possessives.
4. I can write paragraphs and stories.
5. I can follow directions.

My name is
_____

I am _____ years old.

page 1 (one)

I. PART ONE

Page 2: Activity Page

CONCEPTS: *r*-controlled vowels *ar, er, ir, or, ur*

TEACHER GOALS: To teach the children
To recognize the *r*-controlled vowels *ar, er, ir, or, ur*,
To listen to their sounds, and
To find them in words.

VOCABULARY: *r-* controlled vowels

MATERIALS NEEDED: Worksheet 1, magazines, newspapers

TEACHING PAGE 2:

Have the children read the title of the page and say the *r*-controlled vowels. Have them do both exercises on the page. Check by having the children read the words and letters. Give help only if necessary. (church, bird, horn, letter, store, butter, star, shirt, churn, car, acorn, arm)

ACTIVITIES:

1. Do Worksheet 1.

Have the children read the directions at the top of the page. Have them name the pictures and write *ar* on the lines. Have them read the words.

Do the same with *or*.

Have the children read the last direction.

Have them name the pictures and circle all those with the sound made by *er*, *ir*, or *ur*. Check by having the children tell which pictures they circled (toaster, bird, star, curl, horn, skirt, squirrel, finger).

2. Make a chart for each *r*-controlled vowel. Have the children cut out pictures from magazines or catalogs to paste on the chart. Write the name under the picture and underline the r-controlled vowel. List the words that the children will use in their writing but that cannot be pictured in one section of the chart.

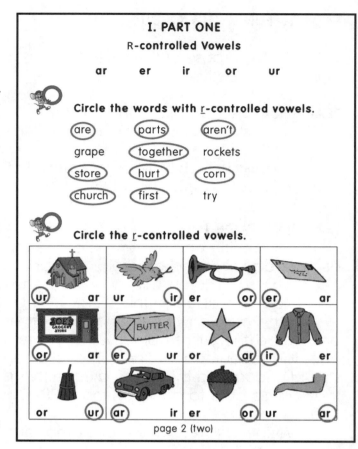

I. PART ONE
R-controlled Vowels

ar   er   ir   or   ur

Circle the words with r-controlled vowels.

page 2 (two)

TEACHING READING:

Read the story "Lion Fun" in *Reader 3*.

Present the words *lion, turtle, scare* and have the children read them several times. Ask the meaning of each word.

Have the children look at the picture. Have several children tell about a time when they saw a lion.

Have the children read the story silently.

Ask these questions:

"Where are the lions sitting?"

"What are some of the things the lions see?"

"What will they do to the bird?"

"What will they do to the turtle?"

"What will they do to the Mother and the child?"

"Why do they like to sit in the grass?"

"What will they do in the grass?"

Have the children find the *r*-controlled words in the story. Write them on the board.

Name _____

Write ar. Read the words.

y __ ar n   b __ ar n

Write or.

c __ or n   f __ or t

Circle the pictures with the er, ir, or ur sound.

Language Arts 106
Worksheet 1
with page 2

Teacher check _____
                    Initial   Date

Page 3: Grouping

CONCEPTS: classifying, *r*-controlled vowels

TEACHER GOALS: To teach the children
To classify words into groups and
To identify and read words with *r*-controlled vowels.

TEACHING PAGE 3 :

Read the sentence and direction at the top of the page with the children.

Work through the entire page with the children. (barn, yarn, car, bird, horn, spur, turtle, churn, corn, jar, horn, store)

Have the children read all the words in the box, circle the three that have the same vowels, and tell which vowel it is by giving the sound of it. Have them tell why the fourth word is different.

Have the children write some sentences using these words. Try to use one statement, one question, one exclamation.

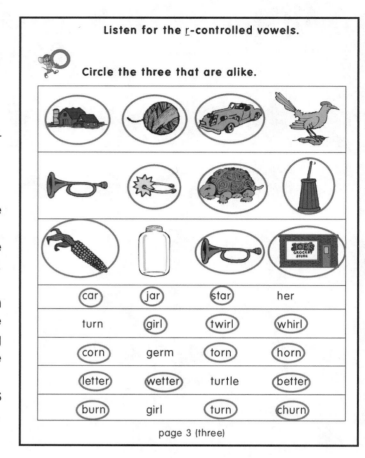

Listen for the <u>r</u>-controlled vowels.

Circle the three that are alike.

car	jar	star	her
turn	girl	twirl	whirl
corn	germ	torn	horn
letter	wetter	turtle	better
burn	girl	turn	churn

page 3 (three)

Page 4: David's Birthday Cake

CONCEPTS: contractions, direct quotations, reading a story, long *a*

TEACHER GOALS: To teach the children
To identify the contractions in the story and give the words for which they stand,
To find the direct quotations in the story,
To read the story by themselves and understand it, and
To identify words with the sound of long *a*.

VOCABULARY: David, birthday,

TEACHING PAGE 4:
Have the children read the title. Ask which word is a possessive and what it means.

Ask a child to tell what a birthday is. Let several tell when their birthdays are.

Write the contractions on the board. Have the children read them and tell what they mean. Write the words behind each contraction as they give them.

(It's	It is
Who'll	Who will
Let's	Let us
They'll	They will
He'll	He will
I'll	I will
We'll	We will)

Have the children read the story silently. *Ask questions similar to these:* "What was David's problem?"

("How did David feel? How would you feel?")

"What did Mother say?"
"What did May say?"
"Who do you think May is?"
"How was David's problem solved"
"How did David feel then?"

Have the children point out the contractions in the story. Have the sentence read using the words instead of the contraction. *(Example:* "It is my

DAVID'S BIRTHDAY CAKE

" It's my birthday, " said David.
" Who'll share my birthday cake? "

" Let's call Grandma and Grandpa, " said Mother.
" They'll share your birthday cake. "

" Let's call your pal, Tim, " said May.
" He'll share your birthday cake. "

" I'll share your birthday cake, " said Father.
" Come and help me, David.
We'll bake a big birthday cake to share!"

page 4 (four)

birthday.") This exercise is a good way to tell whether the children really understand contractions.

Have the children find all the words with the long /a/ sound in the story and read them. Ask which ones rhyme. Find the *r*-controlled vowels.

Tell the children that *David's is* a possessive. Have the children find more possessives in the story. Have the children read them and tell what belongs to the person (my birthday, my birthday cake, your cake).

Have the children read the story aloud. Let one child read the narrator's part, one read David's part, and others read Mother's, Father's, and May's parts. Go through the story with the children first, pointing out the direct quotations, the quotation marks, and when the narrator will read. Then have the story read aloud.

Read the story several times with different children reading the parts.

Do page 5 in the same class period if at all possible.

ACTIVITY:
Ask the children to tell about another David. Read the story of David and Goliath from I Sam. 17.

Page 5: Possessives

CONCEPTS: meaning of Christmas, possessives, recalling details

TEACHER GOALS: To teach the children
To tell the story of the birth of Jesus and what it means to them,
To identify the possessives and tell what they mean, and
To recall details of the story.

BIBLE REFERENCE: Luke chapter 2

MATERIALS NEEDED: Bible

TEACHING PAGE 5:
Read the sentence and question at the top of the page with the children. Let the children tell the story of the birth of Jesus and why we have Christmas.

Write Jesus on the board and have children copy it in the blank space. Let each child tell why he loves Jesus.

Read the next direction with the children. Have the children read each sentence, circle the correct word, and copy it in the blank.

Note: Teach the children to circle the word first in this type of exercise. Then have them read the sentence again using the word they circled. After they have reread the sentence, then copy it in the blank. The children will make fewer mistakes with this method.

Check the work by having the children read the sentences.

ACTIVITIES:
1. Have children draw a picture of the birth of Jesus. They may draw a picture of their own birthday celebration on the other side.

2. Read the story of the birth of Jesus from the Bible or from a Bible story book.

We celebrate a very important birthday on **Christmas Day**.
Do you know whose birthday it is?

_____
It is the birthday of ____ Jesus ____

Tell why you love Jesus.

Write the words.
_____
It is _____ birthday.
~~David's~~ / Dale's

_____
_____ will bake the cake.
Mother ~~Father~~

_____
David will _____ Father.
~~help~~ helps

_____
David _____ share his cake.
~~can~~ can't

page 5 (five)

Page 6: Activity Page

Concept: *r*-controlled vowels *ar, er, ir, or, ur*

TEACHER GOALS: To teach the children
To recognize the sounds of *r*-controlled vowels, and
To write words with *r*-controlled vowels

MATERIALS NEEDED: newspaper, magazine

TEACHING PAGE 6:
Read the direction at the top of the page and have the children repeat it as they follow along. Have the children name the pictures and circle those with the /*ar*/ sound (yarn, car, barn, letter, jar).

Do the same with the other two sections on the page (letter, car, turkey, bird, turtle, ladder, skirt, church, corn, girl, store, horn, fort).

Check by having the children tell which pictures they circled.

Write the words on the board. Have the children practice writing them in their writing tablet.

ACTIVITY:
Give each child a magazine page or a quarter sheet of newspaper on which you have drawn about a six inch circle. Have the children underline all the *r*-controlled words they can find inside the circle. This is a good exercise for the children working in pairs.

TEACHING READING:
Read the story "Rose's Rose" in *Reader 3*.
Present the words *Rose* and *Rose's* and have the children read them several times. Ask the meaning of each.

Have the children look at the picture and tell about it, then read the title of the story.

Have the story read silently.
Ask these questions about the story:

Circle the pictures with the <u>ar</u> sound.

Circle the pictures with the <u>er</u>, <u>ir</u>, or <u>ur</u> sound.

Circle the pictures with the <u>or</u> sound.

page 6 (six)

"Where had Rose's mother been?"
'What did she have for Rose?"
'What color was the rose?"
"How did Rose feel?"
"How would you have felt?"
"Is this story real or make-believe?"
"Could it really have happened?"
Have the children find these things in the story:

a. the possessives and possessive pronouns tell what belongs to each,

b. the words with the long /o/ sound,

c. the direct quotations tell who is speaking,

d. the exclamations, and

e. the words with r-controlled vowels.

Ask a child to be Rose and one to be Rose's mother. Have them read the direct quotations while you read the narration. Encourage good expression.

For a second reading, choose a child to read the narration.

Choose two children to act out the story using an artificial rose. Let them plan their actions. Do not have them read the story, but try to remember the conversation from the story. Let several pairs of children dramatize the story.

ACTIVITIES:

1. Read about the different kinds of roses from seed catalogs.
2. Read the part of "Alice in Wonderland" where the gardeners are painting the roses.

Page 7: Activity Page

CONCEPTS: *r*-controlled vowels, writing a story

TEACHER GOALS: To teach the children
To write sentences with *r*-controlled vowels,
To write a story using paragraphs, punctuation marks, title, and
To understand the main idea of a story.

VOCABULARY: surprise

MATERIALS NEEDED: drawing papers

TEACHING PAGE 7:

Have the children name the three kinds of sentences and tell what each is. Have them tell what the punctuation mark for each is. Ask how the first word in a sentence must begin.

Ask the children to tell what a paragraph is. Ask them to tell what a title is.

Read the direction at the top of the page with the children. Have them read the two words and write a sentence about each on the lines. Let several children read their sentences.

Read the next direction with the children. Read the words and let the children write the sentences in their writing tablets.

The teacher should check the sentences on this page and on the papers. The children should correct their work and recopy the sentences. Remind the children to write neatly and to use good spacing between words.

Read the last directions on the page with the children. This exercise may be done in the same class period or you may give the instructions now and let the children work on their stories when their other work is finished. Set a definite time for the stories to be finished and handed in so you may

Write a sentence for each word.

car

_____

bird

_____

Write a sentence for each of these words in your LIFEPAC Tablet.

star   her   turn   birthday

Write a story about a <u>surprise</u> in your LIFEPAC Tablet. Read your story to your class.

page 7 (seven)

check them and hand them back for recopying. Take one or two class periods to let the children read their stories to the class.

Have the children write at least two paragraphs and make up a title for their story that tells the main idea. You may have some children write only one paragraph, or you may give them more help, if needed.

Go through the rules for telling a story (LH 102, page 20) before the children begin reading their stories to the class.

ACTIVITIES:

1.   Let the children draw or paint a picture to go with their stories. It can be put on an easel or on the chalkboard ledge while the child is reading.

2.   Read stories about birthdays, birds, or any of the other subjects suggested on the page.

TEACHING READING:

Read the story "Working" in Reader 3.

Write the words *work, home, school, yard, to, too, two* on the board and pronounce them. Have the children repeat them after you. Point out the *r*-controlled vowels in *work* and *yard,* the long /o/ sound in *home,* the /k/ sound of *ch* and the double /o/ sound in *school.* Have the children say the words several times.

Tell the children to look at the picture and tell what they see. Most children will realize that the picture shows what the boy is thinking about.

Have the children read the title of the story and tell what kinds of work they see in the picture.

Have the children read the story silently, then have it read aloud. Have the children give kinds of work fathers, mothers, and children do.

Ask how many paragraphs there are. Have a child read each one and tell what the main idea of it is (Fathers and mothers work, I work at school, and I work at home).

Page 8: Working

CONCEPTS: two, to, and too, *r*-controlled vowels, paragraphs

TEACHER GOALS: To teach the children
To tell about many different kinds of work,
To tell the meanings of the words two, to, and too,
To identify words with the *r*-controlled vowels *ar* and *or*, and
To identify paragraphs and tell the main idea of each.

TEACHING PAGE 8:

Write the words *work, yard, to, too, two* on the board and pronounce them. Have the children repeat them after you. Point out the *r*-controlled vowels in *work* and *yard*, the long /i/ sound in *time*.

Have the children read the title and sentence at the top of the page. Talk about them. Tell the children to look at the picture and tell what they see. Most children will realize what the picture shows.

Have the children read the story silently, then have it read aloud.

Ask how many paragraphs there are. Have a child read each one and tell what the main idea of it is (Dad and Jenny will work in the yard, Mom and I will work in the garden, Sis will sit and smile).

Write the word *two* on the board and ask what it means. Tell the children to find two more words in the story that sound the same but are spelled differently. Write them on the board as the children find them. Have a child read the sentence in which they find the word and tell the meaning of it if they can. Tell the children that *to* means toward, and *too* means also.

Point out these words as they occur in the children's reading, or ask the children how they would spell the words they just read in a sentence.

WORK TIME

We will work in the yard.
Dad will cart the trash to the can.
Jenny will carry the basket.
The yard will be nice.

Mom and I will work in the garden.
I will dig.
I will pull weeds, too.
Mom will plant the seeds.
It will be a fun work time.

Sis will help us.
She will do her best.
She will sing.
She will sit and smile.
Sis will be a big help.

page 8 (eight)

Ask which words have *r*-controlled vowels. Remind the children that the *or* in work has the same sound as *er*.

ACTIVITIES:

1. Give a sentence using *to, two,* or *too* and have the children spell the word.

2. Have the children write two sentences for each of the words *two, to,* and *too*. Have them read their sentences to the class and have the class spell the word.

3. Read books and stories about people working, social studies books that have a section on community workers, articles from newspapers, magazines, or encyclopedias about people working, and stories about missionaries.

Page 9: R-controlled Vowels

CONCEPTS: *r*-controlled vowels, writing a story, speaking in a group

TEACHER GOALS: To teach the children
To identify words with *r*-controlled vowels,
To write a story two or three paragraphs in length about their work,
To write a good title for their stories, and
To read their stories to the class.

VOCABULARY: class

MATERIALS NEEDED: drawing paper, crayons or paint, Worksheet 2

TEACHING PAGE 9:

Show the flash cards for the *r*-controlled vowels and have the children give the sound for each. Ask the children to give words for each one. Go through the cards several times.

Have the children read the *r*-controlled vowels and the words for each at the top of the page. As they read the *ar* and the *or*, call attention to the words that have a different sound for the vowel.

Read the sentences with the children and have them read the words.

Have the children read the next direction and underline the vowel and the *r* in each word. Have them read the words.

Have the children read the next section. Talk about each line as they read it and be sure they understand everything they are to do. Tell them they may write a longer story if they wish. Some children should be able to write a two or three page story and should be encouraged to do so. Their story may be about any kind of work they do at home or school.

Remind the children that all the sentences in the paragraph should go together, that the title should be the main

ar	er	ir	or	ur
barn	her	sir	torn	fur
hard	berth	girl	worn	spur
warm	herd	bird	born	hurry
warn	timber	stir	horn	spurt

The <u>ar</u> in <u>warm</u> and <u>warn</u> has the sound of <u>or</u>.

The <u>or</u> in <u>work</u> has the same sound as <u>er</u>, <u>ir</u>, and <u>ur</u>. **Read these words.**

work	worm	worry
word	world	worse

Draw a line under each <u>r</u>-controlled vowel.

h<u>er</u>	t<u>ur</u>n	st<u>ar</u>t	sp<u>ur</u>
f<u>ur</u>	c<u>or</u>n	b<u>ur</u>n	h<u>or</u>n
sk<u>ir</u>t	st<u>ar</u>	cl<u>er</u>k	t<u>er</u>m
b<u>ir</u>d	c<u>ur</u>l	st<u>or</u>m	c<u>ar</u>d

Write a story about your work.
Write a good title.
Draw a picture of your story.
Read your story and show your picture to the class.

page 9 (nine)

idea of the story, that the first word in each sentence must begin with a capital, and that the sentence must end with the proper punctuation mark. Encourage the children to use statements and exclamations in their stories. Tell them not to use questions unless they are direct quotations. Help the children spell unfamiliar words.

Take class time for the children to show their pictures and read their stories. Review the rules for reading and telling stories before they begin.

ACTIVITIES:

1. Do Worksheet 2.

This worksheet is more difficult and some children may need to be guided through it, or you may have them do only the circling.

Have the children read the directions at the top of the page. Have them name the pictures and then circle those with *r*-controlled vowels. Have the children write the letters on the lines under the pictures.

Tell the children to say the names of the pictures and to listen for the *r*-controlled sound before they write any letters or circle any pictures. Remind the children that *er*, *ir*, *ur*, and sometimes *or* all have the same sound, so they will need to remember how the word was spelled.

Have the children name the pictures before they begin (star, corn, house, barn, turkey, dog, skirt, jacket, worm, horn, bird, letter, cow, jar)

Check by having a child name each picture and tell which letters, if any, he wrote under it.

2. Children who have trouble remembering the spelling of *r*-controlled words should work with the *r*-controlled vowel charts. Write the word beneath each picture to help children learn the spellings more easily.

Page 10: R-controlled Vowels

CONCEPTS: short vowel sounds, *r*-controlled vowels

TEACHER GOALS: To teach the children
To say the short sound of all the vowels, and
To recognize the sounds of the *r*-controlled vowels.

TEACHING PAGE 10:
Read the title and the sentences with the children. Ask them to give the short sounds of *a, e, i, o,* and *u.*

Have them point to the *a* and say its short sound. Then have them point to the *ar* and remind them the *r* changes the sound of the *a.* Say *ar* and have the children say it several times.

Do the same with each vowel.

Have the children point to the *ar* at the left of the page. Read the *ar* words and have the children repeat them. Read the entire list again.

Do the same with the *or.* Be sure they know the meanings of all the words. Have them use the words in a sentence .

Read the next sentence with the children. Have them point to the *er* and tell them that all these words must be spelled with the *er.* Read the list with the children.

Do the same with the *ir* and *ur.*

ACTIVITY:
Read one of the words and have the children find it on the page and tell whether it is an *ar, er, ir, or,* or *ur* word.

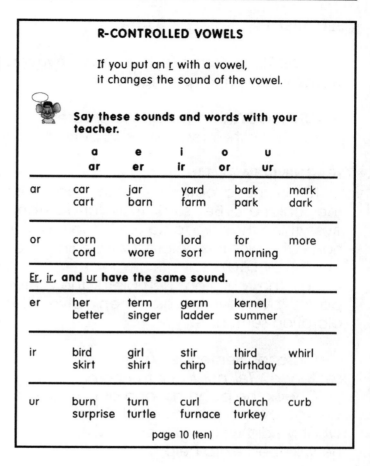

R-CONTROLLED VOWELS

If you put an r with a vowel,
it changes the sound of the vowel.

Say these sounds and words with your teacher.

	a ar	e er	i ir	o or	u ur
ar	car cart	jar barn	yard farm	bark park	mark dark
or	corn cord	horn wore	lord sort	for morning	more

<u>Er</u>, <u>ir</u>, **and** <u>ur</u> **have the same sound.**

er	her better	term singer	germ ladder	kernel summer	
ir	bird skirt	girl shirt	stir chirp	third birthday	whirl
ur	burn surprise	turn turtle	curl furnace	church turkey	curb

page 10 (ten)

SELF TEST 1

CONCEPTS: *r*-controlled vowels, rhyming words, writing and spelling words

TEACHER GOAL: To teach the children
To check their own progress periodically.

TEACHING PAGE 11:
Read the directions on the page with the children. Be sure they understand everything they are to do. Have the teacher name the pictures before they begin (letter, car, turkey, bird).

Let the children complete the entire page by themselves. Then give the dictation sentence.

Dictation Sentence - (Write the sentence.) *Tell her to stir the corn.*

Check the page as soon as possible and go over it with the child. Point out what he did well and then show him where he will need extra help.

ACTIVITY:

1. Children who missed more than one in the *r*-controlled exercise should work with an *r*-controlled vowel chart.

2. Read a list of words that contains about two-thirds *r*-controlled words and one-third other words. Have the children raise their hands when they hear words with the *r*-controlled vowels.

SPELLING WORDS:

car
jar
star
her
germ
stir
whirl
corn
horn
hurt

SELF TEST 1

Circle the pictures with <u>er</u>, <u>ir</u>, or <u>ur</u> sound.

Write rhyming words.

_____   _____
corn_____   star_____

Circle the words with the <u>ar</u>, <u>er</u>, <u>ir</u>, <u>or</u>, or <u>ur</u> sound.

(car)   rockets   (hurt)

(turtle)   (born)   (stir)

(parts)   try   (church)

Write the sentence.

_____
_____
_____
_____

$\frac{14}{18}$ Teacher Check _____
                    Initial   Date
            page 11 (eleven)

II. PART TWO

Page 12: Consonant Blends Review Activity

CONCEPT: consonant blends with *r*

TEACHER GOALS: To teach the children
To understand that in *r*-controlled vowels the *r* always comes after the vowel: *ar, er, ir, or, ur,* and
To understand that *r* can also be part of a consonant blend: *br, cr, dr, fr, gr, tr.*

Vocabulary: hidden

MATERIALS NEEDED: crayons

TEACHING PAGE 12:

Read the title and the sentence at the top of the page with the children. Let them look at the large picture, then read the sentences and name the pictures at the bottom of the page. Have the children circle the things as they find them in the picture. Check by having them tell what they circled and where they found it.

Let the children color the picture.

The children should be able to name the hidden objects for their family and tell the letters in the consonant blend at the beginning of each.

TEACHING READING:

Tell students today they are going to read a story called: "The Cross." (This story and several others have been added to the Language Arts 100 series. If your materials do not include this story in a separate reader, you can check with the customer service department at Alpha Omega Publications to see if they are available.)

Give each student a paper with an open cross shape on it (cardstock paper if possible). Have them color and decorate it to make it special.

Ask them who they think of when they hear about the cross. (Jesus)

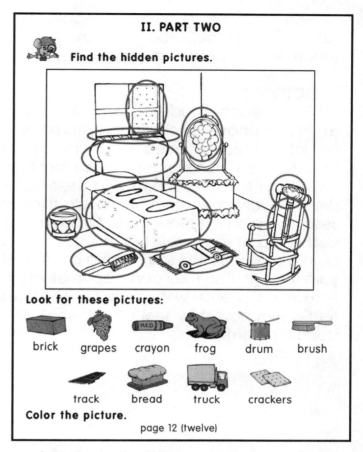

Ask students: "Why was Jesus nailed to the cross?" Give them time for response and discussion.

Tell them the story is about a little boy, Jeffrey-Michael, who wants to know the answer to this question.

Read the story "The Cross" together, then answer the following questions:

"Who is Jeffrey-Michael talking to?" (his mother)

"What did mother say was the reason Jesus was nailed to the cross? (people didn't understand Him)

"Why do you think JM asked if Jesus was mean?" (he may have thought Jesus must have been mean to have such a terrible thing like this happen to Him)

"What was Jesus trying to teach people?" (God and love)

"Did God forgive the people who nailed Jesus to the cross?" (yes)

"Does God forgive us when we do something wrong?" (yes)

"Why?" (because He loves us)

Find long vowel words: (people, nail, Jesus, why, Michael, replied, mean, teach, feeling, confused, ways)

ACTIVITY:

Give each student a nail. With supervision have each student hammer a nail into a piece of wood. Tell them to think about Jesus's sacrifice as they hammer their nail. Help them to understand their nail is like sin. Everytime we sin, we should think of Jesus dying on the cross for us. Punch a hole at the top of the cross students decorated before they read the story. String a piece of yarn through it so they can wear their cross.

Have students write a letter to Jesus telling Him how they feel about what He's done for them.

Page 13: Review Short Vowel Words

CONCEPT: short vowels

TEACHER GOAL: To teach the children
To identify words with short vowels, and
To identify words that look alike but have different meanings.

TEACHING PAGE 13:

Have the children read the direction at the top of the page and the headings in the boxes. Tell them to read each word carefully and to circle those which have the short vowel sounds. Have them say the short vowel sounds. Let the children do the page by themselves.

Check by having the children read the list of words circled in each box. Have them correct any mistakes.

TEACHING READING:

Read the story "Fun With Words" in *Reader 3*.

Note: This page is meant to help children learn that the same word can have several meanings, that sometimes it can be a verb and at other times a noun. Children should learn to really listen to what people are saying and read sentences carefully to be sure they are getting the right meaning of each word that is used.

Have the children read the title. Have them tell where they have seen the same title before (on the Contents page).

Ask a child to tell what it means. Tell the children that on this page they will find that words can be very interesting.

Have the children read the first sentence silently. Then have a child read aloud. Ask where they find bark on a tree.

Have the children read the second sentence silently. Then have a child read it aloud. Ask which word is the same in the first sentence (bark). Ask if it means the same. Ask a child to tell the meaning. Tell the children that the word *bark* has other meanings:

> Circle the words with the short vowel sounds.

short a

⟨can⟩	train	⟨ran⟩
cake	⟨flat⟩	⟨track⟩
⟨plan⟩	plate	snail
⟨band⟩	⟨man⟩	⟨black⟩

short i

⟨pin⟩
⟨sit⟩
pat
bit
bike
⟨him⟩

short e

⟨get⟩
we
⟨pet⟩
⟨went⟩
on
⟨red⟩

short o

⟨on⟩
sat
⟨hot⟩
⟨stop⟩
coat
⟨hot⟩

short u

⟨up⟩
have
⟨run⟩
⟨funny⟩
yes
⟨jump⟩

page 13 (thirteen)

to speak in a very gruff or cross way,
to scrape the skin off your shins,
to cough,
and a ship with three sails.

Ask the children to read the two sentences again and tell in which one *bark* is a noun or naming word and in which one it is a verb or doing word.

Do the other sets of sentences the same way. Other meanings for *cold* which children might use are not friendly and without practice. Other meanings for *train* are long skirt on a wedding gown, any long line of things, and to make a plant go up a wall or trellis.

Have the children read the question at the bottom of the page and give words they know that have more than one meaning.

Examples:

box	play	fly
dress	walk	nail
hand	ring	right
can	band	track

Have children use each meaning of a word in a sentence.

Page 14 : Activity Page

CONCEPT: pronouns

TEACHER GOALS: To teach the children
    To understand the meaning of a
    pronoun, and
    To use pronouns in sentences.

VOCABULARY: pronoun

TEACHING PAGE 14 :

Tell what a pronoun is (a word that is used instead of a name).

Have the children read the direction at the top of the page.

Tell the children to read the sentences carefully and to write one of the words on each line.

Tell the children that the last two sentences are to be done all by themselves. Tell them to think carefully before writing a word on the line. Help the children who seem to be having trouble.

Check by having the children read the sentences. Have them correct any mistakes.

Write the words.

his   their   her

A book that belongs to Jane is __her__ book.

A book that belongs to Dad is __his__ book.

The books that belong to the children are __their__ books.

---

your   my

A book that belongs to me is __my__ book.

A book that belongs to you is __your__ book.

page 14 (fourteen)

Page 15 : Activity Page

CONCEPT: contractions

TEACHER GOALS: To teach the children
To write contractions from words, and
To write words from contractions.

TEACHING PAGE 15:

Have the children read the direction at the top of the page. Tell the children that on the top half of the page they will read the words and write the contraction that can be made by those words, and on the bottom half of the page they will read the contraction and write the words that make up the contraction.

Do the first example in each section with the children, then let them finish the page by themselves.

Check by writing the list on the board and by letting the children check their own papers. The teacher should collect the papers and check them also to see which children still need help with contractions.

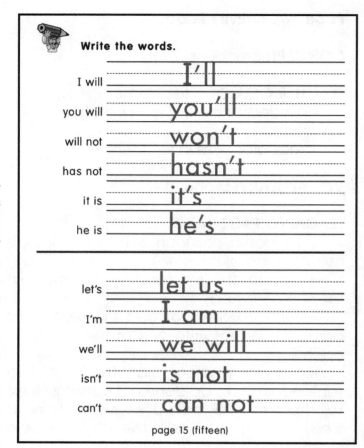

Write the words.

I will	I'll
you will	you'll
will not	won't
has not	hasn't
it is	it's
he is	he's

let's	let us
I'm	I am
we'll	we will
isn't	is not
can't	can not

page 15 (fifteen)

Page 16: Contractions and Sequence

CONCEPTS: sequence, telling a story

TEACHER GOALS: To teach the children
To put three pictures into the order in which they happened,
To tell a story from a series of pictures, and
To write contractions.

TEACHING PAGE 16:

Have the children read the direction at the top of the page. Do the first example together. Have the children read the words, give the contraction, and write it on the lines. Write the correct contraction on the board so the children may check their work. Let the children do the other three items one at a time. Write each on the board for children to check. Point out to the children that in the third and fourth items, the contraction is given and they are to write the words.

Read the direction with the children.

Tell them to look at the three pictures carefully and to point to the one that shows what happened first. Write the number *1* under that picture. Have them point to the picture that shows what happened next and write the number *2* on the line. Write the number *3* under the picture that shows what happened last. Tell the children that first, next, and last is the same as first, second, and third because each series has three pictures.

Let the children finish the page independently. Help the children who seem to be having difficulty. Check by having the children tell which picture is first, next, and last in each series. (Row 1: 1,2,3 Row 2: 1,3,2)

Have the children tell the stories from the pictures. Ask the children to give a title for each story. Ask what has happened before and what might happen after each series. Ask them to tell where each story might have happened.

Write the contraction or words.

he will	he'll
have not	haven't
didn't	did not
I'll	I will

Write 1, 2, 3 for first, next, **and** last.

1 2 3

1 3 2

page 16 (sixteen)

TEACHING READING:

Tell students the name of the story they'll read is: "That Buzzing Sound." (This story and several others have been added to the Language Arts 100 series. If your materials do not include this story in a separate reader, you can check with the customer service department at Alpha Omega Publications to see if they are available.)

Write the word "buzz" on the board. Have students take turns saying it as a real sound. Challenge students to think of things which make a buzzing sound. (stove timer, bees, alarm clock, etc.) List their answers on the board. If the list is long enough, put the items in categories. (inside, outside, electric, non-electric, etc.)

Ask them to tell you what they think the buzzing sound will be. (bees most likely)

Read the story "That Buzzing Sound" then answer the following questions:

"Who are the characters in this story?" (Lin Sue and Janie May)

"What are they going to do?" (play a game)

"What kind of day is it?" (warm or hot, maybe summer)

"Where are they going to play the game?" (in the shade, under the old oak tree)

"What stops them from playing?" (the buzzing sound)

"Where do they look first?" (dad's workshop)

"Where do they look second?" (the beehive)

"Were either of those the buzzing sound they heard?" (no)

"What was the buzzing sound?" (the timer on the oven) Have students explain this answer using clues from the story: (they heard a buzzing sound near the front door, Mom took cookies out of the oven, they didn't look anywhere else, they said they were glad they found the buzzing sound.)

Find long vowel words in the story. (nice, place, old, oak, tree, play, game, right, shade, Sue, Janie, May, laid, blanket, know, find, same, bee, peach, beehive, made, inside, time, smiled, gave, plate, take, outside, these, taste)

ACTIVITY:

Have students do a 5 step sequence activity: Direct them to give you the 5 main parts of the story. They should be the following:

1. Playing the game under the old oak.

2. Looking for the buzzing sound in the workshop.

3. Looking for the buzzing sound at the beehive.

4. Finding the buzzing sound in the house.

5. Eating cookies back under the old oak tree.

Use the sequence steps to act out the story in groups of four. Have students illustrate the 5 steps on paper. Talk about special times like these with a friend. Ask how many have helped bake cookies at home. Look up information on bees – the most famous buzzers of all. Have students do mini reports or stories on bees.

Page 17 : Activity Page

CONCEPTS: plurals, alike

TEACHER GOALS: To teach the children
To write plural words that end in *s*,
To learn about plural words that do not follow the *s* rule, and
To tell why some things are alike and why they are different.

MATERIALS NEEDED: Worksheets 3 and 4

TEACHING PAGE 17:
Have a child read the direction at the top of the page. Have the children read the list of words and give the plural for each. Have them write the plurals on the lines. Write them on the board for children to check.

Read the next direction with the children. Read the list of words. Ask the children if they can think of other words that do not change (sheep, quail, your).

Read the last direction with the children. Read the pair of words and point out changes in each. Have the children write the plural of daddy on the lines.

ACTIVITIES:
1. Do Worksheet 3.
Have the children read the direction at the top of the page. Tell them to look at the things in the rows carefully and choose three that are alike in some way. Have them name the pictures in the first row and tell which three are alike (ball, top, blocks). Ask how they are alike (toys). Ask a child to tell why the spoon is different.

Let the children finish the page by themselves. Check by having the children tell which three they circled and why, and why the other thing in the row is different.

(Row 2 - Three things to wear on the body and one to wear on feet.)

(Row 3 - Three things to put on feet and one to put on head.)

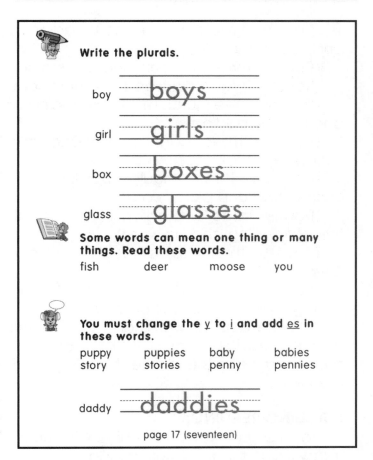

Write the plurals.

boy — boys

girl — girls

box — boxes

glass — glasses

Some words can mean one thing or many things. Read these words.

fish   deer   moose   you

You must change the y to i and add es in these words.

puppy   puppies   baby   babies
story   stories   penny   pennies

daddy — daddies

page 17 (seventeen)

(Row 4 - Three pets and one wild animal.)

(Row 5 - Three fruits and one vegetable.)

(Row 6 - Three children awake and active and one child sleeping.)

2. Do Worksheet 4.
Have the children read the direction at the top of the page.

Tell them to read the words in the first box and to choose the three that are alike in some way (cup, glass, dish). Have them tell how they are alike and why dog is different.

Let the children finish the page by themselves. Move around the room while the children are working and help if needed.

Check by having the children read the three words they circled and tell why they chose them. Have them tell why the other words are not the same.

(Row 2 - Three long *e* rhyming words and one short *i* word.)

(Row 3 - Three plurals made by adding s and one number.)

(Row 4 - Three numbers and one color.)

(Row 5 - Three colors and one number.)

(Row 6 - Three plurals made by adding *es* and one by adding *s*)

(Row 7- Three contractions and one word.)

(Row 8 - Three singular words with y ending and one plural word.)

(Row 9 - Three long *e* rhyming words with the *eet* ending and *oo* word)

(Row 10 - Three possessives and one long *e* word.)

(Row 11 - Three plurals that do not change form and one short *a* word.)

3.   Write a list of words and their plurals on the board such as *child children, man men.* Point out the different endings that are used.

TEACHING READING:

Be sure and wear something with stripes today if possible. If there is a student wearing stripes, do a guessing game with the class. Give them clues about the person (save the stripes for last). If there are several students, vary the game: Give clues but don't mentions stripes. Have all the students you chose stand up and ask the class what they have in common – Stripes! Have students look around the room for things with stripes. Have students think of things that have stripes and list them on the board.

Tell students their story today is called: "I Like Stripes." It is a rhyming story so listen for words that rhyme.

Read the story "I Like Stripes" together, then answer the following questions:

"Who likes stripes?" (the person telling the story – I)

"What animals have stripes?" (tigers, zebra)

"What color are they?" (brown-orange, black-white)

"What food has stripes?" (lollipop, cookies)

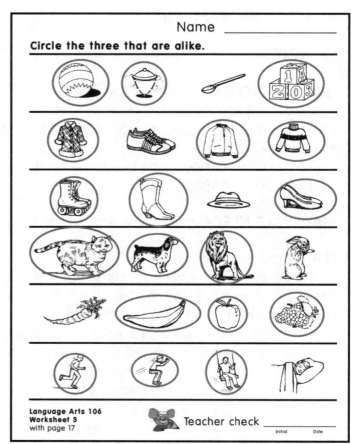

"What color are they?" (rainbow, it doesn't say)

"What other things have stripes?" (flag, popcorn bag, dress)

"What colors are they?" (red-white, purple)

Find the long vowel words (like, stripes, zebra, tiger, white, rainbow, baker's, wide, might). Find the rhyming pairs (black-back, bag-flag, lollipop-shop, dress-guess)

ACTIVITY:

Refer to the list of stripe things students created before reading the story (add any new things from the story). Have students categorize the list (food, animals, people, things). Have students draw a scene with as many striped things in it as possible. (Note: In a scene the objects/people must work together to create the picture.) Give students lengths of yarn or strips of construction paper and have them create a stripe design. Find poetry to share that describes other kinds of things.

Page 18: Activity Page

CONCEPT: plurals

TEACHER GOALS: To teach the children
To change the *y* to *i* before adding *es,*
To change *f* to *v* before adding *es,* and
To learn that some words are the same in singular or plural form.

TEACHING PAGE 18:

Have the children read the direction at the top of the page. Ask what a plural is. Read each of the words and have the children give and spell the plural. Have them write the plural for each of the words on the lines. Write them on the board so that the children may check their spelling. Have them correct any mistakes.

Have the children read the next direction. Read the words in the first column and tell the children that they must change the *y* at the end of these words to *i*, before they add the *es*. Have the children read each pair of words.

Read the words *leaf* and *knife* and tell the children that when the last sound of some words is an /f/ sound, the *f* must be changed to a *v* before the *es* is added. Have the children read the two pairs of words.

Read the word *chief* and tell the children that the *f* in this word is not changed before you add the *s*. Have the children read the two words.

Have the children read all the pairs of words again. Write the plurals for *leaf* and *knife* on the lines. Write them on the board so the children may check their spelling.

Write the plurals for these words.

zebra	house
apple	bee
glass	dish

zebras   houses

apples   bees

glasses   dishes

Read these plurals.

pony	ponies	leaf	leaves
baby	babies	knife	knives
hanky	hankies	chief	chiefs

Write the plurals.

leaf   leaves

knife   knives

page 18 (eighteen)

ACTIVITY:

Dictate these words and have the children write them on a sheet of writing tablet paper.

pony	ponies
baby	babies
leaf	leaves

Write the words on the board so the children may check their spelling.

Page 19: Activity Page

CONCEPTS: titles, plurals, possessives, sequence of events

TEACHER GOALS: To teach the children
To decide what makes a good title,
To find plural and possessive words in sentences, and
To put events in order.

MATERIALS NEEDED: tagboard strips, Worksheet 5

TEACHING PAGE 19:
Have the children read the direction at the top of the page. Ask the children to tell what a title is, and how you decide what would make a good title (A title is the name of the story and should tell the main idea of the story.).

Have the children read the first story silently. Ask a child to tell which title fits the story best. Have the story read aloud, then point out that "Houses" was the best title because that is what the story was about.

Have the children do the rest of the page by themselves. Check by having the children tell which is the best title and why (My Kitten, Leaves, My Mother). Have the stories read aloud.

Have the children tell which of the titles are plurals. Have them find other words in the stories that are plurals.

Ask the children to find the titles that have possessives in them (words which tell that something belongs to someone). Have them write them on a sheet of writing tablet paper (My Dog, etc.). The children should understand that *my* refers to the person who is talking. Have the children read the titles. Have them tell what it is that belongs to the person.

Draw a line under the best title for each story.

We have houses.
Some houses are big.
Some houses are little.
Some houses have trees around them.

Trees
Houses
Cars

I have a pet.
It is a kitten.
My kitten is white.
She likes milk.
She likes to play.

My Dog
My Pets
My Kitten

Trees have leaves.
Leaves can be green.
They can be red,
yellow, or brown.
Leaves fall
from the trees
in the fall.

Trees
Leaves
Colors

My mother helps me.
She makes me
something to eat.
My mother loves me.
I love my mother.

My Father
My Kitten
My Mother

page 19 (nineteen)

ACTIVITIES:
1. Do Worksheet 5.
Have the children read the direction at the top of the page. Tell them to read the sentences carefully, then to write *1* for the first thing that happened, *2* for the second thing that happened, and *3* for the third thing that happened.

Let the children do the entire page by themselves (Row 1: 2, 3, 1; Row 2: 2, 3, 1; Row 3: 3, 1, 2).

2. Have each child write an ownership label for his desk on a strip of tag board (John's desk, Mary's desk, James' desk, etc.). Tape it on the front of the desk so visitors can tell whose desk it is.

Name _____

Write 1, 2, 3 for first, second, and third.

___3___   I ran and ran.

___2___   The bee came after me.

___1___   I saw a bee.

___2___   They take their fish home.

___3___   They eat their fish.

___1___   The boys are fishing.

___3___   I ride my pony fast.

___1___   I have a pony.

___2___   His name is Blackie.

Language Arts 106
Worksheet 5
with page 19

Teacher check _____
                          Initial   Date

Page 20: Tell the Story

CONCEPTS: telling a story, making inferences, predicting outcomes

TEACHER GOALS: To teach the children
To tell a story from a picture,
To make inferences about the picture,
To predict what might happen next in the picture,
To use complete sentences,
To find the main idea of a story,
To note and recall details of stories, and
To speak in a group with confidence.

MATERIALS NEEDED: pictures mounted on tagboard

TEACHING PAGE 20:
Read the title. Have the children repeat it and follow along.

Ask the children to look at the first picture.

Ask questions such as these:
"What is happening in the picture?"
"What do you think is in the box?"
"How does the girl feel?"
"What do you think might have happened just before this picture?"
"What do you think might happen next?"

When the children answer, encourage them to use complete sentences.

Do the same with the other three pictures. Try to get every child to contribute to the discussion.

Let the children choose one of the pictures and write a group story. Write it on the board, then copy it on tagboard for the children to read again.

ACTIVITIES:
1. Paste large pictures of children in many situations on tagboard. Use three or four at a time for the children to tell stories. Some children may be able to write their stories in their writing tablets. Others may dictate their stories to an aide or volunteer.

TELL THE STORY

Tell a story for each picture.

page 20 (twenty)

2. Read stories or books about children doing ordinary everyday things.
3. Use some of the pictures from the Bible booklet to get the children to tell stories.

TEACHING READING:
Ask students to think of BIG things. Have them tell you what they thought of and write it on the board. Categorize the list (animals, buildings, people, etc). Depending on the list, tell students some of the BIG things they thought of will be in their story.

Write these words on the board: dinosaur, whale, hundred, baleen, weigh, earth. Teach students these words before reading the story.

Tell students this story is nonfiction; meaning it tells about something real or true. Pause to get responses after reading the opening question in the story: "Do you know what animal is bigger than any other on earth?

Read the rest of the story "Big Blue" together, then answer the following questions:

"What is the biggest animal on earth?" (the blue whale)

"Is this animal bigger or smaller than the biggest dinosaurs?" (bigger)

"How long is a blue whale?" (100 feet)

"What is 100 feet compared to?" (the length of 3 buses)

"How much can it weigh?" (one hundred tons)

"Do blue whales have teeth?" (no they have baleen)

"What kind of food do blue whales eat?" (tiny fish called krill)

"Why don't we see many blue whales?" (live in the ocean, hunted-few left, accept other reasonable answers)

Find the long vowel words (roamed, alive, blue, whale, weigh, grow, feet, three, teeth, they, baleen, mean, seen, deep, sea, used, day, maybe)

ACTIVITY:

Share additional books about the blue whale. Provide pictures of other kinds of whales. Find a picture which shows the whale's baleen so students will understand how
it is different from teeth.

Take students outside and measure 100 feet to demonstrate the length of the blue whale.

Have students do a water color crayon resist painting of a whale. (Color (heavily) with crayons the objects in the ocean scene, then do a "wash" with blue water color. The paint will resist wherever the crayon is present.)

Do mini whale reports and learn about other whales. Create a 3-D whale using gallon milk or juice jugs.

Write a story about a whale. Choose the setting, characters and problem.

Page 21: Activity Page

CONCEPTS: telephone numbers, verbs

TEACHER GOALS: To teach the children
 To use the telephones with good manners, and
 To identify correct verb forms

VOCABULARY: telephone

MATERIALS NEEDED: real or play telephones, children's phone number

TEACHING PAGE 21:

Have the children read the direction at the top of the page with you. Have each child write his telephone number on the lines. If the child does not know his number, write it on a slip of paper and let him copy it. Have him learn it and tell it to you at later time.

Have the children read the next direction. Tell the children to read each sentence carefully, including the two words under the lines. Have them circle the word that makes sense in the sentence. Have the children read the sentence again using the word they circled to be sure it is right, then copy the word on the lines. Check by having the children read the sentences.

If you have enough telephones, divide the children into their small groups and let them practice conversations they have written, or those you have prepared. Some children may be able to make up their conversations as they go. Encourage the children to use good telephone manners. Have them practice a variety of conversations between adults, children, or children and adults. If you have only two telephones, have them practice before the class. If you are unable to get any telephones at all, let the children pretend they have them.

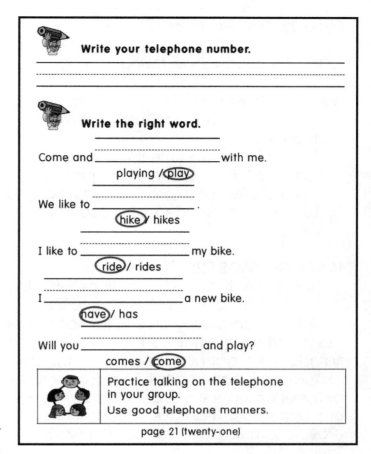

Write your telephone number.

Write the right word.

Come and _____ with me.
 playing / play

We like to _____ .
 hike / hikes

I like to _____ my bike.
 ride / rides

I _____ a new bike.
 have / has

Will you _____ and play?
 comes / come

Practice talking on the telephone in your group.
Use good telephone manners.

page 21 (twenty-one)

Page 22: First, Next, Last

CONCEPTS: sequence, telling a story

TEACHER GOALS: To teach the children
To put three pictures in proper sequence,
To tell a story from the pictures,
To make inferences from the pictures,
To predict what might happen next, and
To tell the main idea of a sequence of pictures.

TEACHING PAGE 22:

Read the title and directions with the children. Discuss each row of pictures.

Ask the children to tell what season of the year it is, what happened just before the first picture, what happened after the third picture, how can you tell it will rain or snow before it actually starts, could you get pears or peaches from an apple tree, and so on (Row 1: 2, 1, 3; Row 2: 3, 2, 1; Row 3: 3, 2, 1; Row 4: 3, 1, 2).

ACTIVITIES:

1. Have children choose one of the sequences and tell a story about it.

2. Some children may write their own stories.

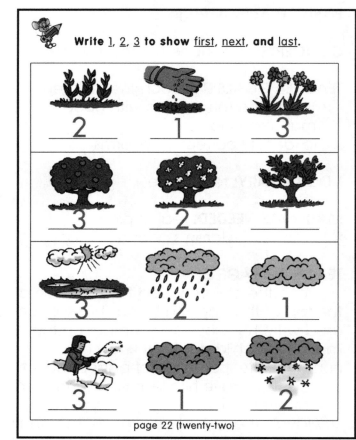

Write 1, 2, 3 to show first, next, and last.

page 22 (twenty-two)

SELF TEST 2

CONCEPTS: contractions, possessives, plurals

TEACHER GOAL: To teach the children
To check their own progress periodically.

TEACHING PAGE 23:

Have the children read the title and tell what it means.

Read all the directions on the page with the children. Be sure they understand everything they are to do on this page. Let them finish the entire page by themselves.

The teacher should check the page as soon as possible. Go over it with the child. Show him what the did well and where he will need to work.

ACTIVITY:

1. Give the children individual help on items missed.

2. If several miss the same kinds of things, work with them in a small group.

SPELLING WORDS:

tar
yarn
herd
term
bird
skirt
for
fort
church
branch

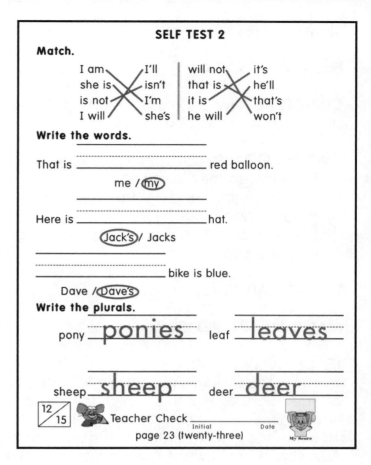

SELF TEST 2

Match.

I am — I'll   will not — it's
she is — isn't   that is — he'll
is not — I'm   it is — that's
I will — she's   he will — won't

Write the words.

_____
That is _____ red balloon.
            me / (my)

_____
Here is _____ hat.
            (Jack's) / Jacks

_____
_____ bike is blue.
            Dave / (Dave's)

Write the plurals.

pony ___ponies___   leaf ___leaves___

sheep ___sheep___   deer ___deer___

12/15   Teacher Check _____
                        Initial   Date
            page 23 (twenty-three)

III. PART THREE

Page 24: I Can Pray

CONCEPTS: saying prayers, leading prayer group, small group discussions

TEACHER GOALS: To teach the children
To make up their own prayers,
To take turns leading the daily prayer group, and
To participate in a small group discussion on what prayers are.

VOCABULARY: pray

MATERIALS NEEDED: Bible

TEACHING PAGE 24:
Have the children read the title and look at the picture. Have a child tell what is happening.

Have the children read the story silently. Ask a child to tell what the first paragraph is about. Ask a child to tell when we should say prayers each day. Have the children tell what we ask God to do. Ask how we know He will be with us if we ask Him to as the Bible says (Matthew 28:20), ". . . and lo, I am with you always, even unto the end of the world."

Have a child tell what the second paragraph is about. Ask how we know God hears our prayers. A discussion on answered and unanswered prayers is good at this point (John 15:7; James 4:3; 1 John 3:22).

Be sure the children understand that our prayers are always heard and are always answered, but not always in the way we might like them to be. God always does what is best for us, not what we want Him to do. Ask why the child says "Thank you" each time he prays.

Have a child read each paragraph aloud.

III. PART THREE
PRAYING

I pray each day.
I ask God to be with me.
I ask God to be with others.
I ask Him to take care of me.

I know Jesus loves me.
I know God hears my prayers.

I say "Thank you" each time I pray.

Pray for someone who is sick or needs help. Tell your group a time you pray at home.

page 24 (twenty-four)

Have the children meet in their small groups after reading the sentences in the box. If you wish, this material may be used for large group discussions. Have the children talk about what prayers are.

ACTIVITIES:
Have the children take turns leading the daily prayer. Encourage them to pray for each other.

Page 25: Activity Page

CONCEPTS: long *e*, pronouns, writing sentences

TEACHER GOALS: To teach the children
To write words with the sound of long *e*,
To identify pronouns, and
To write sentences that make sense with correct punctuation.

TEACHING PAGE 25:
Do this page in the same class period as page 24 if possible.

Have the children read the direction at the top of the page and write the sentence. Let several children read the sentences they have written.

Read the next direction with the children. Tell them to read the story and write the words as they find them. Check by writing the words on the board and having the children check their answers. Have the children read what they have written.

Read the last direction with the children. Tell the children that they should read very carefully and decide who is meant by the words *Him* and *I*. As soon as they know, they should write the names on the lines. Have the children tell what they have written. If they seem to be having trouble, read the sentences aloud and let them tell who is meant. Tell the children that words like these are called *pronouns* and are used instead of saying the noun or name. They mean the same thing as the noun or name.

ACTIVITIES:

1. Write a list of pronouns on the board and have the children use them in sentences.

2. Give a sentence such as "John can run." and have the children give a pronoun that could be used in place of "*John*". Use pronouns such as *I, you, he, him, she, her,* or *they.*

Write a sentence that tells when he prays.

Write the words with the long <u>e</u> sound.

Read the story again.

Him =

I =

page 25 (twenty-five)

---

3. Call attention to pronouns in the children's daily speech. Have the children tell who is meant by the pronoun they are using.

TEACHING READING:
Read the story "Jesus Prays" in *Reader 3.*
The prayer is also found in Matthew 6:9-13.

Tell the children they will be reading a prayer that Jesus prayed.

Have the children talk about the picture. Have them talk abut the clothing and the scenery. Explain the words, *hallowed, debtors, temptation,* and *glory* to the children.

Ask these questions:
"When did Jesus pray this prayer?"
"Who was Jesus talking with in His prayer?"
"What does He want done 'in earth as it is in heaven'?"

"What does He ask about our daily food?"

"Does He want us to forgive others?"

"Where does He ask God to lead us?"

"To whom does Jesus say the kingdom, the power, and the glory belong?"

Have the children read along with you. This story may be difficult for some children. Encourage them to follow along as you read. This will be a good story to come back to again and again.

Page 26: Classification

CONCEPTS: classifying, rhyming words

TEACHER GOALS: To teach the children
To classify pictures and words into groups that are alike in some way,
To tell how the groups are alike, and
To write rhyming words with short *i* and long *e* sounds.

TEACHING PAGE 26:
Put the following rows of words on the board. Have the children read them and tell you which three of the words are alike and how they are alike. Circle the three they chose.

pin	sin	fin	sit	-in
big	pig	pin	wig	-ig
stick	kick	pick	nick	-ick
hat	win	sit	sing	*short i*

Read the first direction with the children. Do the first three rows as a group. Have the children tell why the three are alike. Let them finish the other three rows. Check. Have the children tell why the three words are alike. Row 1: Three things to wear and one container. Row 2: Three parts of the body and one number. Row 3: Three short *i* words and one short *a*. Row 4: Three *ill* endings and one *at*. Row 5: Three capital *T*'s and one lower case *t*. Row 6: Three lower case *s* and one capital *S*.

Have the children read the direction and word endings in the middle of the page and the sentence at the bottom. Have the children give several rhyming words for each pair of endings.

Have the children do the page by themselves and write more rhyming words on the sheet of writing tablet paper. Give help if needed.

Check the first exercise by writing the correct words on the board. Have the

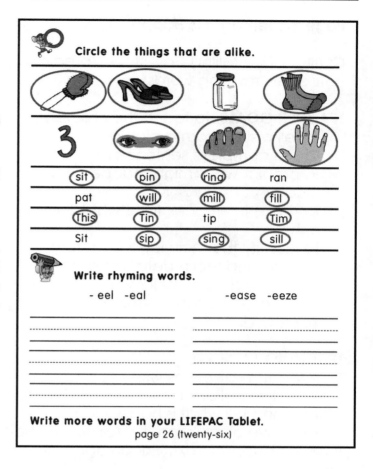

Circle the things that are alike.

sit pin ring ran
pat will mill fill
This Tin tip Tim
Sit sip sing sill

Write rhyming words.
- eel -eal   -ease -eeze

Write more words in your LIFEPAC Tablet.
page 26 (twenty-six)

children check their own papers and correct any mistakes. Have the children read all the words.

Check the rhyming exercise by writing the word endings on the board and by putting the words the children read from their lists under the right ending. Have the children add to and correct their lists. Have them read all the words several times.

The teacher should check this page.

Page 27: Tell What Is Happening

CONCEPTS: telling a story, predicting outcomes, rhyming words

TEACHER GOALS: To teach the children
To tell a story from a picture,
To use complete sentences,
To predict what might happen next in a situation,
To make inferences from what they see or hear,
To identify the main idea of a story,
To note and recall details of a story,
To retell a story in their own words, and
To write words that rhyme with the long /e/ sound.

TEACHING PAGE 27:
Read the directions with the children.
Ask the children to look at the first picture and tell what is happening.
Ask several children to tell what they think will happen next. Encourage different ideas.
Ask questions such as these:
"What do you think happened just before what you see in the picture?"
"What time ot the year is it?"
"What time of the day is it?"
"Is this situation real or a make believe one?"
"Can you tell how old the child (or children) are? How?"
"How do you think the child (or children) feel?"
"How would you feel if this were happening to you?"
Ask the children to think of a good title for each picture. Write several titles on the board and ask the children to read them and to decide which one fits the picture best.
Take time for several children to retell the stories in their own words.

Tell what is happening.
Tell what will happen next.

Write rhyming words.

- een   -ean   -eem   -eam

Write more words in your LIFEPAC Tablet.
page 27 (twenty-seven)

Have the children read the next direction and say the word endings. Have them give rhyming words for each. Have them write on the lines two words for each ending. Then have them write more words on a sheet of writing tablet paper. Check by writing the endings on the board and by putting words the children read from their lists under them. Have the children add to and correct their lists. Have the children read the lists from the board several times. Collect the papers and check them. Have the children correct any mistakes.

ACTIVITIES:
1. Write a sentence on the board and have the children give a sentence that rhymes with it.

Example: This is a bean. (It is big and green.) (Give it to Jean.) (Is it clean?)

Example: We have a team.
(It's on the beam.)
(That was our dream.)

2.   Dictate the following words and have the children write them on a sheet of writing tablet paper.

seen   mean   clean   cream
seem   team   steam
green   bean   dream

(Use each word in a sentence so the children will know which spelling to use for words that sound the same.)

Collect the papers and correct by drawing a line through the incorrect spelling and by writing the correct spelling behind it. Have the children write each misspelled word five times on the back of the paper.

TEACHING READING:

Do not reveal the name of the story yet. Let each student choose a piece of colored construction paper (approx. 4" x 6"). Talk about what most fish typically look like. It would help to have books to look at the variety of colors fish can be. Have students draw, color, paint or glue tissue paper to create a fish on their paper. Collect students' work and display.

Tell students their story is nonfiction. It's about a special kind of fish. This fish doesn't look like most fish and it's name doesn't sound like a fish.

Write these words on the board: catfish, toadfish, whiskers, ocean, wondered, pouch, horse

Read the story "A Sea Horse is a Fish" together, then answer the following questions:

"What kind of fish has whiskers like a cat?" (catfish)

"What kind of fish has a wide mouth like a toad?" (a toad fish)

"Why is it hard to think of a sea horse as a fish?" (fish isn't in it's name, doesn't look like a fish)

"Why is it called a sea horse?" (It's head looks like a horse)

"What does it have that other fish have?" (gills and fins)

"How is a sea horse different from most fish?" (pouch, long tail, hard outer body)

Find long vowel words (maybe, like, toad, wide, easy, these, they, names, sea, closely, see, even, might, babies, tail, weed, bony, change, may, know, really)

ACTIVITY:

Write these headings on the board: Pouch – Long Tail – Bony Outer Body

Have students think of other animals that could be listed under each heading, (i.e. kangaroo, monkey, turtle). Share additional books on sea horses for information and pictures.

Do an acrostic poem: Write SEA HORSE vertically. Have students (whole group or small groups) think of words or phrases which begin with each letter that would tell more about a sea horse. If done in small groups, allow time for sharing.

Write a story: "If I were a sea horse…"(or choose another story starter).

Provide additional books on fish. Do mini reports on fish. Share fiction stories such as "The Rainbow Fish".

Page 28: Tell What Is Happening

CONCEPTS: telling a story, predicting outcomes, rhyming words, pronouns

TEACHER GOALS: To teach the children
　　To tell a story from a picture,
　　To use complete sentences,
　　To predict what might happen next in a situation,
　　To make inferences from what they see or hear,
　　To identify the main idea of a story,
　　To identify and write rhyming words,
　　To note and recall details of a story,
　　To retell a story in their own words, and
　　To write words that rhyme with the long /e/ sound.

MATERIALS NEEDED: pictures, tagboard

TEACHING PAGE 28:
　　Read the directions with the children.
　　Ask the children to look at the first picture and tell what is happening.
　　Ask several children to tell what they think will happen next. Encourage different ideas.
　　Have the children read the next direction and the endings. Have them give several rhyming words for each. Have the children write two of the words on the lines, then write the rest on a sheet of writing tablet paper.
　　Check by having the children read words from their lists for you to put under the right endings on the board. Have the children add to or correct their lists. Read the lists several times. Add words which the children do not have, especially those beginning with consonant blends.

ACTIVITIES:
　　1.　Mount large pictures that tell a story on tagboard. Display two or three and

Tell what is happening.
Tell what will happen next.

Write rhyming words.

- eet　-eat　　　　　　-eech　-each

Write more words in your LIFEPAC Tablet.
page 28 (twenty-eight)

have the children tell the story, including what went before and what will happen next.
　　2.　The children may write their stories or dictate them to an aide or volunteer.

TEACHING READING:
　　Find "My Little Black Pony" in *Reader 3*.
　　Read the title and sentences at the top of the page with the children and talk about them.
　　Have the children read the title of the story and tell what the story will be about. Have them read the story silently.
　　Ask the following questions:
　　"What is the pony's name?"
　　"What color is he?"
　　"What does he eat and why?"
　　"What do the boy and his pony do?"
　　"Where do they ride?"
　　"How does the boy feel about his pony?"

"What do you think the boy does with the pony after their ride?"

"Are apples and grass the only things the pony eats?"

"What is the boy's name?"

"How old do you think the boy is?"

"Where do you think the boy lives?"

"Could this story really happen?"

Have the children find all the words with the long /e/ sound and underline them.

Have the children find words with the short vowel sounds.

Ask how many paragraphs are in the story. Have different children read each paragraph. As the children read each paragraph, ask what the main idea of the paragraph is.

Have the child read the entire story. Ask what the main idea of the story is.

ACTIVITIES:

1.   Have several children tell the story in their own words.

2.   Read stories about ponies or horses.

Page 29: Activity Page

CONCEPTS: recalling details, pronouns, writing stories

TEACHER GOALS: To teach the children
    To recall details from a story,
    To identify pronouns in a story, and
    To write a story using good sentences, correct spelling, good handwriting and to write a title.

VOCABULARY: right

MATERIALS NEEDED: drawing paper, crayons or paints

TEACHING PAGE 29 :
Read the story "My Little Black Pony" in *Reader 3*.

Read the direction at the top of the page with the children. Have them read each sentence silently and write in the words from the story that make the sentence correct. Check by having a child read each sentence. Children should correct any mistakes.

Read the next direction with the children. Tell what a pronoun is (a word that is used instead of a name). Have the children read "My Little Black Pony" again and write the pronouns on the lines as they find them. Write them on the board and have the children check what they have written. Have them correct any mistakes. Have the children tell for whom the pronouns stand.

Have the children read the directions at the bottom of the page. Be sure they understand what they are to do before they begin writing the story. Talk about each sentence.

Correct each child's story as he finishes it. Draw one line through the misspelled word and write the correct word above it. Have the child copy the story over in his best handwriting. Take one or two class

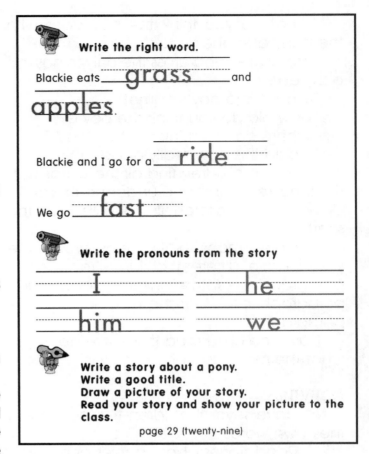

Write the right word.

Blackie eats __grass__ and __apples__.

Blackie and I go for a __ride__.

We go __fast__.

Write the pronouns from the story

__I__   __he__

__him__   __we__

Write a story about a pony.
Write a good title.
Draw a picture of your story.
Read your story and show your picture to the class.

page 29 (twenty-nine)

periods for the children to read their stories and show their pictures. Remind them of the rules for telling or reading stories before they begin.

ACTIVITIES:
Read more stories about ponies or horses.

TEACHING READING:
Ask students what kind of things horses do (give rides, rodeos, work on farms, pull carts, race, etc). List their responses on the board. Have each student draw a picture of a horse "doing" something listed. Divide the list so there are as many different things as possible. Assemble the squares as a quilt and display. Ask students if a sea horse is a horse. (no, it is a fish)

Tell them they'll read another story that tells them more about the sea horse. (nonfiction)

Ask these questions BEFORE reading this time: (You may want to write them on the board).

"What kind of swimmer is a sea horse?"

"Their back fin is like a _____."

"Where do sea horses spend most of their time?"

"How often do sea horses eat?"

Read the story "A Sea Horse is Not a Race Horse" together, then go back and get answers to the questions. (not good swimmers, motor, in the middle of seaweed, all the time)

Ask additional questions:

"How do sea horses move?" (they drift in the water)

"Do sea horses go all over the ocean?" (no, they stay close to home)

"What do they use their tail for?" (wrap around seaweed)

"How did Cindy feel after he told her about sea horses?" (disappointed, discouraged)

"Why didn't Cindy want to be a sea horse anymore?" (wasn't fun sitting all the time)

Find long vowel words (race, sea, Peter, over, ocean, whales, seals, no, why, she, like, dream, go, sometimes, use, motor, tired, takes, time, stay, close, home, most, seaweed, tail, weed, while, eat, meal, way, oh, feel, by, quietly, see)

ACTIVITY:

Put long vowel headings on the board (a, e, i, o, u). Have students work in pairs to put the list of words under each heading. Give each student: a blue piece of background paper, a smaller brown piece of paper and strips of green crepe or tissue paper. Have them create an ocean scene with: a sea horse sitting in the seaweed. Glue onto the blue background piece. Encourage them to add other details with other colored paper or crayons. Ask students why they think Cindy changed her mind to an octopus. Have them write about their reasons.

Write a story about Cindy the Octopus. (What does she look like? What does she do? Who does she see? etc)

Page 30: Activity Page

CONCEPT: following directions

TEACHER GOALS: To teach the children
To follow directions, and
To recall some rules from earlier lessons.

MATERIALS NEEDED: crayons

TEACHING PAGE 30:
Tell the children to look at the picture and find the following things. Have them put their fingers on them when they find them.

Something whose name ends in the long /e/ sound. (Blackie or pony)

Something in which the long /e/ sound is spelled *ie*. (field)

Something that begins with *st*. (store)

Something in which the /k/ sound is spelled *ch*. (school)

Something that has an r-controlled vowel. (corral, store, river, start) Something that is a plural. (trees, apples)

Two things that begin with *tr*. (tractor, trees, trough)

An exclamation point. (on the store)

A word with the *sh* sound. (finish)

Something with the soft /g/ sound. (bridge)

ACTIVITIES:
1.   Color the picture and take it home.
2.   Have the children tell a story from the picture.

Help Blackie get an apple.

page 30 (thirty)

Page 31: Activity Page

CONCEPT: subject-verb agreement

TEACHER GOAL: To teach the children
To select and write singular or plural verbs.

VOCABULARY: correct

TEACHING PAGE 31:

Have the children read the direction at the top of the page. Tell them to read each sentence carefully, including the two words under the lines. Tell them to circle the word that makes sense in the sentence, then read the sentence again to be sure they are right. Then tell them to write the word on the line.

Let the children complete the page by themselves. Check by having the children read the completed sentences. Have them correct any mistakes.

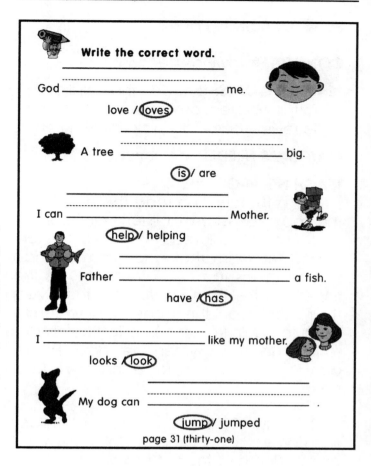

Write the correct word.

God _____ me.
love /(loves)

A tree _____ big.
(is)/ are

I can _____ Mother.
(help)/ helping

Father _____ a fish.
have /(has)

I _____ like my mother.
looks /(look)

My dog can _____ .
(jump)/ jumped

page 31 (thirty-one)

Page 32: Activity Page

CONCEPT: following directions

TEACHER GOALS: To teach the children
To follow directions, and
To review cardinal and ordinal numbers.

MATERIALS NEEDED: crayons

TEACHING PAGE 32:

Have the children read the direction at the top. Tell them to listen very carefully because you will read the directions only once. Tell them that each item will have several things to do. Have them put their fingers on the numbers to help them keep their places on the page and to remind them to begin from the left. Tell the children to look up at you when they have finished drawing the shapes for each row. Read slowly.

Read:

1. Draw 10 circles. (Pause until children finish drawing the circles.) Color the first six circles blue and the last four yellow.

2. Draw 9 squares. (Pause) Color the first, third, fifth, seventh, and ninth squares black.

3. Draw 8 triangles. (Pause) Put green X's on the second, fourth, sixth, and eighth triangles.

4. Draw 7 ovals. (Pause) Draw a red line under the first four ovals. Color the last three purple.

5. Draw 6 rectangles. (Pause) Put a brown X above the first rectangle and an orange circle above the last rectangle. Color the two rectangles in the middle green.

6. Draw 3 large and 2 small circles. (Pause) Put orange X's inside the large circles, and a purple line around the outside of the small circles .

7. Draw 4 squares. (Pause) Color half of each square blue.

8. Draw 3 ovals. (Pause) Put a black square inside the first oval, and a brown X on the third oval.

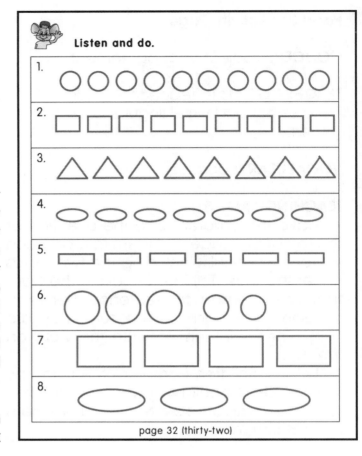

Listen and do.

page 32 (thirty-two)

The teacher should check this page during the class period.

Read the directions over again and have the children look at each row to see if they followed the directions. If several missed the same direction, put examples on the board and let those children do them.

By this time, most children should be able to keep up to four directions in mind without difficulty.

Children who cannot should be given extra help individually or in small groups.

Page 33: Could This Really Happen?

CONCEPTS: real and make-believe, following directions, yes or no

TEACHER GOALS: To teach the children
To read and understand the words *yes* and *no,*
To tell if a pictured situation is real or make-believe, and
To follow directions.

TEACHING PAGE 33:

Write the words *yes* and *no* on the board and ask children to read them. Ask them if they can answer *yes* to a question without saying anything. Ask them to answer *no* without saying anything. Ask if anyone can say *yes* or *no* in another language.

Read the title and direction and have the children repeat. Ask what kind of sentence the title is.

Ask a child to tell what is happening in the first box. Ask the children if this could really happen. How do they know? Have them circle the word *no.*

Tell the children to look at the pictures very carefully. If what they see could really happen, circle the *yes.* If it could not really happen, circle the *no.*

When all have finished marking, have the children tell what is happening in the picture, which word they circled, and why.

ACTIVITIES:

Have the children make up a story for each picture. Include what might have happened before what they see in the picture and what might happen after.

Could this really happen?

Circle yes or no.

yes /(no) yes /(no)

(yes)/ no yes /(no)

(yes)/ no (yes)/ no

page 33 (thirty-three)

SELF TEST 3

CONCEPTS: predicting outcomes, rhyming words, distinguishing between real and make-believe

TEACHER GOAL: To teach the children
To check their own progress periodically.

TEACHING PAGE 34:
Read all the directions on the page with the children. Be sure they understand everything they are to do. Let them do the entire page by themselves.

The teacher should check the page as soon as possible. Go over it with the child. Show him what he did well and where he needs to work.

ACTIVITY:
Give the children individual help on items they missed. If several miss the same things, reteach the skills in small groups.

SPELLING WORDS:

cart
barn
chirp
third
torn
worn
born
fur
trip
trap

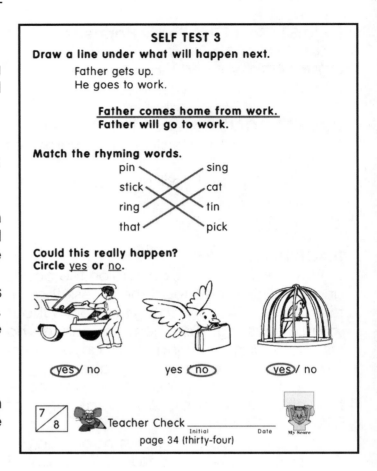

LIFEPAC TEST AND ALTERNATE TEST 106

CONCEPTS: r-controlled vowels, rhyming words, matching contractions, possessives, changing words from singular to plural, and predicting outcomes

TEACHER GOAL: To teach the children
To check their own progress periodically.

TEACHING the LIFEPAC TEST:

Administer the test to the class as a group. Ask to have directions read or read them to the class. In either case, be sure that the children clearly understand. Put examples on the board if it seems necessary. Give ample time for each activity to b completed before going on to the next.

Dictation Sentence-(Write the sentence.)
Bill will stir the corn.

Correct the test immediately and discuss it with the child.
Review any concepts that have been missed.
Give those children who do not achieve the 80% score additional copies of the worksheets and a list of vocabulary words to study. A parent or a classroom helper may help in the review.
When the child is ready, give the Alternate LIFEPAC Test. Use the same procedure as for the LIFEPAC Test. (turtle, ladder, skirt, church)

Dictation Sentence for Alternate LIFEPAC Test-(Write the sentence.)
Will Jill stir the corn?

LANGUAGE ARTS 1 0 6

LIFEPAC TEST

32/40

Name _____
Date _____
Score _____

SPELLING WORDS:

LIFEPAC words	Alternate words
car	cart
star	barn
herd	her
term	germ
stir	chirp
bird	third
corn	torn
born	worn
fur	church
	trip

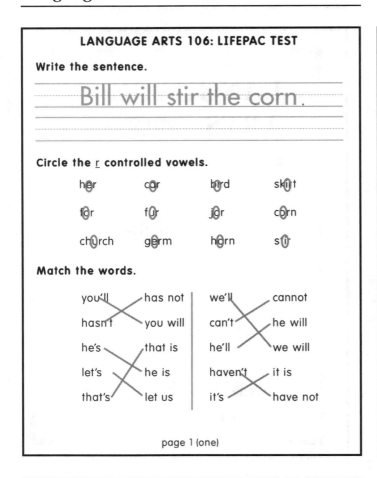

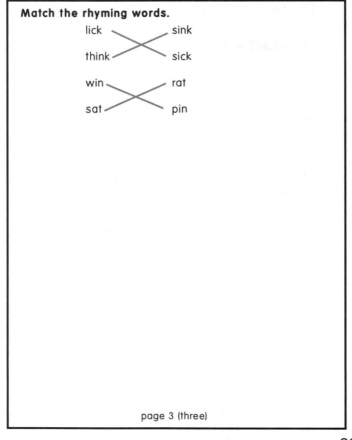

LANGUAGE ARTS 1 0 6

ALTERNATE LIFEPAC TEST

30/38

Name _____
Date _____
Score _____

LANGUAGE ARTS 106
ALTERNATE LIFEPAC TEST

Circle the pictures with the <u>er</u>, <u>ir</u>, <u>ur</u> sound.

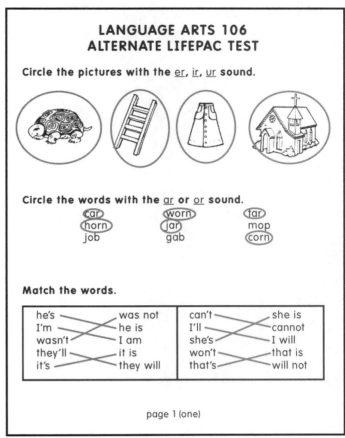

Circle the words with the <u>ar</u> or <u>or</u> sound.

(car)   (worn)   (tar)
(horn)   (jar)   mop
job   gab   (corn)

Match the words.

he's	was not
I'm	he is
wasn't	I am
they'll	it is
it's	they will

can't	she is
I'll	cannot
she's	I will
won't	that is
that's	will not

page 1 (one)

Draw a line under what will happen next.

Jane is playing with her dolls.
Jane's mother is calling her for dinner.
Jane will play with her dolls.
Jane will go to mother.

Write the plurals.

puppy — puppies   story — stories

Write the plurals.

baby — babies   leaf — leaves

sheep — sheep   deer — deer

Write the words.

May's house is yellow.
Mays / May's

Is that ___your___ dog?
you / your

page 2 (two)

Match the rhyming words.

pick — nick
rat — mat
thank — sank
bin — sin

Write the sentence.

Will Jill stir the corn?

page 3 (three)

87

Page 1: FUN WITH WORDS

CONCEPT: purpose of LIFEPAC

TEACHER GOALS: To teach the children
To understand what will be taught in
Language Arts LIFEPAC 107 and
To understand what will be expected of
him in this LIFEPAC.

TEACHING PAGE 1:

Read the page as the children following
along. Talk about each sentence as you
read it so the children understand everything
they will be doing in this LIFEPAC.

Have the children tell what objectives
are and why they need them.

FUN WITH WORDS

You can have fun and learn
by listening, reading, and writing.

In this LIFEPAC
you will learn about vowel digraphs.
You will learn about word endings.
You will learn to spell and
to write more words.
You will learn to write better sentences.
You will learn to write letters and invitations.

 Objectives

1. I can learn words with vowel digraphs.
2. I can write words with new endings.
3. I can tell what comes next in a story.
4. I can tell how many syllables a word has.
5. I can put things in order.
6. I can spell many new words.
7. I can write a good story.

page 1 (one)

I. PART ONE

Page 2: Activity Page

CONCEPTS: Vowel digraphs *ei, ai* and *ay*

TEACHER GOALS: To teach the children

To learn that two vowels together are called vowel digraphs,

To say the long /a/ sound in vowel digraphs *ai, ay,* and *ei,*

To learn that vowel digraph *au* has the sound of *aw,* and

To recall that silent *e* makes the vowel long.

TEACHING PAGE 2:

Read the sentence and the direction at the top of the page with the children. Tell the children to listen for the sound of long *a* in each word.

Tell the children that they have been reading the long vowel words with two vowels together. These are called Vowel Digraphs. Sometimes the two vowels will have a long sound, sometimes another sound. Have them circle every word that has two vowels together. Tell them that in the *ay* words, *y* acts as a vowel. Read the list of *ay* words, then read it a second time and have the children repeat each word after you. Ask which part of the word rhymes.

Do the same for each list of rhyming words. Call attention to the words *they* and *obey* that rhyme with the *ay* words but are spelled differently, to the word *wait* that is different from the *ate* words, and to the words *tale* and *whale* that are different from the *ail* words.

Have the children read the sentence. Discuss the meanings of the vowel digraph *haul.*

Have the children read the direction at the bottom of the page. Tell them to circle all the words that have the sound of long *a.* Check by having the children tell which words they circled.

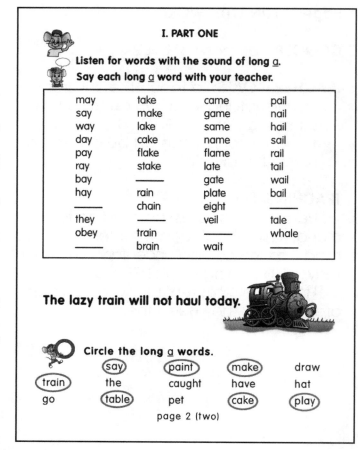

ACTIVITIES:

1. Practice the a, ai, ay, ei, ey, sounds. Be sure they are added to the cards for drill.

TEACHING READING:

Read "Sisters" in *Reader 4.*

Ask the children how many of them have a brother or a sister. Have several children tell about their relationships. Do they get along with their brother or sister? Do they fight?

Have the children read the story silently.

Ask questions similar to these:

"What are some of the things that the sister helps her to do?"

"Is the sister kind to her younger sister?"

"Do the sisters play together?"

"What is a tale?"

"When do the sisters tell tales?"

"Does the sister help her to do what is right?"

"How does the younger sister show her thanks?"

Have the children find the vowel digraph words in the story. Remind them that a vowel digraph will have two vowels together.

Have the children find the words with *ay, ai and ey.* Have them find the long vowel words that end in silent *e.*

TEACHING READING:

Ask children to share what they like to do with Grandma (or Grandpa). Take a poll to see how many have grandmas who live out of state. How many have gone to visit? Does Grandma come to visit you? Share feelings about these visits.

Give students a cloud shaped paper. (Put a plane in the sky.) Have students write one sentence telling their favorite thing to do with their Grandma. (If they don't have a grandma, substitute with another relative.) Display students sentences on sky background.

Show students 3 cut-out dolls: Julie, Grandma Joan and Aunt Sue. Tape the characters to the blackboard so they can be seen. Tell students these are characters mentioned in our story: "Waiting for Grandma".

Write these words on the board and discuss their meaning: replied, exclaimed, flight, delayed, patient, suggested, idea

Read the story "Waiting for Grandma" together, then answer the following questions:

"What is Julie doing?" (waiting for her grandma)

"Who is with her?" (Aunt Sue)

"Where are they waiting?" "How do you know?" (home; later she gets her paints and paper)

"Why is Grandma Joan going to be late?" (it's raining, her flight is delayed)

"How is Julie feeling?" (anxious, impatient)

"What does Aunt Sue suggest she do?" (paint a picture)

"Does Julie like this idea?" "How do you know?" (yes; she had a big smile, "I like that idea.")

Find long a and long i words: (wait, cried, five, plane, fly, rain, flight, delayed, rain, patient, while, trying, why, paint, arrives. like, time, smile)

ACTIVITY:

Go back to the cut-out dolls. Ask students to help you describe each character. Julie: girl, young, anxious, listener... Aunt Sue: older, woman, patient, helpful, kind... Grandma Joan: we don't know about Grandma yet, ...next story!

Give students their own cut-out dolls and have them create the characters. Have students act out the story with the dolls.

Write letters to Grandma or another favorite relative (send them home to be mailed!)

Have students bring in pictures of their grandmas to share.

Get out the paints and have students paint a picture for their grandma (or other relative).

Sing the song: "Mr. Sun" (Raffi) and "Rain, Rain Go Away" (add or change the words to fit the situation) i.e. Rain, rain go away. I want my grandma to come to day.

Page 3: Compound Words

CONCEPTS: compound words, vowel digraphs *ai* and *ay*

TEACHER GOALS: To teach the children
To understand, use, and write compound words, and
To find words with vowel digraphs *ai* and *ay*.

TEACHING PAGE 3:

Read the direction at the top of the page with the children. Have the children read the compound word, and write it on the lines.

When they have finished writing the words, ask them to tell what the words mean and why they think those words were put together.

Have the children read the sentence. Is the sentence real or make-believe? Have them circle any words that include the vowel digraph *ai.*

TEACHING READING:

Carry over activities from the last story. Have students share their paintings and talk about what they painted. Display their paintings. Tape the character cut-out dolls on the blackboard again.

Tell students this is a continuation of the last story they read. Write these words on the board and discuss their meaning: beautiful, special, bright, afternoon, airport, suitcases

Read the story "Julie's Painting" together, then answer the following questions:

"How long did Julie paint?" (an hour)

"What did she paint?" (a rainbow)

"Why did Julie paint a rainbow?" (they made her smile, she wanted Grandma to smile, too)

"What color is on the top of a rainbow?" the bottom? (red, purple)

Write these compound words.

play + mate
playmate

hay + stack
haystack

pay + day
payday

See what happens to my braids.....

when I am afraid!!!

page 3 (three)

"When did Grandma Joan call to say she was at the airport?" (the afternoon)

"Where was Grandma waiting?" (by a bench)

"What did Julie do when she saw Grandma?" (raced down the sidewalk, gave her a bear hug)

"How was she feeling?" (happy, excited)

"What is a bear hug?" (a big hug)

"Did Grandma like Julie's painting?" (yes)

"How do you know?" (she smiled)

Find long a and long i words: painting, rainbow, make, smile, bright, liked, everytime, outside, sky, later, waiting, excited, arrived, raced, sidewalk, gave, replied, gave)

ACTIVITY:

Using from both stories categorize the long a and long i words by phonetic rule.

Give students large pieces of white paper and all the paint colors of the rainbow. Starting with red on top take them through painting a rainbow with the colors in the correct order. Have them cut out their rainbows when dry and glue onto a blue background. Have students get in groups of 3 and role play the two stories.

Have students draw diagrams of an airport. Label the important areas. Make paper airplanes and have a flying contest. Inquire whether your local airport gives organized tours and plan a field trip to the airport.

Page 4: Activity Page

Concepts: vowel digraph *ee,* compound words

TEACHER GOALS: To teach the children
   To say the long /e/ sound in words that have the vowel digraph *ee,* and
   To write words with the long /e/ sound.

TEACHING PAGE 4:
   Read the sentence and direction at the top of the page with the children or have a child read them. Read the letters and ask the children to say the long /e/sound.
   Have the children read each list of words. Ask the children to tell how the words are alike. Have them give the ending for each list. Have the children circle the vowel digraphs.
   Read the next direction with the children. Have them read the first two words and tell what the compound word is. Have them write it on the lines. Ask a child to tell what a wheelchair is.

ACTIVITIES:
   1.   Have the children put together word endings on their desks with alphabet cards. (Have the children make extra vowel cards so they can spell words with double vowels.) Read a word from the list on page 4 and have the children put the beginning sound in front of the correct ending. Have them say the word and spell it before giving the next word.
   2.   Add *ee* to the drill cards.
   3.   Dictate the following words and have the children write them on a sheet of writing tablet paper.

be	glee
he	see
me	wee
we	Lee
she	tree

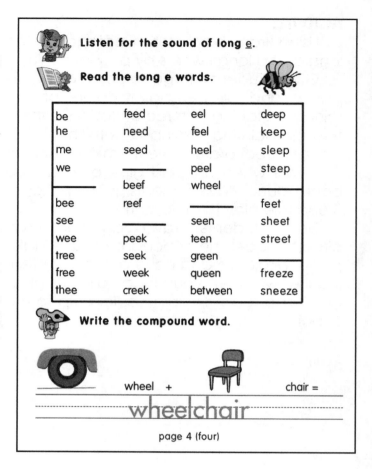

Listen for the sound of long <u>e</u>.

Read the long e words.

be	feed	eel	deep
he	need	feel	keep
me	seed	heel	sleep
we	————	peel	steep
	beef	wheel	
bee	reef		feet
see	————	seen	sheet
wee	peek	teen	street
tree	seek	green	
free	week	queen	freeze
thee	creek	between	sneeze

Write the compound word.

_____   wheel   +   chair =   _____

wheelchair

page 4 (four)

Have the children write the misspelled words five times on the back of the paper.

TEACHING READING:
   Read the story "Sheep" in *Reader 4.*
   Have the children look at the picture. Have them tell about the man holding the sheep.   Have several children tell if the sheep look healthy.
   Have the children read the story silently. *Ask these questions:*
   "Are the sheep happy?"
   "Does the shepherd feed the sheep?"
   "How do you think he keeps them safe?"
   "What might harm the sheep?"
   "Where do you think the sheep will sleep?"
   "How do the sheep act?"
   "Do you think the shepherd is fond of his sheep?"
   Have the children find the words that end in *y* and have the long /e/ sound. Write the words on the board.

Page 5: Activity Page

CONCEPTS: vowel digraphs *ea, ie, ee*

TEACHER GOALS: To teach the children
To say the long e sound in words that have the vowel digraphs *ea, ee,* and *ie,* and
To write words with the long e sound

MATERIALS NEEDED: Worksheet 1

TEACHING PAGE 5:
Add *ea, ie, ee* to the drill cards. Have the children practice the long /e/ sound.

Read the sentence and the direction at the top of the page with the children or have a child read them.

Read the letters and ask the children to give the sound of long e. Have the children read each list of words. Have them give more rhyming words for each list. Have them tell where they hear the sound of long e. Point out that some of the words on this page may sound just like words on page 4. Tell the children that the words sound the same, but are spelled differently and have different meanings. Write several pairs on the board to illustrate. (meet - meat, week - weak)

Have the children give the ending for each list. Have them circle the vowel digraphs.

Read the letters at the bottom of the page. Tell the children these letters also have the sound of long e. Read the words in the box and have the children tell where they hear the sound of long e.

ACTIVITIES:
1. Have the children put together the endings on their desks with alphabet cards. Read a word from the list on page 5 and have children put the beginning letter in front of the ending. Have them say the word and spell it before giving the next word.

2. Do Worksheet 1.

Read the direction at the top of the page or have a child read it. Read the

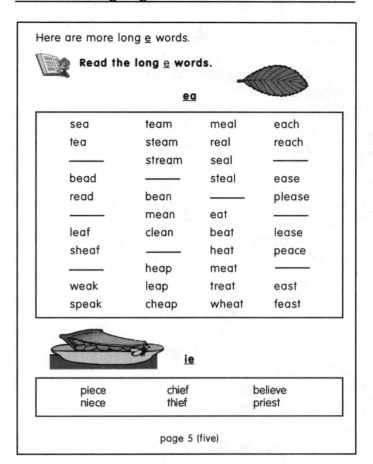

Here are more long e words.

Read the long e words.

ea

sea	team	meal	each
tea	steam	real	reach
——	stream	seal	
bead	——	steal	ease
read	bean	——	please
——	mean	eat	——
leaf	clean	beat	lease
sheaf	——	heat	peace
——	heap	meat	——
weak	leap	treat	east
speak	cheap	wheat	feast

ie

| piece | chief | believe |
| niece | thief | priest |

page 5 (five)

endings and have the children give several rhyming words for each. Call attention to the different spellings for the same sound. Have the children write the rhyming words on the lines, then prepare the sheet of writing tablet paper and put it aside until the worksheet is finished. Have them fold the sheet of paper in half lengthwise, then write the endings at the top.

Have a child read the next direction. Have the children read the four words. Ask them to tell where they hear the long /e/ sound and what the words mean. Have them write the words on the line. Check by having the children read the sentence with the word.

Let the children finish writing the rhyming words. Check by writing the endings on the board and writing words the children give under them. Have the children spell each word after they give it. Have the children add to and correct their lists.

TEACHING READING:

Play "Hide the Object" in the classroom. Send one student out and hide an object. He/she will be the "Finder". Bring the student back in. Tell the "Finder" the class will sing a song (your choice or theirs) while he/she is looking for the object. The class sings louder as the Finder gets close and softer as he/she gets further away.

Take turns choosing a Finder and letting students hide the object.

Tell students today's story is about two brothers, Steven and Taylor. Write their names on the board. Write these words and discuss their meaning: object, decide, clues, piece, fruit, laughs, raisins

Read the story "Steven and Taylor" together, then answer the following questions:

"What game are the boys playing?" (Find the Object)

"Who is older?" (Steven)

"How old is Taylor?" (three)

"How old is Steven?" (eleven)

"How does Steven feel about his little brother?" (enjoys him, thinks he's smart)

"What does Steven do after they play games?" (fixes a snack)

"What is today's snack?" (green grapes)

"Why does Taylor say "gween gwapes"?" (he can't say the r sound)

"Where does Taylor go to eat his snack today?" (outside on the grass)

"What happens?" (Taylor falls asleep)

"Why does Steven say "Maybe tomorrow we'll have 'waisins'"?" (he knows grapes dry out in the sun and turn into raisins, he's talking like Taylor would say it).

Find long e, long a and long i words: (Steven, Taylor, play, games, like, find, decide, hide, sometimes right, away, being, three, might, cheese, piece, green, grapes, "gween", "gwapes", pail, say, he, eat, these, okay, me, please, stay, later, peeked, asleep, smile, maybe, we, "waisins" raisins)

Worksheet

Name _____

Write rhyming words.

_____eed	_____ead	_____eek	_____eak

Write more rhyming words in your LIFEPAC Tablet.

Write the words.

feet	bee	beak	read

I can _____ see _____ .

A _____ bee _____ can sting.

A bird has a _____ beak _____ .

I have two _____ feet _____ .

Language Arts 107
Worksheet 1
with page 5

Teacher check _____
Initial   Date

ACTIVITY:

Have a game day! Students can bring their favorite game to school. Set aside time to allow them to play the games with each other. Serve green grapes and raisins for snacks!

Do a scientific experiment with the green grapes. (Depends on time of year and climate.) Set grapes in a warm, sunny spot and chart how many days it takes for the grapes to become raisins.

Read stories about Arthur and D.W. (big brother-little sister) by Marc Brown. Have students write stories about their younger or older siblings. If a student is an only child, have he/she write about a younger or older friend.

Page 6: Activity Page

CONCEPTS: alike and different, vowel digraphs *ee* and *ie*

TEACHER GOALS: To teach the children
    To tell what is alike and what is different, and
    To read words with vowel digraphs *ee* and *ie*.

TEACHING PAGE 6:

Have the children read the direction at the top of the page. Tell the children to look for three words in each box that are alike in some way (at the beginning, at the end, as the same kind of thing, or as having the same vowel sound). Remind them to read all four words before they circle three. Check by having the children read the three they circled in each box.

Have the children read the next direction and the three words. Ask what the vowel sound is in all the words. Tell the children to read the sentences carefully, to look at the word in the dark print, then to find the word that rhymes with the dark word and to copy it on the line. Remind them to read the sentence over again to be sure the word they wrote makes sense in the sentence. Check by having the children read the sentences aloud.

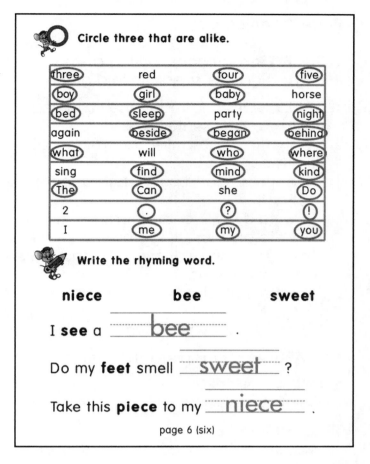

Circle three that are alike.

(three)	red	(four)	(five)
(boy)	(girl)	(baby)	horse
(bed)	(sleep)	party	(night)
again	(beside)	(began)	(behind)
(what)	will	(who)	(where)
sing	(find)	(mind)	(kind)
(The)	(Can)	she	(Do)
2	(.)	(?)	(!)
I	(me)	(my)	(you)

Write the rhyming word.

niece   **bee**   **sweet**

I **see** a ___bee___ .

Do my **feet** smell ___sweet___ ?

Take this **piece** to my ___niece___ .

page 6 (six)

Page 7: Sentences

CONCEPTS: sentences, writing a story, main idea, paragraphs, speaking in a group

TEACHER GOALS: To teach the children
    To tell what a sentence is,
    To write a sentence using good grammar,
    To capitalize and punctuate a sentence correctly,
    To write a well-constructed paragraph,
    To write an interesting story about a kite. The story should be at least three paragraphs long ,
    To write a title that reflects the main idea of the story, and
    To be at ease while speaking in a group.

VOCABULARY: complete, thought

MATERIALS NEEDED: drawing paper, crayons or paint, Worksheet 2

TEACHING PAGE 7:

Read the sentence at the top of the page and talk about it. Give some examples and ask the children to tell whether they are complete thoughts.

Examples:
Where is my
This is fun.
That is a big

Have the children read the directions. Tell them to read the words on each line. If the words are a complete thought or sentence, write *yes* on the lines. If they are not a sentence, write *no* on the lines. Let them do the exercise, then check by having the children read each line and tell if it is a complete sentence. Have the children correct any mistakes.

Have the children read the parts of sentences and make complete sentences out of them.

Have the children read the directions at the bottom of the page silently. Ask one or

---

> A sentence must be a complete thought. Is this a sentence?
>
> **Write yes or no.**
>
> The big dog. — no
>
> I will go home. — yes
>
> We are singing. — yes
>
> Down the street. — no
>
> **Write a story in your LIFEPAC Tablet about a kite.**
> **Write a good title.**
> **Write good sentences.**
> **Draw a picture about your story.**
> **Read your story and show your picture to the class.**
>
> page 7 (seven)

---

two children to tell what they say. Then have the directions read aloud one at a time. Talk about each one. Have the children tell what good titles and sentences are. (The title should tell the main idea of the story in an interesting way, and all sentences must be complete thoughts.)

Encourage the children to write more than three paragraphs and to use statements, exclamations, and direct quotations in their stories.

Have the children draw and color or paint pictures to illustrate their stories.

Take class time for the children to read their stories and to show their pictures. This time is just as valuable as writing the story. Children tend to be more creative in their writing if they know they will be sharing it with others. Review the rules for reading and telling stories for both the reader and the audience before they begin.

ACTIVITIES:

Do Worksheet 2.

Have the children read the directions at the top of the page. Ask the children to tell what a sentence is (complete thought). Tell the children to read each line very carefully and to decide whether it is a sentence. If it is a sentence, write *yes* on the line and put a period behind the last word in the sentence. If it is not a complete sentence, write *no* on the line.

Check by having the children read the lines and tell which word they wrote. Have them make complete sentences out of the parts .

Have the children read the next direction. Tell them to read these sentences carefully, then to write an *S* if the sentence is a statement, a *Q* if it is a question, and an *E* if it is an exclamation. Check by having the children read each sentence and tell which letter they wrote and what it means.

Have the children give more examples of each kind of sentence.

Name _____

Write yes or no. Is this a sentence?

I think I will go to   no

I think I will go, too   yes

Did you see the   no

Where is my big   no

That is mine   yes

Write S by the statements, E by the exclamations, and Q by the questions.

Q   Do you mind if I go, too?

E   Oh, my!

E   Look, look!

S   I am tired.

Q   Did you wind the clock?

S   The lion is in the zoo.

**Language Arts 107
Worksheet 2
with page 7**

Teacher check _____
Initial   Date

Page 8: A Fly by Sy's Pie

CONCEPTS: sound of long *i*, rhyming words, exclamations, direct quotations, contractions, possessives, retelling story

TEACHER GOALS: To teach the children
To identify words with the long /i/ sound made by *y* or *ie* at the end,
To read the pronoun *I* and tell what it means,
To identify rhyming words with the sound of long *i*,
To identify exclamations and read them with good expression,
To identify direct quotations and tell who is speaking,
To identify the contractions and tell the words from which they were formed,
To identify the possessives and possessive pronouns and tell what belongs to each, and
To retell the story in their own words.

A FLY BY SY'S PIE

"Look! Look!" called Sy.
"I have a fly in my pie!
I can't eat this pie.
Look at the fly."

Oh! Oh! Oh!
How the children laughed.
They said "Oh, Sy.
You can eat your pie.
That's a play fly!"

Hee Hee Hee!

"Oh!" laughed Sy.
"A play fly is by my pie!"

page 8 (eight)

VOCABULARY: laughed

TEACHING PAGE 8:
Present the words *Sy, Sy's, laughed, pie,* on the board and have children read them several times. Point out the silent *u* and the /f/ sound of the *gh* in laughed and the /d/ sound for the *ed* ending. Point out the long /i/ sound of the *y* in *Sy* and *Sy's* and the long sound of the *i* with the silent *e* in *pie*.
Have the children read the title and give the rhyming words in it. Ask which word is a possessive and what it is that belongs to *Sy*.
Have the children read the story silently. Let one or two children tell the story in their own words. Let others in the class add details that are left out. Have the children read the story aloud.
Ask these questions:
"Why was Sy upset?"
"Why don't we want flies on our food? "
"Why did the children laugh?"

"How did Sy feel then?"
Have the children find the exclamations in the story and read them aloud. Encourage them to read with expression. Ask what the mark at the end of each sentence is called.
Have the children find and read the direct quotations. Have them tell who is speaking and to whom they are speaking. Ask what the marks are called and where they are found. Ask the children to find the words that tell how the words were said (called, laughed, said). Ask if there would be any difference in how the words were said .
Have the children find the contractions and tell what they mean.
Have the children find the pronouns in the story and tell who is meant by each (*I, they, you*). Then have them find the possessive pronouns and tell what belongs to each (*my, your*).

ACTIVITIES:

1. Have one child read the narrator's part, one child read Sy's part, and two or three children read the children's part together. Remind the children to read only the words inside the quotation marks, the narrator reads everything else. Remind them to read with expression. Let several groups of children read the story this way.

2. Read funny stories or stories in which someone plays a joke on someone else.

3. Dictate the following words and have the children write them on a sheet of writing tablet paper. Collect the papers and correct by drawing a line through each misspelled word and by writing it correctly behind the word. Have the children write each misspelled word five times on the back of the paper.

my	try
by	sky
cry	why

TEACHING READING:

Have students write and complete this line: "When I grow up I will be (occupation or role) because... Have them illustrate a picture to go with their sentence. Share and display.

Tell students their story is about three boys who have ideas what to be when they grow up.

Read the story "What Do You Want to Be?" together, then answer the following questions:

"Which two boys are talking first?" (James and Shane)

"What does Shane want to do when he grows up?" (drive a train)

"What does James want to do?" (fly airplanes)

"Who is Casey?" (Shane's older brother)

"What did he tell the boys?" (he wants to be a teacher)

"What did the young boys think about being a teacher?" (not much fun)

"Why does Casey want to be a teacher?" (so he can learn things and teach others)

"Do you think the boys changed their minds about being a teacher? (no)

"How do you know?" (they shook their heads and left)

Find long vowel words: (drive, train, grow, Shane, told, James. railroad, wave, by, blow, people, miles, away, ride, fly, airplane, be, race, take, high, sky, say, Casey, came, we, teacher, why, seem, like, replied, so, teach, kinds, each, pilot, raced)

ACTIVITY:

Chart long vowel words under vowel category. Make a graph of students choices of what they want to be (opening activity).

Play a game to increase awareness of "grown-up" roles. Have students form groups of 4-6. Give them 5-10 minutes to think of as many adult jobs or roles they can. Compare lists and write answers on the board. Explain to the groups they will only get a point for each role that no one else mentions. If there are duplicates, neither group gets a point.

Have students interview their parents or neighbors about their jobs or roles. Have a sharing time to find out what they learned.

Provide books which give information on occupations. Read or give students opportunities to read and look at them.

Invite parents or other adults in the community to visit the classroom and tell about their job.

Page 9: Activity Page

CONCEPT: subject-verb agreement

TEACHER GOALS: To teach the children
To understand singular and plural verbs, and
To learn about present and past tense in verbs.

MATERIALS NEEDED: Worksheet 3

TEACHING PAGE 9:

Have the children read the direction at the top of the page.

Tell the children to read the first sentence silently and to point to the word that should go on the line. Have a child read the sentence aloud using that word. Have the children circle the word and write it on the line.

Let the children finish the exercise by themselves. Check by having the children read the sentences using the correct words. Have the children correct any mistakes.

Be sure the children understand that teasing and playing jokes on people can be fun, but that some kinds of teasing and jokes are not funny and can be a very mean thing to do. Have them give examples of each kind.

ACTIVITY:

Do Worksheet 3.

Have the children read the direction at the top of the page. Tell them to read each sentence carefully, then to read the two words below the space. Circle the word that is correct and makes sense in the sentence. Remind the children to read the sentence over again before they copy the word on the line.

Check by having the children read each sentence and spell the word they wrote in the space.

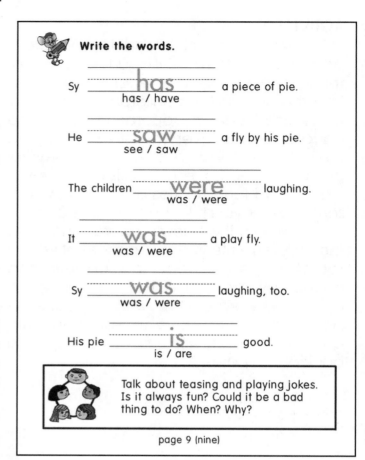

Write the words.

Sy __has__ a piece of pie.
has / have

He __saw__ a fly by his pie.
see / saw

The children __were__ laughing.
was / were

It __was__ a play fly.
was / were

Sy __was__ laughing, too.
was / were

His pie __is__ good.
is / are

Talk about teasing and playing jokes. Is it always fun? Could it be a bad thing to do? When? Why?

page 9 (nine)

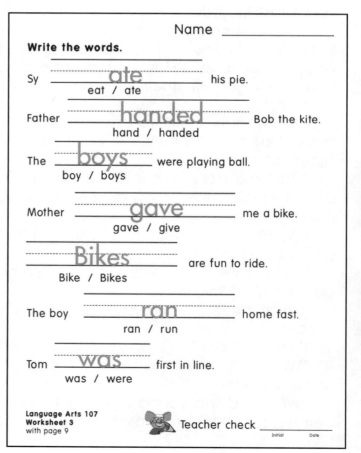

Name _____

Write the words.

Sy __ate__ his pie.
eat / ate

Father __handed__ Bob the kite.
hand / handed

The __boys__ were playing ball.
boy / boys

Mother __gave__ me a bike.
gave / give

__Bikes__ are fun to ride.
Bike / Bikes

The boy __ran__ home fast.
ran / run

Tom __was__ first in line.
was / were

Language Arts 107
Worksheet 3
with page 9

Teacher check _____
Initial   Date

TEACHING READING:

Read "Surprise! Surprise!" in *Reader 4*.

Ask the children if they have ever been surprised. Was it at a party?

Have several children tell about a time when they were surprised.

Present the words *Lila, Lila's, ice cream, surprise, party* on the board and have children read them several times. Point out the long /i/ sound in the words, the long /e/ sound in *cream*, the *r*-controlled vowels in *surprise* and *party*, and the long /e/ sound of *y* in *party*.

Have the children read the story silently. Tell the children that you will talk more about this story in the next lesson.

Page 10: Surprise! Surprise!

CONCEPTS: long *i*, exclamations, contractions, predicting outcomes

TEACHER GOALS: To teach the children
To identify and read words with the sound of long *i*,
To identify exclamations and read them with good expression,
To identify the contractions and tell the words from which they were formed,
To identify the main idea of the story,
To predict what might happen next in the story,
To make inferences from what they read and from what they see in pictures,
To identify the direct quotations in the story and tell who is speaking, and
To retell the story in their own words.

VOCABULARY: surprise

TEACHING PAGE 10:
Read "Surprise! Surprise! in *Reader 4* again. Have the children look at the picture and tell what is happening in it. Have them read the banner in the picture. Have them read the title and see if it changes their idea of what is happening in the picture. Have the children read the story silently.

Read the directions:
"Whose birthday is it?"
"Who's bringing the cake?"
"How old will Lila be?"
"What do you think might be in the boxes by the table?"
"What do you think might happen next?"

Have the children circle the answers. Have them tell what kind of word *Lila's* is and what belongs to her.

Ask the children to find all the contractions in the story. Write them on the board as they read them. Have them tell what each one means. Have them read the list.

Have the children read the exclamations with expression. Have them

Surprise! Surprise!
Circle the word.

Whose birthday is it?
Lila's   Jan's   Dan's   Ty's

Who's bringing the cake?
Jan   **May**   Al   Bob

How old will Lila be?
six   ten   five   eight

What will Lila find in the boxes?
dogs   candles   **presents**

What might happen next?

page 10 (ten)

identify the exclamation point. Ask what other kind of sentences are in the story.

Have the children find the words with the long /i/ sound in the story (Surprise, Lila's, I'll, ice, Mike, Lila). Have a child read them.

ACTIVITIES:
1.   Let the children share their birthday party or surprise party experiences.
2.   Have the children find all the words with *r*-controlled vowels and copy them on a sheet of writing tablet paper. Have them read them.
3.   Dictate the following words and have the children write them on a sheet of writing tablet paper. Correct them by drawing a line through the misspelled word and by writing the correct word behind it. Have the children write each misspelled word five times on the back of the paper.

ice   rice
nice slice
mice price

4. Read stories about birthdays and birthday parties or stories about surprises.

TEACHING READING:

Brainstorm with students about what they think teachers do. List all responses on the board. Have them decide the 5 most important and circle them. Remind students of the previous story, "What Do You Want to Be?" and the writings/illustration they did about their idea. Ask if they remember what each of the boys wants to be. Put the boys' names on the board (Casey, James and Shane) and write the answers (teacher, pilot, train driver). Tell students today's story is called, "Casey's First Lesson".
Ask students to predict what this story might be about.

Read the story "Casey's First Lesson" together, then ask the following questions:

"What is Casey doing at the beginning of the story?" (watching the boys play)

"What did he want to do?" (get them interested in learning)

"How did he do this?" (went to the library and got books)

"Why did Casey sit on the steps?" (so the boys would see him)

"Why did the boys come over to see Casey?" (they were curious about what he was doing)

"Were the boys interested?" (yes)

"How can you tell?" (they didn't run off)

"How long did they look at books?" (two hours)

"Why did Casey smile at the end?" (he knew he was teaching them something)

Find the long vowel words: (Casey, Shane, James, play, driving, train, flying, airplane, he, know, climb, go, teacher, bike, home, read, chose, outside, see, each, time, stayed, maybe, decide, later)

ACTIVITIES:

Choose a group of long vowel words and brainstorm a list of rhyming words with each. Use these words to write poetry. Have a sharing/discussion time: What I learned in school this year (or last). Have students write a letter to last year's teacher telling him/her about something they learned in that grade. Do simple activities where students could take turns being the teacher — (i.e. explaining the steps for a math problem, leading the class in a song, giving spelling words.)

Page 11: Activity Page

CONCEPTS: syllables

TEACHER GOALS: To teach the children
To listen to the parts of words,
To call the parts syllables, and
To identify the number of syllables in words.

VOCABULARY: parts

MATERIALS NEEDED: 3" x 5" cards with 1, 2, and 3 on them (one set for each child), Worksheet 4

TEACHING PAGE 11:
Prepare the sets of number cards.

Tell the children to listen carefully, then to say the word *the*. Ask the children to tell how many parts they heard. Say the following words and have the children tell how many parts they hear in each one: *go, candy, jump, happy.*

Give each child a set of number cards and tell them to hold up the number that tells how many parts each word has. Tell the children that the word parts are called syllables. Remind the children that they must hear a vowel sound in every syllable. Use the word so that children become familiar with it, but do not expect them to be able to read it.

Read these words. Pause slightly between syllables. Some words have just one syllable.

birthday	house	cat
white	ladder	walking
difference	bird	basket
with	happening	mother
child	wonderful	tell

If a child holds up the wrong number, say the word again and have the child repeat it, and hold up the right number card.

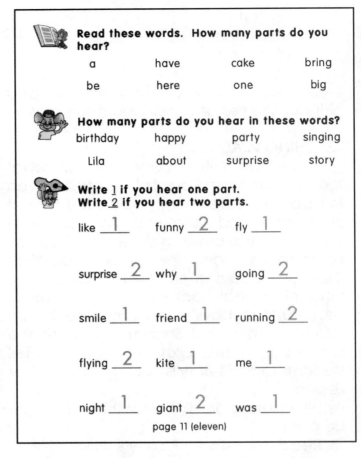

Read these words. How many parts do you hear?

a	have	cake	bring
be	here	one	big

How many parts do you hear in these words?

birthday	happy	party	singing
Lila	about	surprise	story

Write 1 if you hear one part.
Write 2 if you hear two parts.

like 1   funny 2   fly 1

surprise 2   why 1   going 2

smile 1   friend 1   running 2

flying 2   kite 1   me 1

night 1   giant 2   was 1

page 11 (eleven)

Read the list of words again and have the children clap once for each syllable as they repeat the word after you.

Have the children read the direction and question at the top of the page. Have them read each word and tell how many parts it has.

Have the children read the next question. Have them read each word in the list and tell how many parts it has. Read each word again and clap once for the number of syllables in it.

Have the children read the directions in the middle of the page. Do the first two words together, then let the children finish the page by themselves. It may be necessary to work through the entire exercise with some children.

Check by having the children read each word and tell how many syllables it has. Have the children correct any mistakes.

ACTIVITIES:

1. Have the children find and read words in the exercise with the following features:

a. the long /i/ sound (*like, fly, surprise, why, smile, flying, kite, night, giant*)

b. *y* at the end with the long /i/ sound (*fly, why*)

c. *y* at the end with the long /e/ sound (*funny*)

d. Long *i* with silent *e* (*like, surprise, smile, kite*)

e. double middle consonant (*running, funny*)

f. soft /g/ sound (*giant*)

g. Long /i/ sound with two silent letters (*night*)

h. *r*-controlled vowel (*surprise*)

i. *s* with the sound of *z* (*surprise, was*)

j. words beginning with consonant blends (*fly, smile, friend, flying*)

2. Do Worksheet 4.

Have the children read the directions at the top of the page.

Do the first row of words together. Have the children say the word, then tell how many parts they hear in it. Have them write the number on the line. Let the children finish the first exercise by themselves. Check by having the children read the words and tell what number they wrote on the line.

Have the children read the directions for the next two exercises. Read each of the words with the children and have them tell how many parts they hear. Pause slightly between syllables if children have trouble hearing the parts.

Name _____

Write 1 if you hear one part.
Write 2 if you hear two parts.

mind __1__ the __1__ running __2__
wanted __2__ singing __2__ mile __1__
dial __2__ birthday __2__ Sunday __2__
fireman __2__ Bible __2__ slide __1__

Read these words. How many parts do you hear?

minister __3__ contraction __3__
nursery __3__ banana __3__
dictionary __4__ apostrophe __4__

How many parts in these words?

sentences __3__ animal __3__
together __3__ another __3__
butterfly __3__ invitation __4__

Language Arts 107
Worksheet 4
with page 11

Teacher check _____

Page 12: Sentences

CONCEPTS: kinds of sentences, punctuation marks

TEACHER GOALS: To teach the children
To identify and write a statement, a question, and an exclamation;
To identify and write a period, a question mark, and an exclamation point; and
To tell that a statement ends with a period, a question ends with a question mark, and an exclamation ends with an exclamation point.

MATERIALS NEEDED: Worksheet 5

TEACHING PAGE 12:
Write the words *statement, question,* and *exclamation* on the board and have the children read them several times. Ask the children to tell what each one means and give an example of each.

Read the title and sentences at the top of the page with the children. Have the children tell what each kind of sentence does and what the punctuation mark is for each.

Read the direction in the middle of the page with the children. Tell the children to read each sentence carefully, decide whether it is a statement, question, or an exclamation, then put in the proper punctuation mark at the end of each. Check by having the children read the sentence and tell which mark they put in the space. Encourage them to read with expression.

Have the children read the direction at the bottom of the page. Remind them that each sentence must be a complete thought, that the first word must begin with a capital letter, and that the sentence must have the correct mark at the end. Remind them also to write neatly, to space words correctly, to spell correctly, and to write interesting sentences.

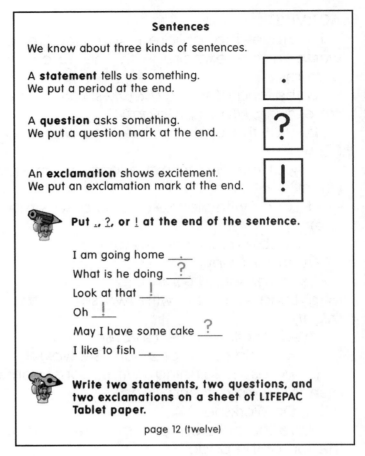

ACTIVITIES:
1.   Do Worksheet 5.
Have the children read the directions at the top of the page. Tell the children to read the sentences carefully and to put the letter for the kind of sentence on the first line and the punctuation mark on the line at the end of the sentence. Check by having the children read each sentence and tell what kind of sentence it is, which letter they wrote on the line at the beginning, and what mark they put at the end.

Have the children read the next set of directions. Tell the children to read each line carefully and decide whether it is a complete sentence. If it is, have them write *yes* on the line. If it is not a sentence, write *no* on the line. Have the children tell why the line is not a sentence, then have them make a sentence out of it. Have them put periods or question marks at the end of the sentences.

2.   Give each child a strip of lined paper (cut sheets of writing tablet paper into strips so that there is a complete set of lines on each strip). Have the children write a sentence on each side of the strip, leaving off the punctuation mark. Have the children exchange strips. Tell the children to read the sentence carefully, decide what kind it is, and write the punctuation mark at the end. You also may have them write *Q* for question, *S* for statement, or *E* for exclamation in front of each sentence. Let the children read the sentences aloud and tell what kind of sentence it is and what the punctuation mark is.

Name _____

Write S by the statements, E by the exclamations, and Q by the questions. Put ., ?, or ! at the end.

____S____ Babies like milk ____.____

____Q____ Did you see my knife____?____

____S____ No, I didn't see it ____.____

____E____ Happy birthday, Lila ____!____

____Q____ Are you eight or nine____?____

Write yes or no. Is this a sentence?

The apples are ripe ____yes____

Find the big yellow ____no____

Bananas are yellow ____yes____

Language Arts 107
Worksheet 5
with page 12

Teacher check _____
Initial   Date

SELF TEST 1

CONCEPT: sentences, punctuation, syllables, long e, and long a

TEACHER GOAL: To teach the children
To check their own progress periodically.

TEACHING PAGE 13 :

Have the children read the title and tell what a self test is.

Read all the directions on the page with the children and be sure they understand everything they are to do on this page. Let the children do the entire page by themselves. Give no help except with the directions.

Check the page as soon as possible and go over it with each child so he can see what he did well and where he needs to work harder. Do not have the children correct their own work (be, happy, eat, read, tree, speak, we, see, ate, take, bait, wait).

ACTIVITIES:

1. Reteach skills the child missed individually or in a small group.
2. If several children miss the same things, reteach the skills in small groups.

SPELLING WORDS:

may
say
way
rain
chain
wait
weight
pail
sail
tail

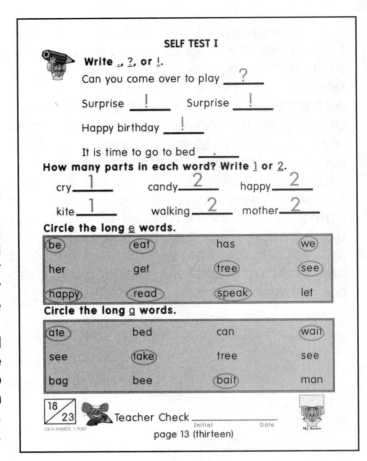

II. PART TWO

Page 14: Ice Cream

CONCEPTS: long *i*, *ea*, questions

TEACHER GOALS: To teach the children
To identify and read words with the sound of long *i* with silent *e*, and
To identify the questions on the page and write answers to them in complete sentences.

MATERIALS NEEDED: Worksheet 6, ingredients for ice cream or prepared ice cream (optional), spoons, dishes (optional)

TEACHING PAGE 14:
Write the words *sometimes, good,* and *spoon* on the board and have the children read them several times. Call attention to the /oo/ sound in spoon, and good, and ask what kind of word *sometimes* is. Ask the children to give other compound words.

Have the children read the title of the story and look at the pictures. Have them name the kinds of ice cream dishes in the picture. Let them share experiences.

Have the children read the first paragraph silently. Ask a child to tell what it says. Have a child read the paragraph aloud.

Have a child read the question and answer it.

Have the children read the second paragraph silently. Ask a child to tell what it says. Have a child read the paragraph aloud.

Have a child read the question aloud and answer it.

Have the children find all the long *i* words, underline them, and read them. Have them find the *ea* words.

Ask the children to tell what the word *it* means in the second sentence in the first paragraph, and the third sentence in the second paragraph.

ICE CREAM

Ice cream is good.
It is very cold.
I like ice cream.

Which kind of ice cream do you like?

I lick my ice cream.
I bite my ice cream.
Sometimes I eat it with a spoon.

How do you eat your ice cream?

page 14 (fourteen)

Have the children read the questions again and write answers to them in complete sentences on a sheet of writing tablet paper. Read the question and have several children read their answers aloud.

ACTIVITIES:
1. Let several children retell the story.
2. Bring an ice cream freezer and make ice cream in the classroom.

Let the children help with the measuring and mixing of ingredients and with the serving when the ice cream is finished (If it is not possible to make the ice cream in class, let children serve prepared ice cream. They could earn money to buy it, or bring money from home).
3. Do Worksheet 6:
Have the children read the directions at the top of the page. Have them read the word endings and give several words that rhyme with each. Ask what the vowel sound is. Have the children write words on the lines,

then prepare the sheet of writing tablet paper and write more rhyming words on it. Check by having the children give rhyming words from their lists for you to write under the word endings you have put on the board. Have the children add to and correct their lists. Have the children read the lists from the board several times, listening for the rhyming parts. Collect the papers and check them over.

Have the children read the direction for the next exercise. Have them read the words in the row. Ask what the vowel sound is. Tell the children to read the sentences carefully and to choose a word and write it on the line. Read the sentence over to be sure the word chosen makes sense. Point out that there are five sentences and only four words. One word will be used twice. Check by having children read the sentences and spell the words they wrote on the lines.

4. Read stories or poems about ice cream or other cold things and stories about snow or ice.

Name _____

Write words that rhyme.

-ice   -ife

_____   _____
_____   _____
_____   _____
_____   _____

Write more rhyming words on a sheet of LIFEPAC Tablet paper.

Write these words.

mice   life   knife   spice

Pepper is a _____ spice _____ .

Jesus gave his _____ life _____ for us.

You cut with a _____ knife _____ .

The _____ mice _____ like to eat.

I give my _____ life _____ to Jesus.

Language Arts 107
Worksheet 6
with page 14   Teacher check _____
                                        Initial   Date

112

Page 15: Activity Page

CONCEPTS: sequence of events, long *i*

TEACHER GOALS: To teach the children
To read and understand the order of events, and
To find words that rhyme with *ike* and *ind*.

MATERIALS NEEDED: Worksheet 7

TEACHING PAGE 15:
Put these sentences on the board and have the children read them and number them in the order in which they happened.

3 Jane began to cry.
1 Jane ran very fast.
2 She fell down.

Have the children read the direction at the top of the page. Tell the children to read the three sentences carefully, just as they did on the board, then to number them in the order in which they happened. Let the children do the exercise by themselves. Check by having the children read the sentences in the order in which they happened. Have the children correct any mistakes (Row 1: 2, 1, 3; Row 2: 2, 3, 1; Row 3: 3, 1, 2).

Have the children read the next direction and the word endings. Have them give several rhyming words for each. Tell the children to write two words that rhyme under each ending and to prepare the sheet of writing tablet paper and write more words on it. Correct by having the children read words from their lists for you to write under the endings on the board. Have the children read the lists several times, listening for the rhyming parts. Have the children add to and correct their lists. The teacher should collect the papers and check them over.

Write 1, 2, 3 for first, second, and third.

_2_ Tom eats his ice cream.
_1_ Tom gets some ice cream.
_3_ Tom's ice cream is all gone.

_2_ We talk to a friend.
_3_ We say, "Goodbye."
_1_ We say, "Hello."

_3_ Surprise! Surprise!
_1_ Let's have a surprise party.
_2_ Here comes Lisa.

Write words that rhyme.
__ike   __ind

Write more rhyming words on a sheet of LIFEPAC Tablet paper.

page 15 (fifteen)

ACTIVITIES:
1.   Do Worksheet 7.
Have the children read the direction at the top of the page. Tell the children to read all three sentences in each set and to number them in the order they happened. Have them read them over again in order to see if they have made any mistakes. Check by having the children read the sentences in order. Have them correct any mistakes (Row 1: 3, 1, 2; Row 2: 2, 3, 1; Row 3: 1, 3, 2; Row 4: 3, 2, 1; Row 5: 1, 3, 2).

Have the children tell the story for each set of sentences in their own words. Ask what the main idea of each set is. Ask what might happen next in each situation.
2.   Dictate these words and have the children write them on a sheet of writing tablet paper. Collect the papers and correct by drawing a line through the misspelled word and by writing the correct word behind it. Have the children write

113

each word they misspelled five times on the back of their paper.

bike   find
like   kind
strike mind

3.   Have children use each of the words on their dictation paper in a sentence. These may be written or oral.

Name _____

Write 1, 2, 3, for first, second, and third.

_3_	I ate all my ice cream.
_1_	I buy some ice cream.
_2_	I begin to eat my ice cream.
_2_	Mother bird sits on her eggs.
_3_	There are four baby birds.
_1_	Mother bird lays four eggs.
_1_	The mice look for food.
_3_	The mice eat and eat.
_2_	The mice find some cheese.
_3_	Ann turns the light off.
_2_	It is light in the room.
_1_	Ann turns the light on.
_1_	Tom has a new toy truck.
_3_	He puts his new truck away.
_2_	He plays with his new truck.

Language Arts 107
Worksheet 7
with page 15

Teacher check _____
Initial   Date

Page 16: Activity Page

CONCEPTS: *nk, ng,* consonant blends, and suffixes

TEACHER GOALS: To teach the children
To write words with *nd, nt, nk,* and *ng* endings, and
To learn how to add *ed* or *ing* to the end of a word.

MATERIALS NEEDED: Worksheet 8

TEACHING PAGE 16:

Have the children read the directions at the top of the page. Tell the children to read the beginning of each word, then put one of the endings on the line to finish the word. Tell them that one, two, or three possible endings will make words. Check by having the children read the word they have made. Write all the possible words on the board for each beginning.

Have the children read the next directions. Have them read the first set of words and listen to the ending sounds. Have the children read the next word *want,* write *ed* behind it to make *wanted,* and write *ing* behind it to make *wanting.* Have the children read all three words. Have each word used in a sentence. Let the children finish the next set by themselves. Have a child read the words. Have each word used in a sentence.

Read the next sentence with the children. Read the row of words and point out the *d* at the end of each. Have the children read the words. Have the children write the *d* at the end of each word in the next row and read the words. Have each word used in a sentence.

Have the children read the next sentence with you. Have them read the words in the row. Write *like* on the board. Erase the *e* and write *ing.* Have the children read the word. Do the same with *wipe, slice,* and *time.*

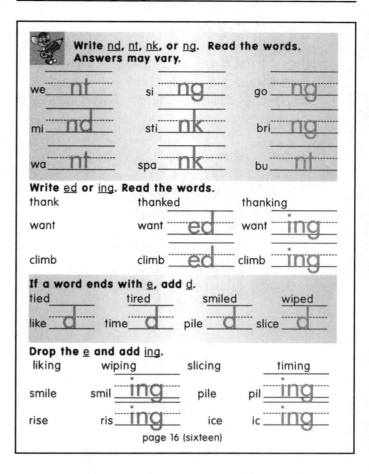

Write **nd**, **nt**, **nk**, or **ng**. Read the words.
Answers may vary.

we	**nt**	si	**ng**	go	**ng**
mi	**nd**	sti	**nk**	bri	**ng**
wa	**nt**	spa	**nk**	bu	**nt**

Write **ed** or **ing**. Read the words.

thank		thanked		thanking	
want		want	**ed**	want	**ing**
climb		climb	**ed**	climb	**ing**

If a word ends with **e**, add **d**.

| tied | | tired | | smiled | | wiped | |
| like | **d** | time | **d** | pile | **d** | slice | **d** |

Drop the **e** and add **ing**.

liking		wiping		slicing		timing	
smile	smil **ing**		pile	pil **ing**		
rise	ris **ing**		ice	ic **ing**		

page 16 (sixteen)

Tell the children to read the pairs of words and to write *ing* on the lines. Have all the words read again. Have the children use each word in a sentence.

ACTIVITIES:

1. Have the children give the correct verb forms for the following words.

sink	(sank, sinking)
think	(thought, thinking)
do	(did, doing)
eat	(ate, eating)
sing	(sang, singing)
find	(found, finding)
drive	(drove, driving)
write	(wrote, writing)
grow	(grew, growing)

2. Correct children after they finish what they are saying, when they use the wrong verb form. Have them repeat the sentence using the correct form.

3. Do Worksheet 8.

Read the words on the worksheet and point out that the *y* must be changed to an *i* before the *ed* is added.

Have the children finish the page and check.

cry   (cried, crying)
fry   (fried, frying)
spy   (spied, spying)
dry   (dried, drying)
try   (tried, trying)
hurry   (hurried, hurrying)
worry   (worried, worrying)
study   (studied, studying)

Name _____

Write the correct word endings.

cry	cried	crying
fry	fri **ed**	fry **ing**
spy	spi **ed**	spy **ing**
hurry	hurried	hurrying
worry	worri **ed**	worry **ing**
dry	dri **ed**	dry **ing**
try	tri **ed**	try **ing**
study	studied	study **ing**

Language Arts 107
Worksheet 8
with page 16

Teacher check _____
Initial   Date

116

Page 17: Activity Page

CONCEPTS: stories, suffixes *ed* and *ing*

TEACHER GOALS: To teach the children
   To understand the meaning of what they are reading,
   To predict how stories may end, and
   To add *ed* and *ing* to the end of verbs.

MATERIALS NEEDED: Worksheet 9

TEACHING PAGE 17:

Have the children read the direction at the top of the page. Have them read the story silently. Have them read the two sentences and decide which one tells what will happen next. Have them draw a line under the right sentence. Check by having a child read the story and the sentence he has underlined. Talk about why that sentence is the best answer. Is it the right thing to do in that situation?

Follow the same procedure for the second story.

Have the children read the directions at the bottom of the page, have them read the four words in the column at the left, have them write the endings on the lines and read each set of words, and have the children use each word in a sentence.

ACTIVITIES:

1.   Do Worksheet 9.

Have the children read the direction at the top of the page. Tell them to read each story, then read the two sentences and draw a line under the one that tells what will happen next. Let the children do both stories at the top of the page. Check by having them read the story and the sentence they underlined.

Have the children read the direction for the last story, and then read the story silently. Have them write a sentence telling what will happen next.

Check by having a child read the story and by having several children read their

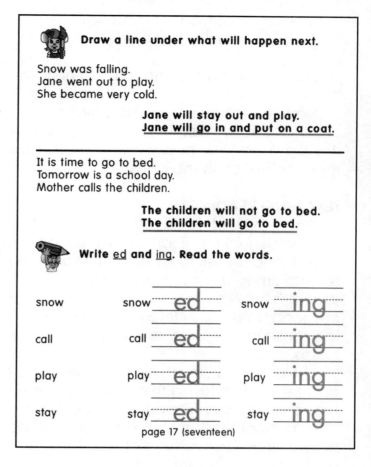

Draw a line under what will happen next.

Snow was falling.
Jane went out to play.
She became very cold.

Jane will stay out and play.
<u>Jane will go in and put on a coat.</u>

It is time to go to bed.
Tomorrow is a school day.
Mother calls the children.

The children will not go to bed.
<u>The children will go to bed.</u>

Write <u>ed</u> and <u>ing</u>. Read the words.

snow	snow *ed*	snow *ing*
call	call *ed*	call *ing*
play	play *ed*	play *ing*
stay	stay *ed*	stay *ing*

page 17 (seventeen)

sentences. Check to see that the sentences are complete, that the first word begins with a capital letter, that the words are spelled correctly, and that the sentence ends with a period.

2.   Write the following list of words on the board and have the children copy them on a sheet of writing tablet paper. Write the endings *ed* and *ing* on the board and have the children add the *ed* and the *ing* to each of the words in the list. Collect the papers and check. Have the children correct any mistakes.

	<u>ed</u>	<u>ing</u>
talk	(talked	talking)
wink	(winked	winking)
back	(backed	backing)
spell	(spelled	spelling)
cry	(cried	crying)
stop	(stopped	stopping)

spot (spotted   spotting)
try   (tried   trying

Some children may need extra help with these.

Have the children choose any three sets of words and write sentences using them on the back of their paper. Have them read their sentences to the class.

TEACHING READING:

Find "The Pet Show" in Reader 4. Write the words *judges*, *Brian*, and *Prize* on the board and have the children read them several times. Point out the long /i/ sounds, the soft /g/ sound in *judges* and the consonant blends in *Brian* and *prize*. Be sure the children know the meanings of the words.

Have the children look at the picture and tell what is happening. Let them share their experiences with pet shows, either real ones or back yard shows. Ask if anyone has won a prize for anything else. Let them tell about it.

Have the children read the story. Tell the children that you will talk more about this story in the next lesson.

Name _____

Draw a line under what happens next.

It is getting light.
The sun is coming up.

We will get up.
We will go to bed.

The sun is going down.
It is getting dark.

We will get up.
We will go to bed.

Write what will happen next.

The house is on fire.
The firemen come.
They put water on the fire.

The fire went out.

Language Arts 107
Worksheet 9
with page 17

Teacher check _____
                         Initial   Date

118

Page 18 : The Pet Show

CONCEPTS: predicting outcome, long *i*, paragraphs, consonant digraphs *wh, th, ch, sh*

TEACHER GOALS: To teach the children
To predict what might happen next in the story,
To identify and read words with the long /i/ sound,
To identify and read words with the *wh, th, ch*, and *sh* sounds,
To identify the possessive pronouns and tell what belongs to each,
To identify and read the questions in the story,
To identify and read the plurals in the story and give the singular form for each, and
To write a well-constructed paragraph in answer to a question.

TEACHING PAGE 18:
Turn to "The Pet Show" in *Reader 4*.
Have the children read the banner above the animals and the title of the story. Have them read the story again silently. *Ask these questions from the LIFEPAC page 18:*
"What are the names of the two children? (Diane and Brian)
"What pet does Diane have?" (rabbit)
"What pet does Brian have?" (kitten)
"What kind of pets are there?" (dogs, cats, fish, birds, rabbits)
Have the children circle the answers. Check.
Have the children find the possessive pronouns, tell whom they refer to, and what belongs to each (her - Diane's rabbit, his - Brian's kitten, their - children's pets).
Ask the children to find all the plurals in the story (many, children, pets, judges, dogs, cats, fish, rabbits, birds). Have the children read them. Have the children tell how each plural was formed.

page 18 (eighteen)

Write the letters *wh* on the board. Have the children go to the board and write all the words in the story that begin with *wh*. Do the same with *th, sh,* and *ch*. Tell the children to look for words with *sh* and *ch* at the end and to write those.

wh	th	sh	ch
Who	their	show	children
What	The	fish	which
Which	think		

Have the children copy the last question in the story on a sheet of writing tablet paper and write a paragraph in answer to it. Have them tell which pet they think will win and why they think it will. Remind them to write at least three sentences, to make each sentence a complete thought, to begin the first word of each sentence with a capital letter, to use correct punctuation, to be neat, and to spell correctly. Collect their papers and correct them. Have the children copy their corrected papers over. Have them draw a picture of the pet they think will win. Take class time for the children to read their paragraphs and show their pictures. Make a wall or bulletin board display with them.

ACTIVITIES:

1.   Have the children write a sentence on a sheet of writing tablet paper for each word in the *wh* and *th* lists they wrote on the board. Have them read their sentences in a small group session.

2.   Read stories about pets or pet shows or articles about caring for pets.

TEACHING READING:

Show students a U.S. map and locate Florida. Have students share anything they know about Florida and/or experiences of those who have lived or visited there. Give students a U.S. map and have them color Florida and their state.

Tell students they'll read a story titled, "Going to Florida". Discuss with students what this story might be about. Put the following words on the board: Florida, family, hurray, except, noticed, castles, ocean, frightened, alligators, especially. Have students read the words and learn their meaning.

Read the story "Going to Florida" together, then ask the following questions:

"Why is Gretchen's family going to Florida?" (vacation)

"What are some things they might do in Florida?" (play on the beach, ocean, see a space shuttle)

"Why isn't Gretchen excited like everyone else?" (she's afraid alligators eat people)

"How does Gretchen show her fear?" (she's pale, tears, body shaking)

"Where did she get this fear?" (from her friend Joey)

"What does Dad suggest?" (they get the real facts from books)

Find long vowel words: (going, to, vacation, told, hurray, old, pale, no, noticed, right, ocean, time, coast, space, take, don't go, cried, rolled, shaking, why, frightened, Joey, eat, people, tight, find, true, okay, wiping)

ACTIVITIES:

Provide nonfiction books on Florida. Have students explore the books to discover all they can about the state. List what is discovered. Assign each student to illustrate and cut out a picture of something on the list. Make a large "All About Florida" collage with their cut-out illustrations.

Write a story of their own titles: Going to Florida. Have them describe what they would do during their visit. Take a poll about alligators. Ask how many believe what Joey told Gretchen. Share the poem: "Alligators Are Unfriendly", by Jack Prelutsky.

Page 19: Activity Page

CONCEPTS: digraph wh, writing a story, punctuation

TEACHER GOALS: To teach the children
To use the correct ending punctuation in sentences,
To review the kinds of sentences, and
To write a story using good sentences, paragraphs, and write a title.

TEACHING PAGE 19:

Write the words *what, which, where, when* on the board and have the children read them several times. Have the children give questions using the *wh* words.

Ask the children to name the three kinds of sentences and give an example of each. Have them tell which punctuation mark goes at the end of each .

Have the children read the direction at the top of the page. Tell them to read each sentence carefully and to put a period at the end of each statement, a question mark at the end of each question, and an exclamation mark at the end of each exclamation. Let the children do the exercise. Check by having a child read a sentence and tell which mark he put behind it. Remind the children to read the sentences with the proper expression.

Have the children read the direction and the titles in the middle of the page. Have them write the title they chose on a sheet of writing tablet paper.

Tell the children to write at least three paragraphs and encourage them to write several pages. Remind them to write complete sentences and to be sure all the sentences in each paragraph are about the same thing. Tell them to write neatly, to space their words well, and to spell correctly. Have children keep a sheet of paper on their desks on which you can write words they cannot sound out or have trouble spelling.

Write ., ?, or !.

What is your name ____?
Which pet will win ____?
I have a pet ____.
No, no, Blackie ____!
Where did he go ____?
Oh, look ____!
When are you coming ____?
Pet shows are fun ____.

Choose a title and write a story.

A Big Surprise

Fun At the Farm

My Pet

Is this story true?
How do you know?
Could this story really happen?

page 19 (nineteen)

Read the material in the box together and talk about it. Encourage every child to contribute to the discussion.

ACTIVITY:

Take class time for children to read the stories they have written. Have them draw and color or paint pictures to go with their stories in an art class. Remind them to choose an important part of the story to draw a picture of, one that illustrates the main idea of the story.

Page 20: Activity Page

CONCEPTS: reading comprehension, like things, drawing conclusions, writing sentences

TEACHER GOALS: To teach the children
To read to find things that are alike,
To read to draw conclusions, and
To understand the meanings of words to build good sentences.

MATERIALS NEEDED: three shoeboxes, 2" x 8" tagboard strips, Worksheet 10

TEACHING PAGE 20:

Write the following sentences on the board. Have the children read all three and decide which two are about the same subject. Have a child draw a line under those two. Have them tell why the third sentence does not go with the other two.

We are in school.
My puppy is brown and white.
We are working hard.

Have the children read the direction at the top of the page. Tell them to read each set of sentences very carefully. Have them draw lines under the two sentences that are about the same thing. Let the children do the exercise by themselves. Check by having children read the two sentences they underlined. Have them tell why the third sentence does not go with the other two. Have the children tell the main idea of the two sentences they chose.

Have the children read the directions at the bottom of the page. Have them write a third sentence for each set that will go with the other two sentences. Then have the children read all three sentences that go together.

Collect the papers and correct. Have the children recopy sentences in which they misspell words or are messy.

Have the children read the sets of sentences aloud.

ACTIVITIES:

1.   Do Worksheet 10.
Have the children read the direction at the top of the page and the headings on the two boxes. Have the children give examples of each.

Have the children cut the bottom part of the paper off on the heavy line. Have them cut the small boxes apart on the lines and paste all the things God made for us in the first box, and all the things people have built or made in the second box.

Check by having the children read what they have put in each box. Have them correct any mistakes.

Bring out the ideas that God created everything in our world and that everything people make is made with things God has created. God also created us.

2.   To help children understand sentence structure, do this exercise. Prepare three shoeboxes (or any three boxes the same size) labeled *Who, What,* and *Where.* Write the following words and phrases on strips of tagboard and have the children put them in the appropriate boxes.

who	what	where
a girl	jumps	in the house
the cat	sings	at school
a fireman	reads	in the garden
a bird	walks	in my book
the rabbit	cries	on the moon
a man	lives	in a box
father	jumps	on his feet
the child	digs	on the table
a fox	runs	on a sign

Have the children choose one strip from each box and put them together to make a sentence. Have them read it to the class. Some of these may be very funny. This exercise is a good way to introduce children to nouns, verbs, and prepositional phrases, and the place of each in a sentence. The children should become aware that they can write a sentence with just a noun and a verb, but that the prepositional phrase makes the sentence clearer and more complete. Begin using the correct names for the parts of the sentence along with such designations as the "*who*", "*what*", or "*where*" words.

Draw lines under the two sentences that go together.

1. <u>I have a pet.</u>
   <u>My pet is a dog.</u>
   Bob is going fishing.

2. <u>Diane has a pet rabbit.</u>
   Zebras live in zoos.
   <u>Brian has a pet kitten.</u>

3. I play with my pets.
   <u>Jesus loves me.</u>
   <u>Jesus is my friend.</u>

4. <u>Ice cream is cold.</u>
   Blackie is a pony.
   <u>Children like ice cream.</u>

Write a third sentence for each set that will go with the other two sentences.

1. _____

2. _____

3. _____

4. _____

page 20 (twenty)

Name _____

Cut and paste.

God made these.	People made these.
trees rocks lakes hills sky stars sun moon plants people animals rain	books streets glasses bridges paper desks sinks pencils cars houses bikes airplanes

trees	paper	plants
books	sky	people
rocks	stars	cars
lakes	sun	houses
streets	desks	bikes
glasses	sinks	airplanes
hills	moon	animals
bridges	pencils	rain

Language Arts 107
Worksheet 10
with page 20

Teacher check _____
                    Initial   Date

123

Page 21: Activity Page

CONCEPTS: reading comprehension: main idea, details; silent *e*

TEACHER GOALS: To teach the children
To read to find the main idea and details in a story, and
To write words with the long *i* sound and silent *e*.

MATERIALS NEEDED: Worksheets 11 and 12

TEACHING PAGE 21:

Have the children read the direction at the top of the page. Ask the children to tell what a title is (a name).

Have the children read the stories and the titles and draw a line under the best title for each story. Have the stories read aloud and have the children tell why the title they chose is the best one. Have them tell why the others are not as good. Bring out the idea that a title should tell the main idea of a paragraph or story.

Discuss each of the stories. Bring out what pets are and how children should care for them. Let the children share their experiences with their pets.

Talk about Jesus. Have the children tell how Jesus is their best friend and how they should act in return. Be sure children know that Jesus hears every prayer and answers it, but that He decides how and when it is answered.

Have the children read the direction in the middle of the page. Have them read the word endings and tell what the vowel sound is and what the *e* does. (Silent *e* at the end makes the *i* have the long sound.)

Have the children give several rhyming words for each ending and write them on the lines. Have them prepare a sheet of writing tablet paper with the endings on the board and have the children read words from their lists for you to write under the endings. Have the children add to and correct their lists. The teacher also should check the papers over. Be sure the children know the meanings of all the words.

ACTIVITIES:

1. Do Worksheet 11.
Have the children read the direction at the top of the page. Ask the children to tell what a title is and how they know if a title is a good one (tells about an important or main part of the story).

Have the children read the first story silently and draw a line under the title they think fits the story the best. Have a child read the story and the title he chose. Ask if anyone has a different title underlined. Ask why they think "What Tom Saw" is the best title for this story.

Have the children do the rest of the page by themselves. Check by having the children read the stories and the titles they chose. Have them tell why those titles were the best.

Have the children tell the stories in their own words. Ask what might happen next in each story. Have several children choose one of the stories to tell and add what they think might happen next.

2. Do Worksheet 12.
Have the children read the direction at the top of the page. Tell them that on this Worksheet they are to read the story very carefully and to write a title for it.

Do the first story as a group. Have the children read the story silently, then think about a good title. Have several children give their ideas. Have a child read the story aloud. Talk about the titles given by the children and let them decide which one is the best. It may help to write the titles on the board as the children give them.

Let the children finish the page by themselves. Check by having a child read the story and by having the children give their titles. Write them on the board and let the children decide which is the very best.

If some of the titles given do not fit the story at all, go through the stories line by line with those children who gave the poor titles. Help them to see that all the lines are about the same thing. Help them to see what that thing is.

3.   Dictate the following words and have children write them on a sheet of writing tablet paper. Collect the papers and correct by drawing a line through the misspelled word and by writing it correctly on the line behind the word. Have the children write each word they misspelled five times on the back of the paper.

pie	ride
tie	side
lie	hide
why	tied
try	tried

Be sure children understand the difference between *tied* and *tide* and that the *y* in *try* is changed to *i* before the *ed* is added.

Draw a line under the best title.

Dogs and cats are pets.
They play.
They have fun.
I like dogs and cats.

Dogs
Cats
Dogs and Cats

Jesus is my friend.
He loves me.
He helps me.
I love Jesus.

Jesus
Love
Help

Write words that rhyme.

_____ie

_____ide

Write more rhyming words on a sheet of LIFEPAC Tablet paper.

page 21 (twenty-one)

Name _____

Draw a line under the best title.

Tom found a box.
He looked in the box.
Guess what he saw.
Nothing!
Nothing at all!

   The Yellow Box
   Tom Guesses
   What Tom Saw

Little Rabbit was lost.
He ran here and there.
He looked for his mother.
He looked and looked.
Where is Mother?

   The Lost Rabbit
   The Last Rabbit
   Mother Rabbit

See my kite.
It is flying.
It goes up.
It comes down.
I hold on to my kite.

   My Kite
   I Can Fly
   My Car

Cows are animals.
They are very big.
They live on a farm.
Cows eat grass.
They give us milk.

   Farms
   Grass
   Cows

Language Arts 107
Worksheet 11
with page 21

Teacher check _____
                    Initial   Date

Name _____

Write a title.

   God is our Father
in heaven.
   He loved us so much
that He sent Jesus
to save us.
   He knows everything
we do or say. He hears
all our prayers.

_____

   Ice is cold. When
we freeze water it
turns to ice.
   We use ice in
iced tea or lemonade
to make it cold.
   We skate on ice
in the wintertime.

_____

   God made two
lights for us.
   The sun gives us
light in the daytime.
At night we have
moonlight.
   When it gets dark
we turn on lights
in our houses.

_____

   We have many kinds
of plants. There are
water plants and
land plants.
   Trees are very tall
plants. Flowers and
weeds are plants.
   Vines are long
creeping plants.

_____

Language Arts 107
Worksheet 12
with page 21

Teacher check _____
                    Initial   Date

Page 22: Activity Page

CONCEPT: contents page

TEACHER GOAL: To teach the children
To read and understand the information on a contents page.

MATERIALS NEEDED: other LIFEPACs and books

TEACHING PAGE 22:

Have the children read the title and the sentences at the top of the page.

Have them turn to the Contents page at the front of the LIFEPAC and read through it. Point out these things as the children read them.
LANGUAGE ARTS 107 - subject area of this LIFEPAC and its number
FUN WITH WORDS - title of this LIFEPAC

CONTENTS-PART ONE, PART TWO, PART THREE

Ask the children to tell how many parts the book is divided into. Have them read the subtitles. Have them tell which of the concepts they have already learned and which ones they will learn next.

Read the material at the bottom of the Contents page to the children. They should understand that the author is the person who writes the book, the editors are people who check the author's work to see that it is correct and that it teaches what the children are supposed to learn. The Copyright 1996 is the year the book was revised, Alpha Omega Publications is the name of the company that revised the book, and "All rights reserved" means that no one else may use anything from this LIFEPAC in their books without permission.

Have the children fill in page numbers and titles on page 22. Tell them to be sure to copy the titles exactly.

Have the children read the sentences in the middle of the page and fill in the answers. Point out that titles have all the important words capitalized, but little words such as *the, on,* or *and* are not capitalized unless they are at the beginning of the title.

ACTIVITY:

Read the contents pages in other LIFEPACs and in other books in the classroom. Have the children tell how they are like the contents page in this LIFEPAC and how they are different. Give the titles and have the children find the page numbers. Give a page number and have the children find the title for that page.

TEACHING READING:

Read the story "Flying My Kite" in *Reader 4.*

Write the words *my, fly, flying, kite, high* on the board and add any words in the story that your children have not had or need to review. Make flash cards for these words .

Read the list of words on the board. Point out the silent *e* in *kite* and the silent *gh* in *high.* Point out the word *fly* and the ending *ing* in *flying.* Have the children read the words several times.

Have the children look at the picture and tell what is happening. Let several children share their kite-flying experiences with their friends.

Have the children read the title. Ask what vowel sound they hear in each word. Ask what letter makes the long /i/ sound in the first two words (*y*).

Let the children read the story silently. *Ask the following questions:*
"Who made the kite?"
"Who is I?" (the person talking)
"Who will help fly the kite?"
"Who is Tim?"
"What is a friend?"
"Why must you have wind?"
"What did Tim do with the kite?"
"Did the kite fly?"
"How do you think the children felt when they saw the kite fly?"

"What do you think might happen next?"

Have the children read the story aloud .

Have the children find all the words that have the long /i/ or long /a/ sound. Have the children find and read the exclamations in the story. Encourage them to read with expression .

Ask the children if they remember what a pronoun is (a word used in place of a name). Have them find the pronouns in the story and tell the person or thing for which each one stands. Ask the children to find the possessive pronoun (*my*) and tell what belongs to the person in each case (*friend, kite*).

Let several children tell the story in their own words. Review the rules for telling stories before they begin.

Note: It helps if the teacher sits in the back of the room while the children are telling or reading stories. By cupping a hand around an ear, she can signal the child to speak louder without interrupting him. A downward motion of the hand can be used to tell the child to put his hands at his sides.

Praise the child for what he did well. Work on improving one thing at a time.

ACTIVITIES:

1. Make kites during the art period. Decorate sheets of wrapping paper or newsprint with paints or crayons and glue them to the frame made of the narrow strips of wood or sticks. Attach a tail made of the strips of cloth and a string. Children could find a how to book in the library that shows how to make a kite before they begin. Fly the kites on a fairly windy day during the noon hour or gym class.

Children could also bring ready-made kites from home to fly.

2. Read how-to books with instructions for making kites, stories or poems about flying kites, or stories about balloons or about flying in hot-air balloons.

Contents Page

Turn to the contents page.
Write the titles and page numbers.

I. PART ONE . . . . _2_
   Vowel Digraphs
   Long a sound
   Long e sound
   Syllables
   Silent e

II. _Part Two_ 14
   Special Consonant Blends
   Verbs Forms
   Plurals
   Sequence

How many parts are in this LIFEPAC? This LIFEPAC has _3_ parts.

PART TWO is on page _14_ .

III. PART THREE . . . . _24_
   Letters
   Invitations
   Friendly
   Business
   Sentence Construction

page 22 (twenty-two)

---

3. Talk about safety rules for flying kites, where are the best places to fly them, and from what you should stay away (power lines, trees, etc).

SELF TEST 2

CONCEPT: predicting outcomes, verb forms, plurals, sequence

TEACHER GOAL: To teach the children
To check their own progress periodically.

TEACHING PAGE 23:

Have the children read the title and tell what it means. Have the children read all the directions on the page. Be sure they understand everything they are to do. Let the children do the page by themselves. Give help only with directions.

Check the page as soon as possible and go over it with each child. Show him what he did well and where he needs more work. Have him give the correct answers for any items he missed. (ORDER: 3, 1, 2)

ACTIVITIES:

1. Give the child individual help on the kinds of things he missed.

2. If several children miss the same things, reteach them in a small group.

SPELLING WORDS:

cry
bike
fire
find
sink
free
beach
real
thief
chief

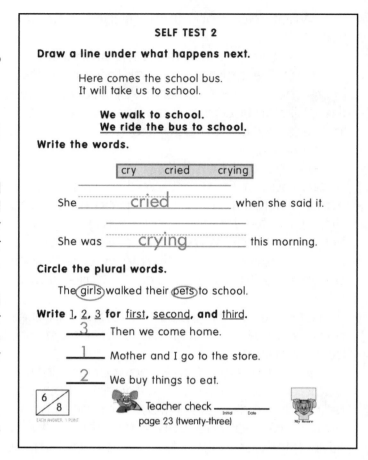

SELF TEST 2

Draw a line under what happens next.

Here comes the school bus.
It will take us to school.

We walk to school.
We ride the bus to school.

Write the words.

cry   cried   crying

She _____cried_____ when she said it.

She was _____crying_____ this morning.

Circle the plural words.

The (girls) walked their (pets) to school.

Write 1, 2, 3 for first, second, and third.

___3___ Then we come home.

___1___ Mother and I go to the store.

___2___ We buy things to eat.

6/8
EACH ANSWER, 1 POINT

Teacher check _____
                 Initial   Date
page 23 (twenty-three)

III. PART THREE

Page 24: Jane's Party

CONCEPTS: letters and invitations, outcomes, inferences, possessives

TEACHER GOALS: To teach the children
To tell the difference between a friendly letter and an invitation,
To tell how letters are sent and received,
To predict what will happen next in the story,
To make inferences from the picture and the story,
To identify the possessive, *Jane's,* and tell what belongs to her in each instance,
To identify and read words beginning with the *wh* sound, and
To tell the story and the contents of the invitation.

VOCABULARY: who, what, where, why

TEACHING PAGE 24:

Have the children read the title and sentences at the top of the page and talk about them.

Have the children read the title of the story. Tell them to look at the pictures carefully and tell what is happening in each. Have the children read the story silently, then have a child read it aloud.

Have the children read the four *wh* words aloud. Have them read the entire invitation silently. Ask the children to give the answers to the *wh* words. Have the invitation read aloud. Ask a child to tell what it says in his own words.

Ask questions similar to the following:

"Where does Jane live, in the city or in the country?" "How do you know?"

"Is it a large city or a small town?" "How do you know?" (Small towns usually do not have mailboxes on street corners or very large apartment building like this.)

"How will the mail get to the Post Office?" (trucks)

III. PART THREE

You can write words and sentences.
Now you will have fun writing
letters and stories.

JANE'S PARTY

Jane is going to have a party.
She wants her friends to come.
Her friends will get the letters.
Look at what the letters will say!

What?	A party
Where?	At Jane's house
When?	Tomorrow at three
Why?	It's Jane's birthday

Please come!

page 24 (twenty-four)

"How does Jane get her mail?" (carrier)

"How did the mail get to the boy in the other picture? (rural carrier) "Where does the boy live?" "How can you tell?"

"Who do you think the boy is?" (friend, cousin, one-time neighbor) "How do you think the boy will get to Jane's party? "

"How else could Jane have asked the boy to come to her party?" (telephone or in person)

"What is an apartment building?" "Have you ever lived in one?"

Ask the children to read the possessive in the title and tell what belongs to Jane. Have them find two more Jane's on the page and tell what belongs to her in each instance (house, birthday). Ask if anyone can find a possessive pronoun and tell what belongs to the person (her friends).

Ask if the word *it's* is a possessive.

Ask the children to tell what it means. Remind them that the possessive *its* does not have an apostrophe.

Have the children underline all the words beginning with *wh*. Have them read them aloud.

Have several children tell the entire story in their own words.

ACTIVITIES:

1. Have the children bring invitations they have received or sent from home and make a bulletin board display with them.

2. Read stories about parties or invitations to parties.

3. Let the children share experiences either sending out invitations for their own parties, or receiving invitations for someone else's party.

Page 25: Activity Page

CONCEPTS: letters: invitation, friendly, business

TEACHER GOALS: To teach the children
To identify invitations, business and friendly letters, and
To answer questions by writing complete sentences.

VOCABULARY: invitation, business, friendly

MATERIALS NEEDED: sample business letters, friendly letters

TEACHING PAGE 25:

Write the vocabulary words on the board and pronounce them for the children. Have them repeat them. Have the children give the meaning of each or use it in a sentence.

Have the children read the direction at the top of the page. Have the children read the questions aloud but give no answers. Tell the children to think about the answers.

Read the rest of the page with the children. Have them answer the question and tell about their invitations.

Read two or three examples of actual business or friendly letters to the children and have them tell which type each letter is. Talk about why people send letters. Have the children tell about business or friendly letters they have received.

Have the children write the answers to the questions at the top of the page on a sheet of writing tablet paper. Tell them to read the invitation on page 24 if they cannot remember, but to try to answer the questions by themselves if they can. Remind them to write their answers in complete sentences, to use their best writing, and to spell correctly. Ask them to tell how a sentence should begin and how statements should end.

Write the answers on a sheet of LIFEPAC Tablet paper.

1. What is Jane having?

2. Where will the party be?

3. When is the party?

4. Why is Jane having a party?

This kind of letter is called an **invitation**.

Have you ever gotten an invitation? _____

Tell about it.

Two other kinds of letters are **business** letters and **friendly** letters.

Some of the letters your mother and father get are **business** letters.

Letters that you and your parents get from friends and relatives are **friendly** letters.

page 25 (twenty-five)

To check, have one child read the question and another read his answer. Have the children correct any wrong answers. Collect the papers to see how well the children did.

ACTIVITY:

Put the business and friendly letters on the bulletin board with the invitations and label each section. You may have children bring letters from home to put on the bulletin board. Check the contents of each one before displaying it.

Page 26: Thank-You Letters

CONCEPTS: parts of a letter, thank-you letters

TEACHER GOALS: To teach the children
To identify a thank-you letter,
To name the parts of the letter and tell where each is found and what its purpose is, and
To write a thank-you letter.

VOCABULARY: (speaking vocabulary—heading, salutation, body of letter, closing, signature), thank-you

MATERIALS NEEDED: thank-you letters

TEACHING PAGE 26:

Read the paragraph at the top of the page with the children. Ask if any of the children have written or received thank-you letters. Let several tell about them.

Have the children read the direction in the middle of the page. Read the letter with the children, pointing out the parts of the letter as you read them. Talk about what the letter says.

Write the parts of the letter on the board and have the children read the name of each part, find it in the letter, and read that part of the letter.

Have the children read the direction at the bottom of the page and name the parts of a letter.

Note: Since this is just an introduction to the parts of a letter, do not expect children to remember all the names. They will learn more about them in later LIFEPACs.

Children should learn to write letters and to know the correct place for each part on the page.

Read the thank-you letters you had prepared earlier, or brought in, to the children and have them tell what the parts of the letter are. Have them tell why the person is saying, "Thank-you."

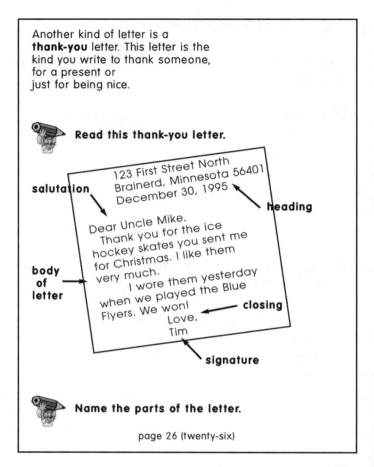

Another kind of letter is a **thank-you** letter. This letter is the kind you write to thank someone, for a present or just for being nice.

Read this thank-you letter.

salutation

123 First Street North
Brainerd, Minnesota 56401
December 30, 1995

heading

Dear Uncle Mike,
Thank you for the ice hockey skates you sent me for Christmas. I like them very much.
I wore them yesterday when we played the Blue Flyers. We won!
Love,
Tim

body of letter

closing

signature

Name the parts of the letter.

page 26 (twenty-six)

ACTIVITIES:

1. Write a class letter to thank someone for something they have done for the class or for the school. Write the letter on the board as the children give the information for the parts. Use the correct letter form. Write all sentences the children give on the board. Then read through them and choose the ones that will make the best letter. Have all the children copy the letter in their best writing and send the letters to the person.

2. Write a letter similar to the one on page 26 on a large sheet of paper or tag board and label the parts of the letter. Post where the children can see it while they are writing letters. Put the labels in a different color and have the children read them from time to time for review.

3. Add the thank-you letters to the bulletin board display from page 25 and label them.

Page 27: Envelopes

CONCEPTS: addressing an envelope, writing a letter

TEACHER GOALS: To teach the children
To identify the address and return address on an envelope, and
To write a letter and address an envelope.

VOCABULARY: (speaking vocabulary— address, return address, stamp, envelope)

MATERIALS NEEDED: used addressed envelopes, blank envelopes or papers (4" x 6")

TEACHING PAGE 27:
Prepare the paper to be used for envelopes if the children are not writing letters to be sent by mail.

Have the children read the sentence at the top of the page and look at the envelope.

Read the envelope to the children pointing out the various parts of the address and the return address.

Show the children the used addressed envelopes and point out the same parts on each of them. Try to get envelopes with rural addresses as well as city addresses. Point out the stamp and cancellation mark and explain what they are. Point out the zip code and the abbreviation for the name of the state.

Write the vocabulary words on the board and have the children read them.

Draw a rectangle on the board and address it as on page 27. Explain each part as you write (name, street address, etc.). Have the children repeat each line after you as you write it.

Erase everything inside the rectangle and write an address and a return address using local addresses. Have the children tell what each line is.

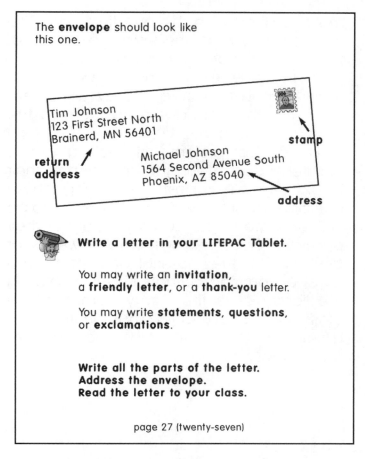

The **envelope** should look like this one.

Tim Johnson
123 First Street North
Brainerd, MN 56401

return address

stamp

Michael Johnson
1564 Second Avenue South
Phoenix, AZ 85040

address

Write a letter in your LIFEPAC Tablet.

You may write an **invitation**, a **friendly letter**, or a **thank-you** letter.

You may write **statements**, **questions**, or **exclamations**.

Write all the parts of the letter.
Address the envelope.
Read the letter to your class.

page 27 (twenty-seven)

Have the children read the directions on the rest of the page. They may write make-believe letters or they may write letters that will be mailed to someone. Talk about the kinds of things they may write about that will be interesting to the person receiving the letter. Encourage them to write at least two paragraphs.

Have them address an envelope if the letter is to be mailed, an envelope sized piece of paper if it is not.

Correct each child's letter and have him copy it over neatly. Have the children use the back of the letter for the first writing of the address on the envelope, then correct it before it is copied onto the envelope or paper.

Have each child read his letter and envelope to the class.

ACTIVITIES:
1. If the letters are mailed out, have the children bring in the answers to them and

make a display on the bulletin board. The children may read the letters to the class, then put them on the bulletin board .

2.   If the letters are not to be mailed, make a bulletin board display with them after the children have read them to the class.

For a class project, write to authors of children's books telling them which of their books you like best, or asking them questions about how the books came to be written. Write to the authors in care of their publishing house. Allow four to six weeks for answers. Put the material and letters you receive from the authors into a display in the library or in the library corner of the classroom. Each child may write to a different author, or the class may write to one author.

PAGE 28: Activity Page

CONCEPT: verb tenses: present and past

TEACHER GOAL: To teach the children
To identify verbs in their present and past tense.

VOCABULARY: different

TEACHING PAGE:

Have the children read the direction at the top of the page. Have them read the pairs of sentences and tell when the activity happened. Point out that to show when the activity is over, many words have an *ed* at the end (work—worked). With many other words, the word we use to show something is all finished or over is very different from the now word or the present tense.

Have the children read the next sentence and the pairs of sentences. Ask which word they would use to tell what is happening now, and which word they would use to tell what happened after it was finished.

Note: Using the words *now* for the present and *after* for the past tense may be easier for some children to remember. Use the terms past and present also so children become familiar with them.

Have the children read the directions for the bottom section. Have them read the words in the first set and tell which ones go together. Have them draw lines between them. Have the children read the pairs of words again.

Let capable children finish the page by themselves. Work through each set with children who need more help. Check by having the children read the pairs of words. Have them tell which word is the *now* word or present tense, and which word is the *after* word or past tense. Have the words used in sentences.

Write the following list of words on the board and have the children write a

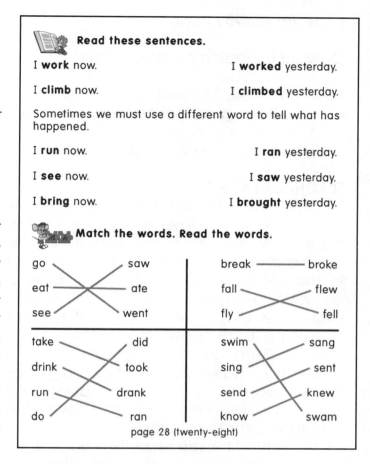

sentence for each word on a sheet of writing tablet paper. Collect the papers and correct the sentences. Have the children recopy any sentences in which mistakes were made.

is	were
are	has
was	have

Page 29: Activity Page

CONCEPT: reading comprehension, long *i*

TEACHER GOAL: To teach the children
To write a good sentence using words they understand, and
To write long *i* words ending with silent *e.*

TEACHING PAGE 29:

Have the children read the direction for the first exercise. Have them read all the parts of sentences in the first set silently. Have a child read the first line and the part in the second group that would make a complete sentence. Have other children match endings with the other two beginning parts. Have the children draw lines between the matching parts.

Let the children do the other two groups by themselves. Check by having the complete sentences read. Have the children correct any mistakes.

Have the children read the direction for the next exercise. Have them read the word endings and tell what the vowel sound is. Ask what the letter is at the end of each ending (silent *e*). Have the children give several rhyming words for each ending. Have them write words on the lines then prepare the sheet of writing tablet paper and finish writing the rhyming words on it. Write the words on the board as the children give them. Have the children add to and correct their lists. Have them read the lists and listen for the rhyming parts. Check their papers over to see who needs more help.

Dictate the following words and have the children write them on a sheet of writing tablet paper. Collect the papers and correct by drawing a line through the misspelled word and by writing it correctly on the line behind it. Have the children write each word they misspelled five times on the back of the paper (file, pile, tile, mile, pine, mine, whine, dine, line, fine).

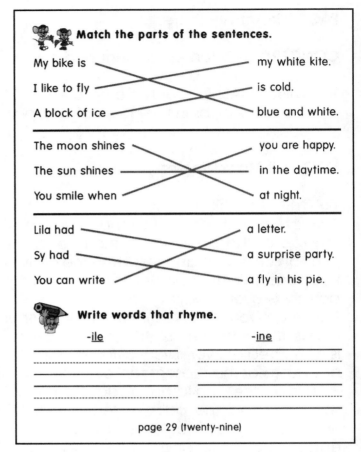

Match the parts of the sentences.

My bike is — blue and white.
I like to fly — my white kite.
A block of ice — is cold.

The moon shines — at night.
The sun shines — in the daytime.
You smile when — you are happy.

Lila had — a surprise party.
Sy had — a fly in his pie.
You can write — a letter.

Write words that rhyme.

-ile   -ine

page 29 (twenty-nine)

Be sure children know the meaning of each word.

Have the children write a sentence on a sheet of writing tablet paper for each word in the list. Collect the papers and correct. Have the children write all words they misspelled five times each on the back of the paper.

Page 30: Fun with Words

CONCEPTS: homonyms, word meanings, reading comprehension, nouns, verbs

TEACHER GOALS: To teach the children
That a word may have more than one meaning,
That some words sound alike but are not spelled the same way, and
That a word may be pronounced in more than one way.

MATERIALS NEEDED: Worksheet 13

TEACHING PAGE 30:
Note This page is meant to help children learn that the same word can have several meanings, that sometimes it can be a verb and at other times a noun. Children should learn to really listen to what people are saying and read sentences carefully to be sure they are getting the right meaning of each word that is used.

Have the children read the title. Have them tell where they have seen the same title before (on the Contents page).

Ask a child to tell what it means. Tell the children that on this page they will find that words can be very interesting.

Read the first sentence. Ask the children if they have ever attended a school play. Read the second sentence. Ask which word is the same in the first sentence (play). Ask if it means the same. Ask a child to tell the meaning. Tell the children the word *play* has other meanings:

to act the part as if on a stage, (He played a clown.)

to act in a certain way, (You must play fairly.)

to give forth or make music. (He will play the piano.)

Ask the children to read the two sentences again and tell in which one *play* is a *noun* or *naming word* and in which one it is a *verb* or *doing word.*

MORE FUN WITH WORDS

Fun With Words

We will go to the school **play**.
The cat will **play** the fiddle.

She has a pretty **ring** on her finger.
The cow's bell will **ring**.

Please **hand** the paper to me.
Humpty Dumpty cannot lend a **hand**.

 Finish the dot-to-dot picture.

page 30 (thirty)

Do the other sets of sentences the same way.

Other meanings for *ring* which children might use are

a circle with an empty center, (Tell them to hold hands and form a ring.) and

an enclosed area in which events occur. (The lions are in the circus ring.)

Other meanings for *hand* are

a round of applause (Give them a hand!) and

a pointer that moves around a circular dial, as on a clock. (The big hand is pointing to 9, so it is nine o'clock.)

Have the children give words they know that have more than one meaning. Examples:

box	play	fly
dress	walk	nail
hand	ring	right
can	band	track

Have children use each meaning of a word in a sentence.

Have the children finish the picture.

ACTIVITIES:

1. Do Worksheet 13.

To help the children learn about words that sound alike but are spelled differently, have the children read the words and tell what they mean. Have them use each word in a sentence.

plane-plain, tail-tale, right-write, sail-sale, to-two-too, die-dye, see-sea, be-bee
ate-eight, meet-meat, tied-tide, main-mane

2. To help the children learn about words with the same spelling but different pronunciations, write these words on the board. Have the children read them and give their meanings. Have each word used in a sentence.

wind (that blows)	read (the book)
wind (the clock)	read (finished reading)
live (animals)	bow (to a lady)
live (many years)	bow (of ribbon)

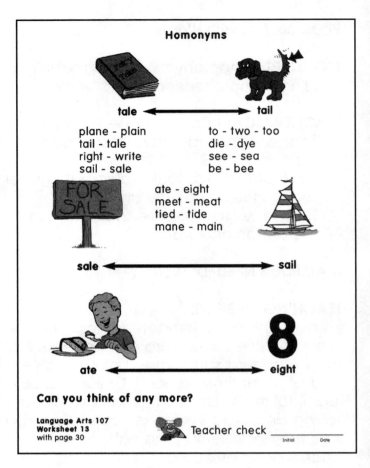

Homonyms

tale ←————→ tail

plane - plain	to - two - too
tail - tale	die - dye
right - write	see - sea
sail - sale	be - bee

FOR SALE

ate - eight
meet - meat
tied - tide
mane - main

sale ←————————→ sail

ate ←————————→ eight

8

Can you think of any more?

Language Arts 107
Worksheet 13
with page 30

Teacher check _____
Initial   Date

Page 31: Activity Page

CONCEPT: sentence types, long *i*

TEACHER GOAL: To teach the children
To identify statements, exclamations, and questions,
To write the correct punctuation, and
To spell long *i* words with *ight* and silent *e* endings.

TEACHING PAGE 31:

Have the children read the directions at the top of the page. Have them tell what each kind of sentence does, and what the punctuation mark is for each.

Tell the children to read each sentence carefully, to put S, E, or Q on the line in front of the sentence, and to put the proper punctuation mark behind it. Check by having a child read each sentence, tell what kind of sentence it is, what letter he wrote, and what punctuation mark he wrote.

Have the children read the direction for the last exercise. Have them read the word endings and give several rhyming words for each.

Check by having the children read words from their lists for you to put under the word endings you have written on the board. Have the children add to and correct their lists. Have them read the lists from the board several times, listening for the rhyming parts. Collect the papers and check them over. Be sure the children have drill cards for igh and ight.

TEACHING READING:

Read the story "The Lazy Little Train" in *Reader 4*.

Ask the children to tell what they see in the picture. Ask if the picture shows something real or something make believe. How can they tell?

Have the children read the title. Ask if the picture fits the title.

Let the children read the story silently. Help sound out words with the children if

they need help. (You might want to present the words *lazy* and *soon* before they begin if they have not had these words in their reading yet.)

Ask what was wrong with the little train and what he decided to do. Ask why the little train decided to go back to work.

Ask the children to tell if they think it is fun to be lazy. Ask them if being lazy instead of getting their work done is doing God's will.

Ask the children to find the contractions in the story. Have them read them and tell what the words are. Ask what letters were left out and why the apostrophe is used.

Have the children read the sentences that tell what the little train said. Tell the children the part of the sentence that tells what someone said is called a *direct quotation*. There will always be a quotation mark at the beginning and another one at the end.

Put S by the statements, E by the exclamations, and Q by the questions. Put ., ?, or ! at the end.

E	Oh, look	!
S	Mother is not home	.
Q	Where are you going	?
E	No, no, no	!
Q	What will you do now	?
S	I know who you are	.
E	Surprise	!
Q	Is that a train	?

Write words that rhyme.

-**ight**   -**ire**

Write more rhyming words on a sheet of LIFEPAC Tablet paper.
page 31 (thirty-one)

Write the sentences on the board and have the children point to the quotation marks and show which part of the sentence the little train said. Have the children read the story aloud .

Ask the children how many paragraphs are in the story. Ask the children to tell what each paragraph is about. Point out that each paragraph is about something different about the train, yet all the paragraphs tell a story about the train.

ACTIVITIES:

1. Have the children tell the story in their own words. Go through the Rules for Telling Stories chart before they begin.

2. Let one child be Little Train and read what Little Train says while the rest of the class reads the story.

3. Read stories and articles about real and make-believe trains.

Show films, filmstrips or videos about trains.

Read "The Little Engine That Could" or other stories about lazy people, especially those who changed for the better, and "The Grasshopper and the Ant."

SELF TEST 3

CONCEPT: rhyming words, kinds of sentences, punctuation of sentences, sentence completion

TEACHER GOAL: To teach the children
To check their own progress periodically.

TEACHING PAGE 32:
Have the children read the title and tell what it means.

Have the children read all the directions on the page. Be sure they understand everything they are to do.

Let the children do the page by themselves. Give help only with the directions. Do not have the children check this page.

Check the page as soon as possible. Go over it with each child and show him what he did well and where he will need to work.

ACTIVITIES:
1. Give individual help on items missed.
2. If several children miss the same things, reteach the skills in small groups.

SPELLING WORDS:

beef
weep
sleep
sheep
sweep
cheek
hire
fire
fight
might

SELF TEST 3

Write words that rhyme.

night _____   pie _____

tire _____   ride _____

Write S, Q, or E and ., ?, or !.

_Q_ What is in the box _?_

_E_ Oh, mother _!_

_S_ That is my house _._

_E_ Run, run _!_

_Q_ Which car is yours _?_

Draw lines to make sentences.

Jane is going	her friends to come.
She wants	get letters.
Her friends will	the letters will say.
Look at what	to have a party.

14 / 18
EACH ANSWER, 1 POINT

Teacher check _____
page 32 (thirty-two)   Initial   Date

My Score

141

LIFEPAC TEST AND ALTERNATE TEST 107

CONCEPTS: long a, sequence, vowel digraphs, predicting outcomes, syllables, verb forms, statements, questions, exclamations, and rhyming words

TEACHER GOAL: To teach the children
To check their own progress periodically.

TEACHING the LIFEPAC TEST:

Administer the test to the class in a group. Ask to have directions read or read them to the class. In either case, be sure that the children clearly understand. Put examples on the board if it seems necessary. Give ample time for each activity to be completed before going on to the next.

Correct immediately and discuss with the child.

Review any concepts that have been missed.

Give those children who do not achieve the 80% score additional copies of the worksheets and a list of vocabulary words to study. A parent or a classroom helper may help in the review.

When the child is ready, give the Alternate LIFEPAC Test. Use the same procedure as for the LIFEPAC Test.

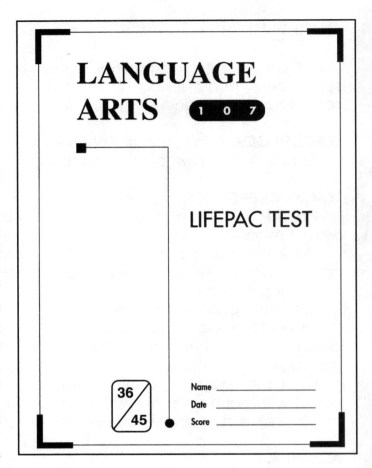

LANGUAGE ARTS 1 0 7

LIFEPAC TEST

36/45

Name _____
Date _____
Score _____

SPELLING WORDS:

LIFEPAC words	Alternate words
may	way
rain	wait
bee	weight
teach	beach
chief	real
sheep	thief
seek	sleep
fine	dine
hire	wire
right	fight

LANGUAGE ARTS 107: LIFEPAC TEST

Circle the long a words.

(sail)	(quail)	(bait)
has	got	bad
(wait)	hide	(wail)

Put 1, 2, 3 for first, second, and third.

1 Mother makes a cake.

3 We eat the cake.

2 Mother cuts the cake.

---

3 I found my dog.

2 I looked for my dog.

1 My dog was lost.

Circle the words with the vowel digraphs.

(speak)	bet	(wait)
cat	(read)	get
(bait)	(meat)	(see)

page 1 (one)

Draw a line under what will happen next.

It is dark.
I am getting ready for bed.
I say my prayers.

I will go to school.

I will go to bed.

How many parts in each word? Write 1 or 2.

happy _2_   sad _1_   slip _1_

cake _1_   bump _1_   swimming _2_

watching _2_   singing _2_   rough _1_

Write the words.

try	tried	trying

Bob _tried_ to wash his pet.

Jill is _trying_ to help him.

Circle the plural words.

The (hamsters) are in the (cages)

page 2 (two)

Write S by the statements, E by the exclamations, and Q by the questions. Put ., ?, or ! at the end.

Q Why are you here ?

S I am at school .

E Jump, Tom !

Q What is your name ?

S This is my bike .

Match the rhyming words.

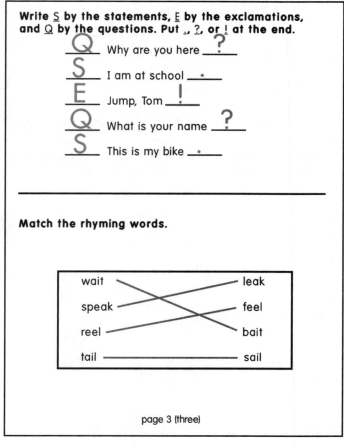

wait	leak
speak	feel
reel	bait
tail	sail

page 3 (three)

143

LANGUAGE ARTS 1 0 7

■

ALTERNATE LIFEPAC TEST

33 / 41

Name _____

Date _____

Score _____

LANGUAGE ARTS 107
ALTERNATE LIFEPAC TEST

Circle the long a words.

(sail)	(bait)	(wait)
has	bad	(quail)
(wail)	got	hide

Put 1, 2, 3, for first, second, and third.

2 ___ We work hard at school.

3 ___ We come home from school.

1 ___ We go to school.

---

1 ___ I asked Mike to go with me.

3 ___ Mike and I go for a ride.

2 ___ Mike said he would go with me.

page 1 (one)

Match the rhyming words.

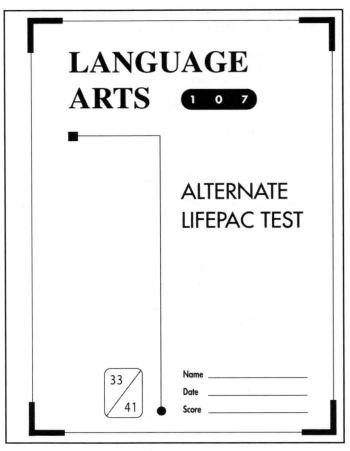

mail	week
teach	preach
wait	bait
seek	wail

Draw a line under what will happen next.

It is dinnertime.
Mother makes something to eat.
She calls the children.

The children will go away.

The children will eat.

How many parts in each word? Write 1 or 2.

summer __2__   singing __2__   laugh __1__

walking __2__   mad __1__   jump __1__

page 2 (two)

Write the words.

sing	sang	singing

They will ___*sing*___ in the morning.

We ___*sang*___ at lunch on Monday.

Write S by the statements, E by the exclamations, and Q by the questions. Put ., ?, or ! at the end.

E ___ Look, Mother, look __!__

S ___ Give me that book __.__

Q ___ Where is my hat __?__

E ___ Run, run __!__

S ___ Yes, he is __.__

Circle the vowel digraphs.

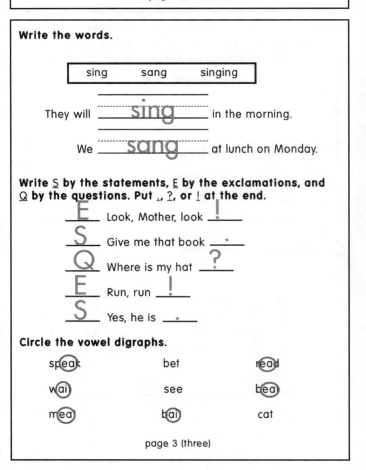

sp(ea)k	bet	r(ea)d
w(ai)l	see	b(ea)
m(ea)	b(ai)l	cat

page 3 (three)

144

Page 1: Self Awareness

CONCEPTS: self-awareness, membership

TEACHER GOALS: To teach each child
That he is a person created by God,
That no other person is exactly like him,
That he is a member of many groups (family, school, church, state, country),
That as a member of many groups he has both privileges and obligations,
That he can write his name and age and the names of his teacher, his school, and his church, and
That being a Christian is very important.

BIBLE REFERENCES: Genesis 2:7, Ephesians 6:1 through 4

TEACHING PAGE 1:

Ask the children to write their first, middle, and last names, and their ages on the lines. Help only if necessary.

Read the rest of the page together, and have the children write in the names of the teacher, school, and church. Help those who need help with spelling.

Have the children tell what being a member of a group means to them. Talk about all the groups they belong to. Talk about the privileges and the obligations they have as part of a group.

Have them tell what they receive from their parents and what their parents expect from them. Have them tell what they do at home to help. Read the Bible verses and discuss them.

Talk about privileges and obligations for their school and church groups.

Have the children tell what it means to be a Christian. Have them tell how a Christian should act in his groups.

I am _____
_____
_____
_____

I am _____ years old.

I go to _____ School.

My teacher is _____
_____

My church is _____
_____

page 1 (one)

ACTIVITY:

Have each child tell what his name is, how old he is, and what church he attends. Have each one tell a little about his family.

Page 2: FUN WITH WORDS

CONCEPT: purpose of the LIFEPAC

TEACHER GOALS: To teach the children
To understand what they will learn in the LIFEPAC, and
To read the objectives.

BIBLE REFERENCE: Proverbs 22:6

TEACHING PAGE 2:

Have the children look at the pictures at the top of the page. Ask them to name each one and to give the vowel sound they hear. (rose, book, cube) Write the words on the board and have the children read them. Put the word *boot* on the board. Point out the difference in the *oo* sound in *book* and *boot.*

Have the children read the title and the top part of the page. Talk about the sentences so the children will know what they will be expected to learn in this LIFEPAC. Have the children close their LIFEPACs and ask them to name all the things they will be learning.

Have the children read the title and tell what objectives are. Have them read each objective and discuss it. Ask the children to tell why the objectives are there. Ask the children to tell how many accomplished the objectives for LIFEPAC 107. Ask them to tell how they will accomplish the objectives for LIFEPAC 108.

Have the children write the objectives in their writing tablets.

FUN WITH WORDS

Listening, reading,
and writing can be lots of fun.
In this LIFEPAC
You will learn about main ideas.
You will learn new sounds for letters.
You will learn to spell and
write new words.
You will learn to listen and
follow directions.
You will learn to write longer stories.

 Objectives

1. I can write words with the long i sound.
2. I can write words with the long o sound.
3. I can write words with the oo sound.
4. I can write words with the long u sound.
5. I can write contractions.
6. I can write possessives.
7. I can write interesting stories.

page 2 (two)

I. PART ONE

Page 3: Activity Page

CONCEPTS: long *i*, vowel digraph *ie*, syllables

TEACHER GOALS: To teach the children
To review the sounds of long *i*, soft *g*, silent *b, e, g, gh, u*, and the *ight* words,
To review contractions,
To learn that the *ie* has the sound of long *i* or long *e*, and
To count the number of syllables in words.

MATERIALS NEEDED: Worksheet 1

TEACHING PAGE 3:
Hold up the card for *i* and ask for the long sound. Have the children give words which have the long sound of *i* at the beginning, in the middle, or at the end.

Have the children read the direction at the top of the page. Read each set of words in the box and have the children repeat them. Have the children tell what the rhyming part of the words is. Ask the children to give the meaning of each word.

Have the children give more words that rhyme with each group.

Point out the soft /g/ sound in *giant*, the silent *b* in *climb*, the silent *e* in the *ie* words, the silent *gh* in *sigh* and the *ight* words, the silent *g* in *sign*, and the silent *u* in *buy*. Point out that *wind* has two meanings and two pronunciations. Have the children read the words in the box again.

Have the children read the contractions and tell from which words each was formed. Have them use each one in a sentence.

Tell the children that the vowel digraph *ie* sometimes makes the long *e* sound.

Read the last direction.

Have the children read the *ie* words. Have them use the words in sentences.

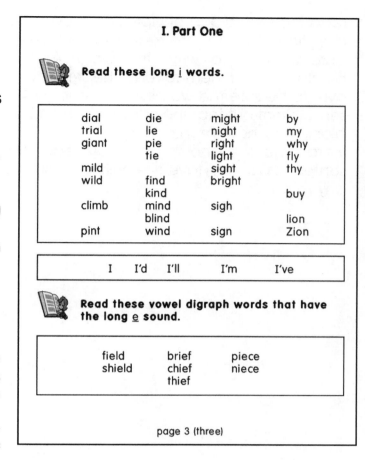

I. Part One

Read these long i words.

dial	die	might	by
trial	lie	night	my
giant	pie	right	why
	tie	light	fly
mild		sight	thy
wild	find	bright	
	kind		buy
climb	mind	sigh	
	blind		lion
pint	wind	sign	Zion

I	I'd	I'll	I'm	I've

Read these vowel digraph words that have the long e sound.

field	brief	piece
shield	chief	niece
	thief	

page 3 (three)

ACTIVITIES:
1.   Say several long *i* words from the lists on page three and have the children make them on their desks with alphabet cards. Have them say the word and spell it before you give the next word.
2.   Dictate the following words and have the children write them on a sheet of writing tablet paper. Collect the papers and correct by drawing a line through the misspelled word and by writing the word correctly on the line behind it. Have the children write each misspelled word five times on the back of the paper (die, lie, pie, by, my, why).
3.   Do Worksheet 1.

Have the children read the directions at the top of the page. Have them read the lists of words silently and write the number of syllables they hear in each word on the line behind it. Some children may need help sounding out the words. Have the children read the next group of words and read the directions. Tell them to read the sentences carefully and to write the words in the blanks. Remind them to read the sentences over to be sure the words they chose make sense. Point out that the number behind the blank tells how many syllables are in the word. Check by having children read the sentences aloud. Have the children correct any mistakes.

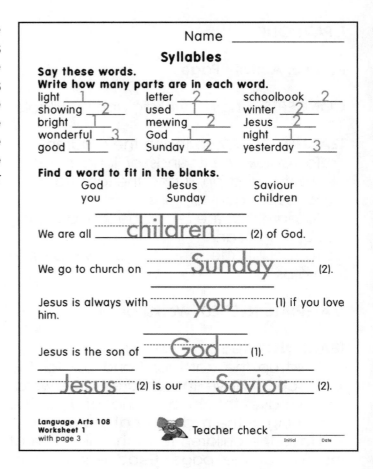

Name _____

Syllables

Say these words.
Write how many parts are in each word.

light ___1___   letter ___2___   schoolbook ___2___
showing ___2___   used ___1___   winter ___2___
bright ___1___   mewing ___2___   Jesus ___2___
wonderful ___3___   God ___1___   night ___1___
good ___1___   Sunday ___2___   yesterday ___3___

Find a word to fit in the blanks.

| God | Jesus | Saviour |
| you | Sunday | children |

We are all _____children_____ (2) of God.

We go to church on _____Sunday_____ (2).

Jesus is always with _____you_____ (1) if you love him.

Jesus is the son of _____God_____ (1).

_____Jesus_____ (2) is our _____Savior_____ (2).

Language Arts 108
Worksheet 1
with page 3

Teacher check _____
                          Initial   Date

PAGE 4: Activity Page

CONCEPTS: reading comprehension: sequence of events, possessives

TEACHER GOALS: To teach the children
To review the long sound of *ie*,
To read to understand the sequence of events, and
To write words showing possession.

MATERIALS NEEDED: Worksheet 2

TEACHING PAGE 4:
Read the first direction. Have the children circle the word with the long *e* sound. Remind them that *ie* can sound like long *e*.
Have the children read the next direction. Tell them to read all three sentences and to point to the one that happened first. Have a child read it. Have the children read the other two sentences and number them in order. Have the children read them. Have a child read all three sentences in order.
Let the children do the other set of sentences by themselves. Check by having the children read the sentences and tell which number they put in front of each. Have a child read all three sentences in order (group 1: 3, 2, 1; group 2: 2, 1, 3).

ACTIVITY:
Do Worksheet 2.
Have the children read the directions and the groups of words. Tell them to read each sentence carefully and to write in the missing word. Remind them to read the sentences over to be sure the words they chose make sense. Check by having them read the sentences aloud.
Have the children write a sentence in their writing tablets for each word in the list at the bottom of the page. Collect the papers and correct for spelling, capitalization, structure, and content. Have

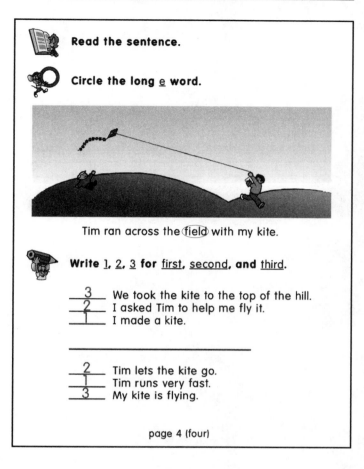

Read the sentence.

Circle the long e word.

Tim ran across the field with my kite.

Write 1, 2, 3 for first, second, and third.

__3__ We took the kite to the top of the hill.
__2__ I asked Tim to help me fly it.
__1__ I made a kite.

__2__ Tim lets the kite go.
__1__ Tim runs very fast.
__3__ My kite is flying.

page 4 (four)

the children recopy sentences in which they have made mistakes. Let the children read several of their sentences aloud.

Name _____

Write the possessives.

his	her	your	my

I have ___my___ Bible.

Joy has ___her___ Bible, too.

Do you have ___your___ Bible?

Tony will let you share ___his___ Bible.

our	their	children's	classes'

This is our Sunday School ___classes'___ room.

All the children have ___their___ books.

We all have ___our___ lessons done.

Soon the ___children's___ mother will come.

Write a sentence for each of these possessives in your LIFEPAC Tablet.

God's	my	mother's
Jesus'	our	their

Language Arts 108
Worksheet 2
with page 4

Teacher check _____
Initial   Date

Page 5: Long o

CONCEPTS: sound of long *o*, vowel digraphs *oa, ow*

TEACHER GOALS: To teach the children
To read words that have the long /o/ sound,
To learn the sound of *oa* and *ow*, and
To review compound words.

TEACHING PAGE 5:

Read these lists of words to the class and have the children tell which long vowel sound they hear.

Review sounds:

make	bike	grapes
peel	cry	train
wheat	white	me

New sounds:

go	you	home
few	cue	don't
gold	chose	fuel

Have the children read the sentence at the top of the page. Ask the children to tell what they are to listen for.

Have the children name the pictures and give the vowel sound for each.

Have the children read the list of words. Help them sound out any words with which they have trouble. Point out the variations of long *o* in the words (*o, oa,* silent *e, ow*). Be sure the children know the meaning of each word. Have them use each in a sentence.

Have the children read the next direction. Have them look at the picture and read the words. Ask a child to tell what the word *checkerboard* is.

Tell the children to look at the pictures on the page, to read the words, and to put the words together to get a compound word. Have them write the words on the lines.

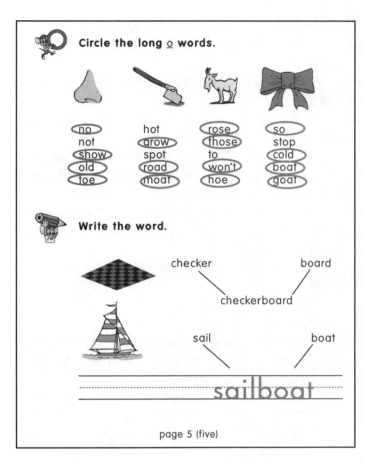

Circle the long <u>o</u> words.

no	hot	rose	so
not	grow	those	stop
show	spot	to	cold
old	road	won't	boat
toe	moat	hoe	goat

(circled: no, show, old, toe, grow, road, moat, rose, those, won't, hoe, so, cold, boat, goat)

Write the word.

checker   board
checkerboard

sail   boat
sailboat

page 5 (five)

Let the children finish the page by themselves. Check by having the children read the compound words. Write them on the board as they read them. Have the children read them again.

Have the children give other compound words and add them to the list.

TEACHING READING:

Tell students this next story is a continuation of the last story. Have them share what they remember about "Going to Florida". What was Gretchen going to do at the end of the story? (find books about alligators) Share nonfiction books or other resources about alligators. Specifically look for information about alligators and people.

Write these words on the board: whole, learning, adventure, decided, library, exercise, computer, huge, humans, quietly. Have students read the words and learn their meanings.

Read the story "No More Alligator Fear" together, then answer the following questions:

"Who went to look for books about alligators?" (the whole family)

"Where did they go?" (to the new library)

"How did they get there?" (they walked)

"Why did they walk?" (it was close to home and a nice day)

"What worried Gretchen when she got to the library?" (so many books, how to find the right ones)

"Who helped her?" (Her big brother, Alan)

"What did he show her?" (how to use the computer to find the books)

"Why did Gretchen think Joey might be right when she was looking at the books?" (alligators have big mouths)

"What did Alan find that took away her fear?" ('alligators do not harm humans')

"Why did everyone say 'hurray' quietly?" (they were in the library)

"What will Gretchen do next?" (tell Joey)

Find long vowel words: (whole, they, decided, library, be, close, home, why, don't nice, day, she, so, we, find, by, showed, use, computer, typed, screen, came, titles, see, he, told, wrote, piece, paper, like, huge, Joey, right, humans, wait, away, quietly)

ACTIVITIES:

Read the Jack Prelutsky poem, "Alligators Are Not Friendly" again. Have students put some motions with the words. Write individual, small group or class poems/songs about alligators. Make alligator hand puppets to act out songs and poems. Take a trip to the library and use the computer to find books on other topics. Take a walking tour of the library making observations of what else the library offers. Have students share experiences with a big brother or sister (or older friend) who helped them learn something. Have students write a note or card to someone who has helped them learn something.

Page 6: oo sounds

CONCEPTS: *oo* sounds, rhyming words

TEACHER GOALS: To teach the children
To identify and read words with the sound of *oo* as in *balloon* and as in *book,* and
To write rhyming words for *soon* and *cook* .

MATERIALS NEEDED: Worksheet 3

TEACHING PAGE 6:
Ask the children which letters they see at the top of the page. Have the children tell what the pictures are and read the words under each. Ask the children if the *oo* has the same sound in *balloon* and *book.*

Have the children look at each picture, write *oo,* and read the word. Tell them to listen carefully for the *oo* sound.

Have the children sound out the words in the lists. Tell them the sound of *oo* will be the same as in the picture above it.

Ask the children to read the next direction. Have them read the words. Ask for more examples of rhyming words for each of the words. Have the children read the direction at the bottom of the page. Have them finish the exercise independently.

Check by writing the words on the board and by having the children read rhyming words from the lists on their papers. Have the children add to and correct their lists.

ACTIVITIES:
1. Do Worksheet 3.
Ask the children to tell what the letters are at the top of the page and give both sounds for them. Have them tell what the pictures are and read the words underneath. Have the children read the directions. Be sure they understand what they are to do.

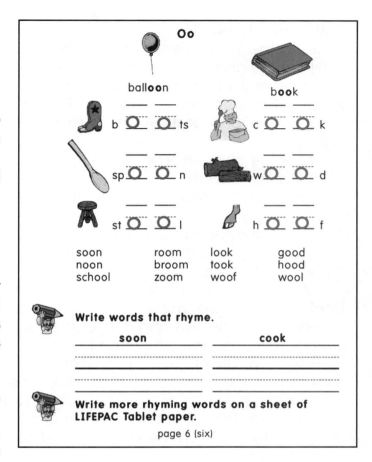

Oo

balloon   book

b oo ts   c oo k

sp oo n   w oo d

st oo l   h oo f

soon	room	look	good
noon	broom	took	hood
school	zoom	woof	wool

Write words that rhyme.

soon	cook

Write more rhyming words on a sheet of LIFEPAC Tablet paper.

page 6 (six)

Let them finish the exercise by themselves. Check by having the children read the word and tell which number they wrote on the line.

Have the children read the last direction and write the words for the pictures. Check by having the children name the picture and spell the word they wrote on the lines (book, hook, spool, spoon, moon, school).

2. Dictate the following words and have the children write them on a sheet of writing tablet paper. Correct their papers and have the children write each misspelled word five times on the back of the paper.

book	soon
cook	moon
good	school
look	room
wood	spoon

TEACHING READING:

Read the story "Friends" in *Reader 4*.

Have the children talk about lunch time. Allow several children to talk about their favorite foods to eat for lunch. Ask how many like apples best. Ask how many like oranges.

Have the children read the story silently.

Ask questions similar to these:

"What will the girls put away before they eat?"

"What kinds of fruit are in their lunches?"

"Will the girls trade food or be thankful for what they have?"

"What will the girls remember to take back to the classroom?"

Have the children find the compound word in the story. Write it on the board.

Have the children find the *oo* words as in *took*. Write them on the board under the word *took*.

Have the children find the *oo* words as in *boot*. Write them on the board under the word *boot*.

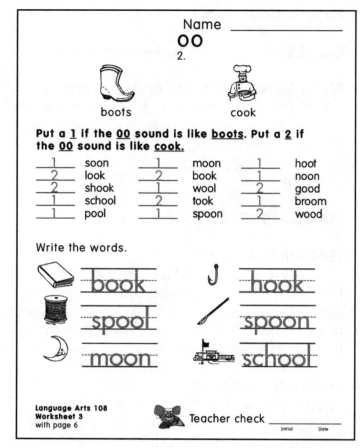

Name _____

OO
2.

boots   cook

Put a <u>1</u> if the <u>OO</u> sound is like <u>boots</u>. Put a <u>2</u> if the <u>OO</u> sound is like <u>cook</u>.

1	soon	1	moon	1	hoot
2	look	2	book	1	noon
2	shook	1	wool	2	good
1	school	2	took	1	broom
1	pool	1	spoon	2	wood

Write the words.

book   hook

spool   spoon

moon   school

Language Arts 108
Worksheet 3
with page 6

Teacher check _____
Initial   Date

Page 7: Long *u*

CONCEPTS: sound of long *u*, vowel digraphs *ou, ew*

TEACHER GOALS: To teach the children
　To read words that have the long /u/ sound, and
　To learn the sounds of *ou* and *ew*.

TEACHING PAGE 7:
　Have the children read the direction and circle the words. Help them sound out any words with which they have trouble.
　Tell the children that they have been reading long vowel words with two vowels together. These are called *vowel digraphs*. Sometimes the two vowels will have a long sound, sometimes, another sound.
　Point out the variation in letters making the sound of long *u* (silent *e, ou, ew*).
　Have the children read the directions. Help them sound out and read the words in the lists. Have them listen carefully for the long /u/ sound. Point out the various spellings.
　Have the children read the next direction. Have the children read the sentences aloud, then underline the long *u* words. Have different children read the sentences the second time. Practice the vowel digraphs with the drillcards.

TEACHING READING:
　Tell students this next story is going to give facts Gretchen learned about alligators in the books she read. Before reading, have students tell you what they know about alligators (either from previous knowledge or new learning from the stories and books shared in class) Make a chart of their answers.
　Write the following words on the board: wild, facts, realized, information, swamps, Everglades, reptile, favorite. Have students read the words and learn their meaning.

Circle the long u words.

fuse	fun	you	us
up	cute	cut	fuel
pew	sun	view	done
run	mule	use	usual

Read these words with your teacher.

Listen for the long u sound.

united	cube	fume	use
usual	cute	fuse	you
museum	mule	fuel	pew
music	view	humor	mew

Read these sentences.

Does the car need <u>fuel</u>?
There are a <u>few</u> <u>cute</u> kittens left.
We can <u>view</u> the valley.
Will you <u>use</u> the cube?

page 7 (seven)

　Read the story "A Little About Alligators" together, then ask the following questions:
　"What did Gretchen learn about wild animals?" (to leave them alone)
　"What did she learn about what Joey told her?" (some was true)
　"Where do alligators live in Florida?" (swamps, rivers, lakes, Everglades) Locate the Florida map or books to show location and pictures of the Everglades.
　"How big are alligators?" (8-10 inches as babies; over 20 feet as adults)
　"What do alligators eat?" (insects, small animals, fish, soft-shelled turtles, water snakes, birds)
　"Why does Gretchen want to take the books home?" (to read more about alligators)
　"Why do you think she hopes there is an alligator zoo?" (varied answers; she'll feel safer)

Find long vowel words: (library, day, afraid, wild, leave, alone, realized, lakes, mostly, Everglades, state, sometimes, places, true, seeing, right, told, reptile, today, babies, grow, over, feet, eat, eaters, favorites, snakes, these, read, home, like, see)

ACTIVITIES:

Discuss with students the idea of fearing what's unknown — We are more afraid when we don't know the truth. Relate this idea back to the story about Andrew getting lost in the woods.

"Why wasn't he afraid?" (He knew the Truth about Jesus-he read it in the Bible).

"Why has Gretchen's fear about alligators changed?" (She read about the facts —-she learned what was true and untrue). Use the nonfiction books to do mini reports about alligators. Use the factual information about size to measure how big alligators can be.

Have students draw and color alligator shapes on large pieces of butcher paper, cut out a front and back, stuff with paper scraps and staple around the edges to create a pet alligator. Write an imaginary story about having an alligator for a pet. Give students a paper plate and have them create a meal for an alligator (refer to the information in the story)

Page 8: Activity Page

CONCEPT: reading comprehension: real or make-believe

TEACHERS GOALS: To teach the children
To read to understand if something is real or make-believe, and
To write words with the sound of long *o*.

TEACHING PAGE 8:

Have the children read the direction at the top of the page. Tell them to read each sentence carefully and to decide whether it is true or false. Tell them, if they think the sentence is true, to circle the *yes* at the end. If they think the sentence is not true, circle the *no*. Remind them to read each sentence over after they have marked their answer to be sure they marked the right one.

Have each sentence read aloud and have the children tell whether it is true or false.

ACTIVITIES:

1. Read stories that are obviously either real or make-believe.
2. Dictate these words and have the children write them on a sheet of writing tablet paper. Correct the papers and have the children write each misspelled word five times on the back of the paper.

old	goat
cold	told
coat	boat
vote	sold
hold	tote

 Circle <u>yes</u> **or** <u>no</u>.

Blue is a color.	(yes)	no
A fox is a bird.	yes	(no)
A duck is a bird.	(yes)	no
Birds have two feet.	(yes)	no
All dogs are brown.	yes	(no)
Fish live in the water.	(yes)	no
Fish have two legs.	yes	(no)
Four comes after five.	yes	(no)
Ice cream is cold.	(yes)	no
My sister is a boy.	yes	(no)
We talk to God in our prayers.	(yes)	no
God hears us pray.	(yes)	no
We should do bad things.	yes	(no)
Jesus is with us now.	(yes)	no
Boats are good to eat.	yes	(no)
Goats are animals.	(yes)	no
Goats like green grass.	(yes)	no

page 8 (eight)

Page 9: Activity Page

CONCEPT: possessives

TEACHER GOAL: To teach the children
To select the possessive form of nouns and pronouns.

TEACHING PAGE 9:
Have the children read the direction at the top of the page. Ask the children to tell what possessives are and to give some examples.

Tell the children to read each sentence carefully. Have them circle the word that goes on the line and copy it neatly. Check by having the children read the sentences.

Ask them to tell what it is that belongs to each person.

Write the words.

That is _____ coat.
me / (my)

Please give _____ book to them.
(your) / you

_____ cat is black.
Tobys / (Toby's)

There is _____ house.
(their) / there

These are _____ toys.
(Tippy's) / Tippys

_____ sister is not home.
She / (Her)

_____ father is at work.
(Our) / Out

Those are _____ toy trucks.
him / (his)

page 9 (nine)

Page 10: Activity Page

CONCEPT: verb forms

TEACHER GOALS: To teach the children
To write verbs with *s, ed,* and *ing* endings, and
To write the correct verb form in sentences.

TEACHING PAGE 10:

Have the children read the directions for each section. Have them write words with the *s, ed,* and *ing* endings in the first exercise. Have them choose the correct verb form and copy it in the blank space in the second exercise. Have them circle the correct word before they copy it. Check by having the children read the words and sentences.

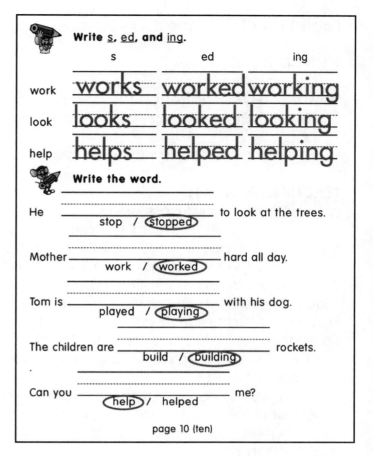

Write s, ed, and ing.

	s	ed	ing
work	works	worked	working
look	looks	looked	looking
help	helps	helped	helping

Write the word.

He _____ to look at the trees.
    stop / (stopped)

Mother _____ hard all day.
       work / (worked)

Tom is _____ with his dog.
       played / (playing)

The children are _____ rockets.
                 build / (building)

Can you _____ me?
        (help) / helped

page 10 (ten)

Page 11: Activity Page

CONCEPT: possessives

TEACHER GOALS: To teach the children
To match meanings with possessives, and
To write sentences using possessives.

TEACHING PAGE 11:
Review the word *possessive*.

Have the children read the direction at the top of the page. Have the children read the meanings and possessives in the first half of the exercise. Have the first meaning read aloud and ask which possessive matches it. Have the children draw a line, then let them finish the rest of the exercise. Check by having the meanings and possessives which match read aloud.

Do the second half of the exercise as a group and talk about each possessive and its meaning after the children have matched them.

ACTIVITIES:

1. Have the children use each of the possessives in the right-hand column on the page in a sentence. Have them write the sentences on a sheet of writing tablet paper. Let each child read several of his sentences aloud.

2. Read stories about Sunday school and church attendance and stories about Jesus.

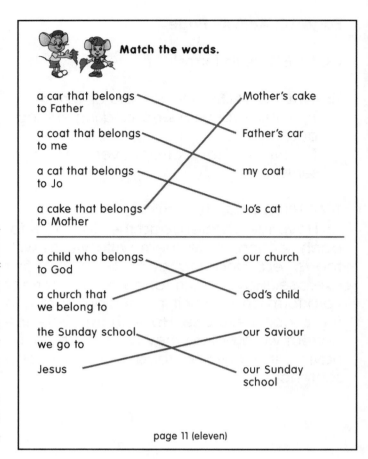

Match the words.

a car that belongs to Father

a coat that belongs to me

a cat that belongs to Jo

a cake that belongs to Mother

Mother's cake

Father's car

my coat

Jo's cat

a child who belongs to God

a church that we belong to

the Sunday school we go to

Jesus

our church

God's child

our Saviour

our Sunday school

page 11 (eleven)

Page 12 : Activity Page

CONCEPT: alphabetical order

TEACHER GOAL: To teach the children
To put letters and words in alphabetical order.

VOCABULARY: alphabet, alphabetical

MATERIALS NEEDED: alphabet cards and charts, Worksheet 4

TEACHING PAGE 12 :

Present the word *alphabet* and ask the children what it is. Have the children say the alphabet. Tell them that when you put the letters of the alphabet into the order in which you say them, it is called *alphabetical* order. Have the children repeat it several times and tell what it means.

Put four or five letter cards on the chalk tray or on a table and ask a child to put them in order. Be sure an alphabet chart is where the child can see it. Do this with different groups of letters until you have used all the letters in the alphabet. Have some groups of letters close to each other in the alphabet, and others with the letters widely separated.

Examples: (d f a c b) (g z m a r)

Write a letter on the board and ask the child to come up and write the letter that comes before it and the letter that comes after it. Give each child a chance to do this at least once.

Write two words on the board and ask the children to tell which one would come first in the alphabet.

Examples:

boy	zoo
fur	yes
joy	old
butter	went

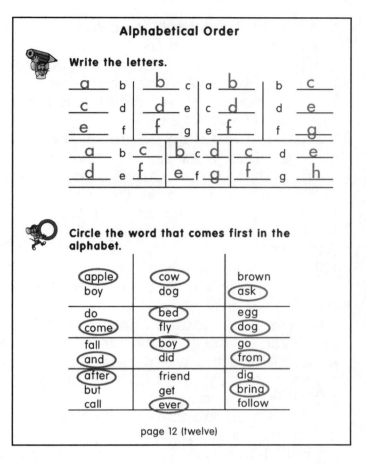

Write the following sets of words on the board.

can	jump	this
class	jar	these
glass		which
girl		why

Ask if anyone can tell which word will come first in the alphabet. Someone may know that you look at the second or third letter in the word if the first or the first and second letters are the same. If not, tell them and show them with the words written on the board. Do not expect all the children to remember this. Only a few may be ready to learn it.

Have the children read the title and the first direction. Tell them to look at the letter carefully. If the line is in front of the letter, write the letter that comes before the letter in the alphabet. If the line is behind the letter, write the letter that comes after it in the alphabet. Do the first two examples of each kind with the children, then let them finish the exercise. Check by having the children read each set aloud. Have them correct any mistakes.

Ask the children to read the next direction. Do the first set with them, then let them finish the page. Check by having the word that would come first read aloud. Have the children correct any mistakes.

ACTIVITIES:

1. Do Worksheet 4.

Have the children read the directions at the top of the page. Do the first three examples together, then have the children finish the page. Check by having the children read the words in the order they come in the alphabet. Do this page with the slower students.

The starred exercise is more difficult. The children must put these words in alphabetical order by the second letter. You may wish to have some children work through this part with your help, or omit it.

2. For a short, time-filling drill say "before j" or "after d" and have the children give the letter you are asking for.

3. Say two words and have the children tell which one comes first in the alphabet.

Name _____

Number the words in the order they come in the alphabet.

1	apple	3	girl	1	bird
2	boy	1	egg	3	zoo
3	cow	2	farm	2	help
2	doe	3	stone	2	look
3	hoot	2	moon	1	foot
1	cone	1	joy	3	pool
2	you	2	queen	3	other
1	wood	3	toe	1	end
3	zoom	1	note	2	ill
2	out	1	how	3	use
1	kick	3	vow	2	mule
3	root	2	now	1	ask
H 1	back	2	clock	3	tube
3	big	3	crow	1	table
2	bed	1	can	2	took

Language Arts 108 Worksheet 4 with page 12

Teacher check _____
Initial   Date

SELF TEST 1

CONCEPTS: long *i*, long *o*, long *u*, vowel digraphs, possessives, and alphabetical order

TEACHER GOAL: To teach the children
  To check their own progress periodically.

TEACHING PAGE 13:

Have the children read all the directions on the page. Be sure they understand exactly what they are to do. Let them complete the page independently.

Correct the page as soon as possible. Go over it with the child so he can see what he did well, and where he needs more work. Have him correct any mistakes as you are going through the page.

ACTIVITIES:

1. Reteach concepts the child has missed.

2. If several children miss the same things, work with them in a small group session.

SPELLING WORDS:

pie
lie
tie
die
might
night
right
light
guy
buy

II. PART TWO

Page 14: Joan's New School

CONCEPTS: introductions, contractions

TEACHER GOALS: To teach the children
To make simple introductions,
To introduce themselves to others,
To introduce their friends to each other, and
To understand contractions and their uses.

TEACHING PAGE 14:

Present the new words *Joan* and *school*. Have the children repeat them several times and use each in a sentence.

Ask the children to look at the picture and tell what they think is happening.

Have the children read the title aloud. Let them read the story silently.

(Ask the children to find and read sentences that answer these questions:)

"How did Joan feel at first?"

"Why did she feel this way?"

"What did the other children do? Then how did Joan feel?"

Let several children each read a paragraph aloud. Have the children find and read the contractions in each paragraph. Be sure the children understand where *Joan's* is a contraction, not a possessive. Have the children circle the contractions. Have the children tell what the original words were for each contraction.

Have the children draw a line under each word that contains an *oo* or *oa* vowel digraph.

Ask the children to tell how Joan got to know the other children. Tell them that when someone tells someone else their name, they are introducing themselves. Have the children give examples of how they think this could be done. Teach the children that

II. PART TWO

JOAN'S NEW SCHOOL

Joan wasn't very happy.
She didn't like her new school.
She didn't know any of the children.

The children told Joan their names.
They asked her to play with them.
They worked and played all day.

Quite soon it was time to go home.
Joan's happy now.
She likes her new school, and
    she has many friends.

page 14 (fourteen)

the best way is simply to say, "Hello, my name is Mary Smith." Give the children a chance to introduce themselves to several other children for practice.

Children should also practice introducing one friend to another. The most effective way for younger children is: "Mary, this is John." *or* "Mary, this is my friend, John." The proper responses would be, "Hello, John." *and* "Hello, Mary."

Only two rules need to be stressed at this point: always introduce the boy or man to the girl or woman; and always introduce the younger person to the older person.

ACTIVITY:

Set up situations requiring introductions and let the children practice introducing people correctly. Use situations similar to these:

a. your friends to your mother,
b. your mother to your teacher,
c. your friend to your pastor, and
d. your friend to an older friend.

TEACHING READING:
Have the children read the story "Joan's New School" from *Reader 4* silently.

Page 15 : Activity Page

CONCEPTS: contractions, oral expression

TEACHER GOALS: To teach the children
To match contractions and their meanings, and
To learn to speak clearly and in complete sentences.

MATERIALS NEEDED: Worksheet 5

TEACHING PAGE 15:

Have the children read the directions on the page. Have them do the contraction exercises by themselves. Check by having the words and contractions read in the first exercise. In the second exercise, have the children write the contractions on the board. Have the children correct any mistakes.

Have the children read what is in the discussion box and talk about it. Choose a child to lead the discussion under your supervision. Encourage every child to participate. Help the leader keep the discussion on the subject. Remind him to ask questions to get every child involved. Every child should have a chance to lead a discussion during the year.

ACTIVITIES

1. Do Worksheet 5.

Have the children read the directions for each section. Have them do the exercises by themselves. Give help only if necessary. Check by having the children read the words and contractions. The teacher should collect the papers and check the spelling and placement of the apostrophe for each.

2. Use small group discussions for book reports, show and tell, planning parties or programs, planning art or social studies projects, science projects and experiments. Sessions should be ten minutes or less. The

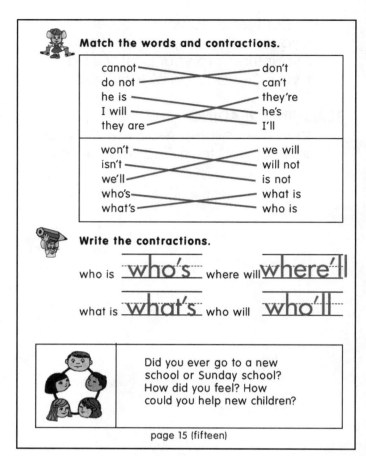

Match the words and contractions.

cannot	don't
do not	can't
he is	they're
I will	he's
they are	I'll

won't	we will
isn't	will not
we'll	is not
who's	what is
what's	who is

Write the contractions.

who is ___who's___ where will __where'll__

what is ___what's___ who will __who'll__

Did you ever go to a new school or Sunday school? How did you feel? How could you help new children?

page 15 (fifteen)

teacher, aide, or parent volunteers may supervise, but the teacher should meet with each group at least once every month.

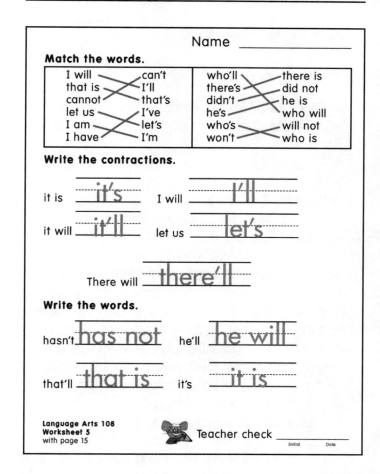

Name _____

Match the words.

I will ⟍ ⟋ can't
that is ⤫ I'll
cannot ⟋ ⟍ that's
let us ⟍ ⟋ I've
I am ⤫ let's
I have ⟋ ⟍ I'm

who'll ⟍ ⟋ there is
there's ⤫ did not
didn't ⟋ ⟍ he is
he's ⤫ who will
who's ⤫ will not
won't ⟍ ⟍ who is

Write the contractions.

it is ___it's___   I will ___I'll___

it will ___it'll___   let us ___let's___

There will ___there'll___

Write the words.

hasn't ___has not___   he'll ___he will___

that'll ___that is___   it's ___it is___

**Language Arts 108
Worksheet 5
with page 15**

Teacher check _____
Initial   Date

167

Page 16: Activity Page

Concepts: *qu* and *squ*

TEACHER GOALS: To teach the children
To understand the sounds of *qu* and *squ*, and
To write *qu* and *squ* in words.

TEACHING PAGE 16:

Write the letters *qu* on the board. Ask the children to read them. Tell them the sound for *qu* is the same sound as they make for *kw*. Have the children say it several times. Tell the children that in the words they will be reading, the *q* and *u* are always found together. They may be at the beginning of a word or in the middle, but never at the end.

Have the children read the direction at the top of the page. Help them sound out and read the words. Have them underline or draw a circle around the *qu* in each word.

Have them read the next direction. Have them name the pictures, write *qu* under each picture on the lines, and then read the words.

Have the children read the next direction. Help them sound out and read the words. Have the children read the next direction. Have them name the pictures, write *squ* under each picture on the lines, and then read the words.

Have the children read the last direction, and then use each of the words in a sentence. These may be oral or written.

TEACHING READING:

Teach students a chant: "Buzzing bee, buzzing bee, why are you chasing me?" (say twice) Choose one student to be the "bee". This "bee" will answer the question after students have chanted the question. Take turns choosing students to be the bee. Determine a good time to stop, then discuss the reasons the bees came up with for chasing. List them on the board.

Read these words.

quite   quiet   quick   quack

Write qu. Read the words.

queen   quail   quarter   quilt

Read these words.

squeak   squat   squirt   squeal

Write squ. Read the words.

square   squirrel   squash

Use each of the qu and squ words in a sentence.

page 16 (sixteen)

Introduce the next story: The Bee Chase

Write these words on the board: quickly, queen, quietly. Have students read the words and learn their meaning.

Read the story "The Bee Chase" together, then ask the following questions:

"Why was Trudy yelling 'help?'" (a bee was chasing her)

"Why did Trudy change the subject?" (answers varied; didn't want to admit that she bothered the bee)

"How was Mother feeling about her changing the subject?" (not too pleased)

"What did Trudy finally admit?" (she made the bee mad)

"Why did she shoo the bee away?" (she wanted the yellow flower it was sitting on)

"What will Trudy do next time?" (leave the bee alone)

"What did Trudy give to her mother at the end?" (the yellow flower)

Find qu words: (quickly, queen, quietly). Find long e and long u words: (bee, Trudy, me, mean, usually, queen, see, agree, be)

ACTIVITIES:

Make a garden of flowers. (Students can each make a flower or use die-cut shapes) Have each student draw, color and cut out a bee to add to the class picture. Share the poem: "Chirp and Buzz" by David Byrn, Who Sat On My Sandwich? Initiate a discussion on being truthful. What were some of the reasons Trudy's mother knew she wasn't being truthful? (she got quiet, she changed the subject, Mother knew bees don't usually bother us). Relate this story to Gretchen's learning about wild (alligators) animals.... "leave them alone." Have students make a list of wild animals. Make posters relating the message to leave wild animals alone.

Page 17: Activity Page

CONCEPT: reading comprehension: main idea

TEACHER GOALS: To teach the children
To define a sentence and a paragraph,
To read to find the main idea, and
To write complete sentences with correct punctuation.

MATERIALS NEEDED: Worksheet 6

TEACHING PAGE 17:

Have the children read the direction at the top of the page. Have them tell what a sentence is (a group of words that make a complete thought).

Have the children read each group of sentences and decide what the main idea is. Have them write it in a complete sentence on the lines.

Note: Some children may still be writing very large. You may wish to have them use a sheet of writing tablet paper, instead.

Do the first example with the children.

Check by having children read the sentences they wrote. Have the children correct any mistakes.

Ask the children to tell what a group of sentences about the same thing is called (paragraph). Ask the children to tell whether or not all the sentences in each group should be there.

ACTIVITY:

Do Worksheet 6.

Have the children read the direction at the top of the page. Have them read each story carefully and write a complete sentence telling what the story is about.

Collect the papers and check for spelling, punctuation, capitalization, sentence structure, and content. Have the children recopy sentences in which they made mistakes.

Let the children read their sentences aloud.

Write what the sentences are about.

Jo has a new coat.
It is red and black.
She likes her new coat.

The boys were running.
The girls were running.
The cats and dogs were running, too.

We like to go to school.
We work hard in school.
We have fun, too.

Cats are good pets.
They must have food and water.
We have fun with cats.

page 17 (seventeen)

Name _____

Write what the story is about.

Little Rabbit ran this way and that way. He found something to eat. Then he went home and went to sleep.

Tony's dog was lost. Tony was looking for him, but he could not find him. Where could Tony's dog be?

Jim had a new coat. It was red. Mother and Father gave Jim his new coat. Jim liked his coat.

**Language Arts 108
Worksheet 6
with page 17**

Teacher check _____
Initial   Date

Page 18: Activity Page

CONCEPTS: short *u*, plurals

TEACHER GOALS: To teach the children
   To review the sound of short *u*, and
   To form plural words.

TEACHING PAGE 18:

Hold up the flash card for the letter *u* and ask for its name and short sound. Ask the children to give words beginning with the sound and words having it in the middle.

Have the children read the direction at the top of the page. Do the first example together. Have them look at the picture of a cup, read the words, look at the two cups, and trace the word, then write it.

Have the children tell what kind of word *cups* is (plural). Ask what it means. Review all the plurals on the page.

Have the children read the words which have the short *u* sound.

Let the children finish the page by themselves. Check by having them read the line and speak the word they wrote on the lines. The teacher should collect the papers and check them. Have the children correct any mistakes.

ACTIVITY:

Have the children select three words from the page and write one sentence for each word.

Write the words.

one cup	two	cups
one pup	three	puppies
one duck	two	ducks
one cuff	two	cuffs
one truck	two	trucks
one drum	three	drums

page 18 (eighteen)

Page 19: Brown Pony

CONCEPTS: listening, recalling a story

TEACHER GOALS: To teach the children
To listen,
To recall the story with accurate recall of details and sequence of events, and
To use the information in the story to illustrate the events.

TEACHING PAGE 19:

Tell the children to listen very carefully because you are going to read them a story only once. They must answer some questions about it.

Read this story:

Once there was a brown pony. He was not very big, but he was very strong. His owner took good care of him and gave him plenty of food and water.

One day when the pony was in the barn eating some hay, a fire started in the grass outside the barn. It spread fast and soon the pony smelled the smoke.

The pony pushed against the barn door. He pushed and pushed. Suddenly the barn door opened and the pony ran outside. He was safe.

Soon some men came and put the fire out.

Have the children read the directions. Tell them to read the first part of the sentence carefully. Have them read the two words at the end of the sentence and circle the one that finishes the sentence the way they heard it in the story. Have the children read the directions at the bottom of the page and do what it says to do.

ACTIVITY:

Have a pet show. This show could be just for your class or for the entire school. Let your class plan it and manage it. It could be held in connection with a science fair or parent-teacher meeting.

Listen to the story.

Circle the right answers.

This story is about.............. (a pony) / a horse.

The pony was.......................... gray. / (brown)

The pony was...................... (small.) / large.

The fire began in the........... (grass.) / glass.

The fire got............................ (bigger.) / better.

The pony smelled.................. small. / (smoke.)

The pony ran......................... our. / (out.)

He was.................................... (safe.) / some.

Draw a picture of this story.

Color your picture.

page 19 (nineteen)

Page 20: Activity Page

CONCEPT: reading comprehension: sentences that make sense

TEACHER GOALS: To teach the children
To think about what they are reading, and
To decide if what they are reading makes sense.

TEACHING PAGE 20:
Have the children read the direction at the top of the page. Tell the children to read the words at the top of each set of sentences. Then have them read both sentences and copy the words into the blanks so that the sentences make sense and sound right. Let them finish the page by themselves.

Check by having the children read the sentences with the correct words.

The teacher should collect the papers and check them. Have the children correct any mistakes.

Have the children use the same words in sentences of their own.

ACTIVITIES:
Have the children draw a picture and write a paragraph about a truck.

The children may show their picture and read their paragraphs to the class.

Note: Always take time as soon as possible after the children finish their writing to let them read it to the class. This helps them learn to stand in front of a group and speak. It will also encourage them to be more creative in their writing and drawing because they know they will be sharing it with their classmates.

Some children should be encouraged to write longer, more detailed stories.

Write the words.

truck	trucks

I have a toy ___truck___ .

The ___trucks___ are big.

---

is	are

Tom and Jack ___are___ running.

That ___is___ my dog.

---

run	ran

I will ___run___ fast.

The boys ___ran___ to school.

page 20 (twenty)

Page 21: Activity Page

CONCEPTS: reading comprehension: sentences that make sense, recalling details

TEACHER GOALS: To teach the children
To decide if what they are reading makes sense, and
To read for understanding and to recall details.

TEACHING PAGE 21:

Have the children read the direction and the two words at the top of each section. Tell them to read the sentences carefully and to write the correct word on the line. Remind them to read the sentence again after they have written the word and to see if the sentence makes sense and sounds right.

Check by having the children read the sentences. Collect the papers and correct. Have the children correct any mistakes.

TEACHING READING:

Read "Baby Zebra" in Reader 4.
Write the words _cold, Zebra, sneezed, hanky, again,_ and _parachute_ on the board, pronounce each one and have the children repeat it. Point out the parts of the words that might cause problems: long _o_ in cold, long _e_ in Zebra and sneezed, capital _Z_ in Zebra because it is a name in this story, the ending on sneezed, the _nk_ and _y_ with the long /e/ sound in _hanky, ai_ with the sound of short _e_ in _again,_ and the /sh/ sound for _ch_ in parachute. Be sure the children know the meanings of the words. Have them repeat the list several times.

Have the children look at the picture and tell what they think is happening. Ask if anyone has seen a zebra and where. Have the children read the title. Ask where they hear the long /e/ sound in the words.

Have the children read the story silently, then have it read aloud.

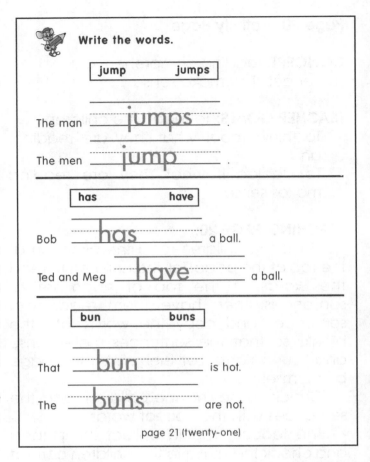

page 21 (twenty-one)

Ask questions such as these:
"What was wrong with Baby Zebra?"
"Where do you think he caught the cold?"
"What was the sound of the sneeze?"
"Why should you always use a hanky when you sneeze?"
"Why did Baby Zebra think he had a parachute?"
"Could this story really happen?" "Why not?"
"Could Baby Zebra clap his hands?" "Why not?"
"What do you think will happen next?"
Have the children read the words with the long /e/ sound in the story.

Have the children find the pronouns in the story and tell for whom each one stands. Have them read the sentence using the name instead of the pronoun.

Ask the children to find exclamations and read them with expression. Ask which exclamation is also a direct quotation. Ask the children to tell what a direct quotation is and where the quotation marks are.

Ask if there are other places in the story where a direct quotation might have been used. Have the children tell what could have been said. (Baby Zebra could ask for a hanky, or Mother Zebra could say, "Here is your hanky.")

Have several children tell the story in their own words.

ACTIVITIES:

1.   Write the word *hanky* on the board and underline the *nk.* Tell the children that *n* and *k* together have a little different sound, almost as if a *g* were put in between them and the word was spelled *hangky.* Say the sound several times and have the children repeat it. Write these words on the board and have the children find the sound and say the words several times (think, sink, bunk, bank, clink, dunk, thank, rink, spank, blank).

Be sure children know the meanings of all the words. Have children use each one in a sentence .

2.   Have the children make parachutes. Tie strings to all four corners of a handkerchief and tie the other end of the strings to a washer. Throw the parachute up in the air and watch it come down. Use a very lightweight washer or the parachute will come down too fast.

3.   Read stories about zebras or other zoo animals and articles about zebras from science books or encyclopedias or books on wild animals.

Page 22: Activity Page

CONCEPTS: verb tenses, recalling details

TEACHER GOALS: To teach the children
To review subject-verb agreement, in sentences,
To review present tense (what is happening now) and past tense (if something is already done), and
To recall details of a story.

TEACHING PAGE 22:

Read "Baby Zebra" again.

Have the children read the direction at the top of the page. Tell the children to read the sentence carefully, including the two words under the lines, then circle the correct word. Tell the children to read the sentence again with the word they have circled to see if the sentence makes good sense. Then have them copy the word on the line.

Let the children do the page by themselves. Give help only if needed.

Check by having the children read the sentences. The teacher should also check this page.

ACTIVITIES:

1. Write the word *begin* on the board. Read the word and tell the children we say *begin* when we are starting now, as "Begin your work." Ask what the word would be when we have already started. Write the word *began* behind *begin* and say both words several times.

Do the same with the following words. Write the word you would use if it were happening now and ask children to give the word they would use if it were already done.

blow	blew	grow	grew
break	broke	know	knew
bring	brought	run	ran
come	came	see	saw
do	did	send	sent

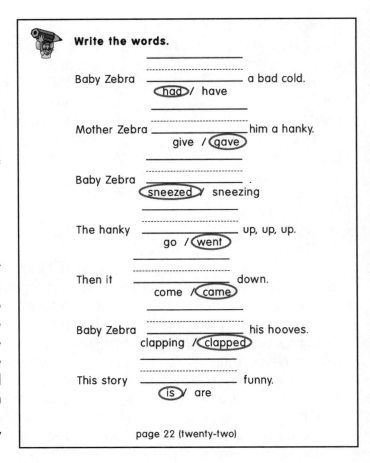

Write the words.

Baby Zebra _____ a bad cold.
had / have

Mother Zebra _____ him a hanky.
give / gave

Baby Zebra _____ .
sneezed / sneezing

The hanky _____ up, up, up.
go / went

Then it _____ down.
come / came

Baby Zebra _____ his hooves.
clapping / clapped

This story _____ funny.
is / are

page 22 (twenty-two)

draw	drew	sing	sang
drink	drank	ring	rang
drive	drove	speak	spoke
eat	ate	swim	swam
fall	fell	take	took
fly	flew	throw	threw
freeze	froze	wear	wore
sneeze	sneezed	sit	sat
go	went		

2. Another good way for children to learn these forms is to say a sentence similar to this to themselves:

I (take) it now. I (took) it yesterday.

Do exercises like this often. Correct the children when they have finished speaking. Tell them the correct word and have them repeat the sentence.

Page 23: Plurals

CONCEPTS: plurals, writing sentences

TEACHER GOALS: To teach the children
To identify and write plurals, and
To write a complete sentence for each plural.

MATERIALS NEEDED: Worksheet 7

TEACHING PAGE 23:
Ask the children to read the title. Have them read the lists of plurals and give the singular for each. Have the children tell how each plural was formed .

Have the children read the next direction. Tell them to read the word carefully. Have them write its plural on the lines. Write the list on the board and let the children correct their spelling .

Have the children read the next directions. Review what a complete sentence is.

Collect the papers and check for correct use of the plural, spelling, sentence structure, capitalization, and punctuation. Give them back to the children for correction. Let each child read two or three sentences aloud.

ACTIVITIES:
1.   Do Worksheet 7.
Have the children read the directions and complete the page by themselves. Check by having the children read the singular and plural words.

If your class has not had any experience with crossword puzzles yet, put this diagram on the board and print the definitions on each side. Work through it with the children and leave it on the board while they are doing the worksheet.

2.   Write these plurals on the board or duplicate copies to give to the children. Have them write the singular for each.

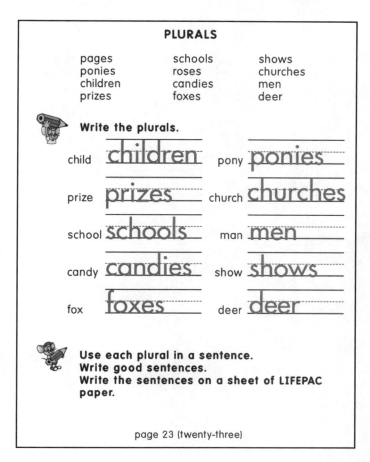

babies (baby)	women (woman)	
boxes (box)	moose (moose)	
flies (fly)	bunches (bunch)	
days (day)	sheep (sheep)	
houses (house)		

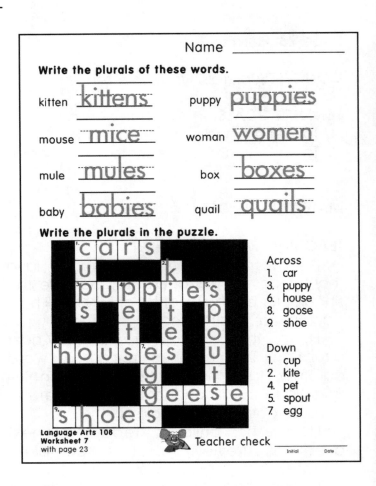

Name _____

Write the plurals of these words.

kitten kittens   puppy puppies

mouse mice   woman women

mule mules   box boxes

baby babies   quail quails

Write the plurals in the puzzle.

Across
1. car
3. puppy
6. house
8. goose
9. shoe

Down
1. cup
2. kite
4. pet
5. spout
7. egg

**Language Arts 108
Worksheet 7**
with page 23

Teacher check _____
Initial   Date

Page 24: Activity Page

CONCEPT: long *u*

TEACHER GOALS: To teach the children
To review the sound of long *u*, and
To learn proper use of the telephone.

VOCABULARY: underline

TEACHING PAGE 24:

Discuss the picture at the top of the page. Have the children read the sentence. Have them underline words that have the long *u* sound.

Have the children read the last direction on the page. Have a child read each word and give a rhyming word. Have the children write a word for each word. The starred words are more difficult. You may wish to do the entire exercise with the children.

TEACHING READING:

Read the story "Playing" in *Reader 4*.

Write the words *hello, Jeannie, Dee Dee, oh, good-bye* on the board and pronounce them. Have the children repeat them several times.

Have the children read the title and tell what is happening in the picture. Ask if anyone can guess what the girls are talking about. (The bike formed by the telephone wire might give someone a clue.)

Have the children read the conversation silently. Ask who is talking, who is she talking to, and what did she ask Jeannie to do. Ask what Dee Dee has that is new and what it is like. Ask what Jeannie decided to do and how Dee Dee feels. Have a child read the page aloud.

Read what Dee Dee says and have the children give Jeannie's answers. Write the answers on the board. Let one child read each part using the telephones. If you have dial phones, make up a number and have the child dial it before he begins reading.

Jan will walk on cue to humor us!

Underline the words with the long <u>u</u> sound.

Read the sentences again.

Write a word that rhymes.

muse	_____	tube	_____
you	_____	plume	_____
H cue	_____	H you'll	_____

page 24 (twenty-four)

The child playing Jeannie could also answer "Hello" before Dee Dee begins talking.

Let several pairs of children act out the conversation. Boys may use names with the long /e/ sound such as Bobby, Ronnie, or Dean.

Talk about good telephone manners. Children should know how to answer the phone politely. Answering "Hello" in a cheerful voice is acceptable, but answering "Johnson's residence", is much better. Teach whatever is the accepted practice in your community.

Teach the children to end the conversation with "Good-bye". Tell them that just hanging up the phone is very rude.

Children should be taught how to take a message for someone else. Tell them to write the message down, to be sure they have times and places right, and to ask the person to repeat if they do not understand, or to spell names to be sure they have it right. *Have the children practice conversations such as this:*

Child: "Jones' residence."

Caller: "This is Mrs. Smith. May I speak to your mother, please?"

Child: "I'm sorry, Mrs. Smith, my mother can't come to the phone right now. May I take a message for her?"

Caller: "Yes, please tell her to call me when she comes home. My number is 555-5516."

Child: "Would you repeat your number again, please?"

Caller: "Yes, my number is 555-5516."

Child: "Thank you, Mrs. Smith. I'll have my mother call you as soon as possible. Good-bye."

Caller: "Thank you. Good-bye."

Have the child playing Ann actually write down Mrs. Smith's name and phone number. Let several children act out this conversation or write similar ones using their own names.

Note: Some telephone companies have real phones with dials and ringers which can be borrowed by schools. Some also have booklets on telephone manners which the children may use.

If you cannot get real telephones, ask children to bring play phones from home (take any batteries out). Two telephones for each small group would be ideal.

ACTIVITY:

Let the children work in pairs and write their own conversations. Let the children act them out in front of the class or in their small group.

Page 25: Activity Page

CONCEPTS: verb forms, long *o*, writing a story

TEACHER GOALS: To teach the children
To use correct verb forms, to review silent *e* and vowel digraph *oa*, and
To write a story using complete sentences and paragraphs.

VOCABULARY: interesting

MATERIALS NEEDED: drawing paper, crayons or paint, Worksheet 8

TEACHING PAGE 25:

Have the children read the directions at the top of the page. Have them read the endings.

Do the first example as a group. Have the children read the first word. Ask which ending will go in the blank behind the next word. Have them write it in. Have them read the new verb form. Ask the children to use each word in a sentence to show when this would happen. Let the children finish the exercise, then check.

Have the children read the next direction and the endings. Have them give rhyming words for the endings and write two words for each ending on the lines. Have them write more words on a sheet of writing tablet paper. Write the endings on the board and put rhyming words under them as the children read from their lists. Point out the different spellings for the same sounds. Have the children add to and correct their lists.

Have the children read the last set of directions. Tell the children to reread "Flying My Kite" in *Reader 4*. Tell them to write a story about a kite. Remind them to use complete sentences and good paragraphs. Have them draw a picture to go with their story.

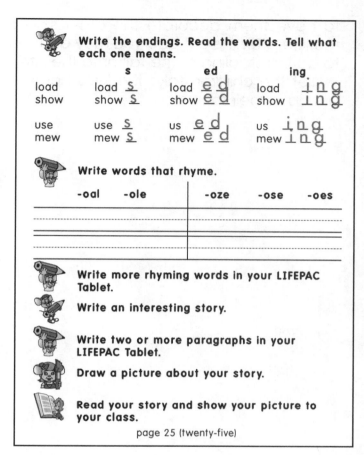

Write the endings. Read the words. Tell what each one means.

	s	ed	ing
load	load **s**	load **ed**	load **ing**
show	show **s**	show **ed**	show **ing**
use	use **s**	us **ed**	us **ing**
mew	mew **s**	mew **ed**	mew **ing**

Write words that rhyme.

-oal	-ole	-oze	-ose	-oes

Write more rhyming words in your LIFEPAC Tablet.

Write an interesting story.

Write two or more paragraphs in your LIFEPAC Tablet.

Draw a picture about your story.

Read your story and show your picture to your class.

page 25 (twenty-five)

Correct each child's story for spelling, punctuation, capitalization, sentence structure, paragraphing, and interesting ideas. Have him recopy it before he reads it to the class.

Take class time for each child to read his story and show his picture. Go over the rules for good speakers and good audiences; before you begin.

ACTIVITIES:

1.   Dictate these words and have the children write them on a sheet of writing tablet paper. Correct the papers and have the children write each misspelled word five times on the back of the paper (rose, pole, froze, coal, toes, goes, roll, stole, mole, hose).

2.   Do Worksheet 8.

Have the children read the titles and tell what they mean.

Read the directions with the children, then let them make the kite. You may wish to have them decorate the other side of the kite after it is cut out. You may also wish to do the stapling of the tail onto the kite.

Let the children take the kites home to put up in their rooms.

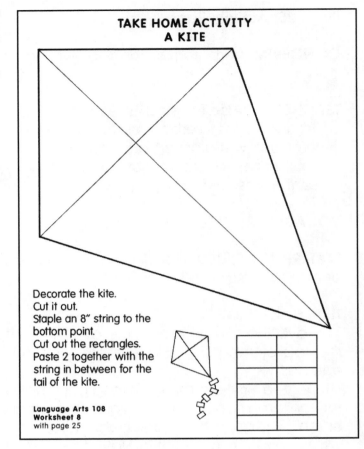

**TAKE HOME ACTIVITY
A KITE**

Decorate the kite.
Cut it out.
Staple an 8" string to the bottom point.
Cut out the rectangles.
Paste 2 together with the string in between for the tail of the kite.

**Language Arts 108
Worksheet 8**
with page 25

Page 26: Activity Page

CONCEPT: long *e*

TEACHER GOALS: To teach the children
To review vowel digraphs *ee, ea, ie,* and
To write words that rhyme with the sound of long *e*.

TEACHING PAGE 26:

Have the children read the direction at the top of the page. Have them read each word and give several rhyming words. Accept any words that rhyme even if they have different spellings (feed, read). Have the children write one or more rhyming words on each line. Have the children read the words they have written.

Have the children read the direction and the words in the middle of the page. Ask them to tell which letters make the long /ē/ sound in each word. Have them read the words again.

Tell the children to read the sentences and to write one of the words on the line. Tell them to choose the word that makes sense in the sentence. Have the children read the sentences. Be sure the children know the meanings of the words.

The teacher should check this page and have the children correct any mistakes.

ACTIVITIES

1.   Play a rhyming game. The teacher says a word from one of the lists on this page to the first child. He gives a word that rhymes and also gives its meaning. That child says a word to the next child and the next child gives a rhyming word and its meaning. Each child must give a word with an ending different from the one he just received from the previous child.

2.   Dictate the following words and have the children write them on a sheet of writing tablet paper.

Write rhyming words.

feed _____

peak _____

wee _____

east _____

Write the words. Read the sentences.

| chief | seen | read |

Do you see the __chief__ ?

I can __read__ a book.

Have you __seen__ Tom?

page 26 (twenty-six)

---

read	beak
week	feed
bleed	speak
lead	cheek
peak	peek

(Use each word in a sentence so children will know which spelling to use for words which sound the same.)

Collect the papers and correct by drawing a line through the incorrect spelling and writing the correct spelling behind it. Have the children write each misspelled word five times on the back of the paper.

TEACHING READING:

Ask students what they know about bees. List their responses on the board. Share experiences with bees.

Tell students they'll read a story and learn more facts about bees.

Write these words on the board: colony, hive, combs, hatch, female, waxy, pollen, nectar, guard, survive, hundreds, drones. Have students read and learn the meanings of these words before reading the story. Extra time and vocabulary activities may be necessary since many are new words.

Read the story "Busy Bees" together, then ask the following questions:

"How do bees live?" (in a hive, colony)

"What is the hive made up of?" (waxy combs)

"What does each comb look like?" (it has six perfect sides) *Draw the shape on the board, show pictures from books.

"What are the waxy combs use for?" (food, eggs, bedrooms, storage)

"What bees are the worker bees?" (the females)

"What do they do?" (everything! - care for the queen, eggs, and male bees, build the hive, collect pollen, guard)

"Could the hive survive without the worker bees?" (no!)

"What do we know about the queen bee?" (she's the biggest, she lays the eggs, there is only one in each hive)

"How many eggs can the queen lay each day?" (hundreds)

"What happens to the male bees after they mate?" (they die)

"What does it mean if someone tells you 'you're as busy as a bee'" (you're very busy, working hard)

Find long vowels words: (seen, bee, home, hive, made, combs, each, sides, open, used, hold, like, female, queen, male, over, most, so, time, survive, only, lays, may, day, feed, drones, mate, die, my, today)

ACTIVITIES:

Give each student 2-3 six sided shapes to cut out and color yellow. Glue each shape on a large piece of butcher paper creating a hive. Make sure shapes are touching each other as the hive is built. Use pictures from books to help students understand the idea. Using the facts from the story, make a booklet about bees. (The pages could be shaped like a hive) Choose 3-5 facts about bees. Write a sentence for each fact and have students copy each one on a booklet page in their best handwriting. Have students illustrate a picture for each fact (page). Share several nonfiction books about bees to increase their knowledge and interest. Make up finger poems or songs to familiar tunes:

One, little two, little three busy bees,
Four, little five, little six busy bees
Seven, little eight, little nine busy bees,
Buzzing all around!

SELF TEST 2

CONCEPTS: contractions, plurals, subject-verb agreement, verb forms

TEACHER GOAL: To teach the children
To check their own progress periodically.

TEACHING PAGE 27:

Have the children read the directions on the entire page. Be sure they know exactly what they are to do in each section. Let them complete the page.

Correct the page as soon as possible. Go over it with the child so he can see what he did well, and where he needs more work. Have him correct any mistakes as you are going through the page.

ACTIVITIES:

1. Reteach concepts the child missed.
2. If several children miss the same things, work with them in a small group.

SPELLING WORDS:

road
toad
load
good
hood
cook
book
spoon
moon
soon

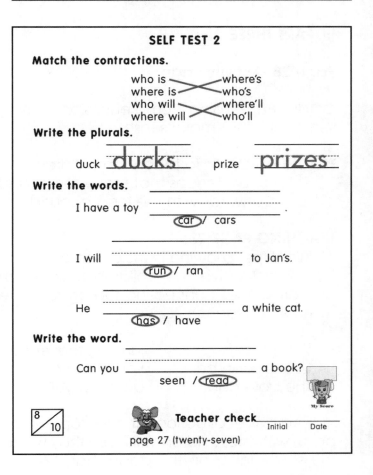

SELF TEST 2

Match the contractions.

who is ——— where's
where is ——— who's
who will ——— where'll
where will ——— who'll

Write the plurals.

duck ducks   prize prizes

Write the words.

I have a toy _____ .
car / cars

I will _____ to Jan's.
run / ran

He _____ a white cat.
has / have

Write the word.

Can you _____ a book?
seen / read

8/10   Teacher check _____
page 27 (twenty-seven)   Initial   Date

III. PART THREE

Page 28: Activity Page

CONCEPT: reading comprehension: writing sentences that make sense

TEACHER GOALS: To teach the children
To write sentences that make sense, and
To write words with the long _e_ sound.

TEACHING PAGE 28:
Write the following parts of sentences on the board. Have the children read them and draw lines connecting the parts of the same sentence.

Where are	jump in the leaves.
Leaves can be	you going?
The boys can	green or yellow.

Read the direction at the top of the page with the children. Tell them they will do the same thing on this page that they just did on the board.
Tell the children to read the parts of the sentences very carefully before drawing any lines. Let the children do both sets of sentences by themselves. Help those who need help. Check by having children read both parts of the sentence. The teacher should check this page .
Have the children read the next direction and the word endings. Call attention to the two ways to spell the long /e/ sound. Tell the children that even though the endings are spelled differently, they are pronounced the same, so they rhyme. Have the children give words that rhyme for each ending. Have them write two words for each on the lines, then write the endings at the top of a sheet of writing tablet paper and write more words.
Write the endings on the board and have the children read words from their lists for you to put under each.

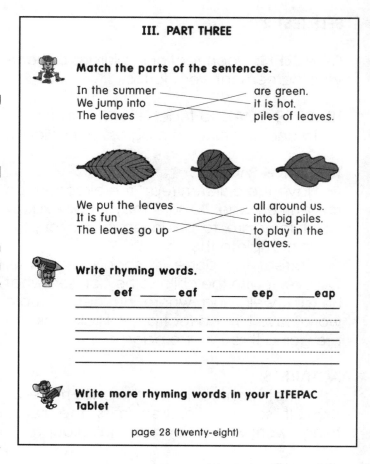

III. PART THREE

Match the parts of the sentences.

In the summer ———— are green.
We jump into ———— it is hot.
The leaves ———— piles of leaves.

We put the leaves ———— all around us.
It is fun ———— into big piles.
The leaves go up ———— to play in the leaves.

Write rhyming words.

_____ eef _____ eaf _____ eep _____eap

Write more rhyming words in your LIFEPAC Tablet

page 28 (twenty-eight)

Read the lists several times. Have the children add to and correct their lists.

ACTIVITIES:
1. For the children who had trouble with the sentence matching, write five or six sentences on strips of writing tablet paper. Cut them in half and let children match them up on their desks. Write the sentences so that only one ending will make sense with the beginning .
2. Dictate the following words and have the children write them on a sheet of writing tablet paper.

leaf	leap
beef	deep
cheap	reef
keep	steep
peep	heap

(Use each word in a sentence.)

Collect the papers and correct them by drawing a line through the misspelled word and writing the correct spelling behind it. Have the children write each misspelled word five times on the back of the paper.

TEACHING READING:

Read the story "Leaves" in *Reader 4*.

Have the children read the title. Ask one child to tell what the story will be about. Have the children read the story silently. The teacher should move around the room as the children read to help children sound out words that cause difficulty.

Ask questions such as these:
"Do all trees have leaves?"
"Which do not?"
"What do leaves do for the tree?"
"What color are leaves in summer?"
"When do they turn color?"
"What colors?"
"When does it start getting cold?"
"What happens to the leaves?"
"What did the children do with the leaves?"
"Have you ever done this?"
"Was it fun?"
"How did it feel?"
"What do you think will happen next?"

Let the children read the story aloud. Read one of the questions above and ask the children to find and read the sentence that answers it. Ask what kind of sentences are in the story. Have them find long *e* words and read them.

Ask the children to find the plurals in the story and tell how they were made.

Ask the children to find the pronouns in the story and tell for whom or what they stand.

Let the children share their experiences with leaves.

Have several children tell the story in their own words.

ACTIVITIES:

1. Have the children draw a leaf shape and cut it out. Have them trace the leaf many times in all positions on a sheet of drawing paper, overlapping the shapes. Color each section a different color. Use the autumn colors of red, orange, brown, and yellow.

2. Read poems about falling leaves or autumn or sing songs about falling leaves or autumn.

Page 29: Activity Page

CONCEPTS: reading comprehension, oral expression

TEACHER GOAL: To teach the children
To decide if what they are reading makes sense, and
To learn to speak clearly and in complete sentences.

TEACHING PAGE 29:

Read the direction at the top of the page with the children. Have the children read each sentence, circle the correct word, then write it on the line. Do the first example together. Check by having the children read the sentences. The teacher should check this page. Have the children correct any mistakes and read the sentences over again.

The material in the box is to be used for a discussion. Tell the children that the symbol of the heads connected by lines will mean that they will be talking about what is in the box.

You may use this material for a class discussion if you wish, but it is important for the children to learn to speak in small groups as well as large groups. They should also learn to lead the discussion in a small group, and to keep the discussion on the subject.

If possible have only five or six in a group. The teacher should work with the group while the rest of the class is busy with something else. An aide can also take a group.

After all the groups have finished their discussions bring the groups together to tell what they talked about or what conclusions they reached.

ACTIVITIES:

1. Have the children draw a picture of the things in our world that God has made. Or have the children make a mural to be

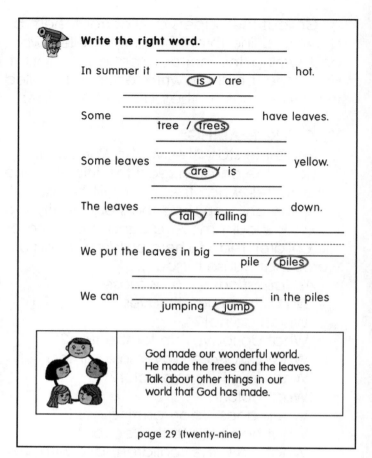

Write the right word.

In summer it _____ hot.
(is) / are

Some _____ have leaves.
tree / (trees)

Some leaves _____ yellow.
(are) / is

The leaves _____ down.
(fall) / falling

We put the leaves in big _____
pile / (piles)

We can _____ in the piles
jumping / (jump)

God made our wonderful world. He made the trees and the leaves. Talk about other things in our world that God has made.

page 29 (twenty-nine)

put up in the library or a hallway where the entire school could enjoy it. A class essay could be written to go with the mural.

2. Read the Creation story from the Bible.

TEACHING READING:

Choose coloring pages or pictures from old magazines or calendars. Cut each picture in 4-6 pieces. Give students in groups (4-6) each a piece of one picture. Ask students to look at their piece. Ask them if they can tell what the whole picture will look like. (no) Tell them they only have one piece of the picture and aren't able to know exactly how it will look until it gets back together. Tell them to work in their group and put the pieces together to make a picture. Give them time to see the other groups' pictures and respond.

Introduce today's story: The Quilt. Ask how many know what a quilt is. Give time for responses and discussion. If you have a quilt of your own, you may want to share it.

Write these words on the board: quilt, square, patterns, fabric, stitched, patient. Have students read and learn the meanings of the words.

Read the story "The Quilt" together, then ask the following questions:

"Who is making a quilt?" (Mrs. Sanders and Melissa's mother)

"What are they using to make the quilt?" (squares with different patterns and colors)

"How big will the quilt be?" (it will fit a small bed)

"When did Mrs. Sanders and Melissa's mother work on the quilt?" (every afternoon)

"What would Melissa do?" (watch)

"What was Melissa hoping?" (it would be for her)

"When will she know if it will be for her?" (don't know, quilts take a long time, they haven't decided)

Find squ word: square – think of more you know

Find the qu word: quilt – think of more you know

ACTIVITIES:

Give each student a square of paper to decorate. When completed arrange the squares to make a classroom quilt. If possible, use fabric squares and ask a parent to sew them together. Find books with pictures of quilts to show students there are many kinds of quilt patterns. Invite others to share quilts they have at home (with parental permission, of course). Have a discussion about being patient (experiences, difficulties). List students responses of times they had to be patient on the board. If it isn't mentioned,

at the end add "waiting for Jesus". Discuss how God asks us to trust Him by being patient.

Part 30: Activity Page

CONCEPT: reading comprehension: sequence of events

TEACHER GOALS: To teach the children
To read to understand, and
To put sentences in order of events

VOCABULARY: next

TEACHING PAGE 30:

Have the children read the direction at the top of the page. Tell them to read all three sentences carefully. Then have them write a *1* on the line in front of the sentence that tells what happened first, a *2* in front of the sentence that tells what happened next, and a *3* in front of the sentence that tells what happened last. Read the sentences again in order to see if they are right. Check the first group with the children by having them read the sentences in order.

Let the children finish the page by themselves, then check. Have the children correct any mistakes.

TEACHING READING

Ask students to share experiences where they have been afraid. Allow time for discussion on this topic. Have students draw a picture of their experience.

Put the following words on the board. Read and discuss their meaning. squirrel, field, nearby, thought, shelter, protect, practice, verse

Tell students the name of their story is, "I Am Always With You".

Read the story "I Am Always With You" together, then ask the following questions:

"Where does Andrew go every afternoon after school?" (the big field behind his house)

"What does he do there? (watch the gray squirrels)

Write 1, 2, 3 for first, next, and last.

2	The tree has big green leaves.
1	The tree has very little leaves.
3	The tree has red or brown leaves.

3	The leaves go up all around us.
1	We put the leaves in big piles.
2	We jump in the leaves.

2	He goes for a ride.
3	He gets off his pony.
1	The boy gets on his pony.

1	Dad helped Lee make a tree house.
3	Tippy wants to get in, too.
2	They sit in it and talk.

page 30 (thirty)

"Why do you think he doesn't go far from the field?" (varied answers; doesn't want to get lost)

"What is the name Andrew gave the littlest squirrel?" (Squirt)

"Why did he name the other one Squirmy?" (it never stands still)

"Why did Andrew end up getting lost in the woods?" (he followed the squirrels)

"Why couldn't he find his way out?" (trees surrounded him, everything looked the same, it was raining)

"What did Andrew find in his pocket?" (paper with his memory verse)

"Why wasn't Andrew afraid when he was lost?" (he remembered Jesus was always with him)

Find words with: ew, oo (Andrew, knew, afternoon, school) Find words with long vowels: (field, behind, goes, he, home, likes, gray, sometimes, names, trees, seeds, find, awhile, chase, each, like game, play, realize, rain, know, way, take, reason, afraid, piece, paper, Bible, week, peace, Jesus, keep, safe) Find words with squ: squirrel, Squirmy, Squirt)

ACTIVITIES:

Have students get with a partner and recite the memory verse: "I am always with you" – Matthew 28:20 Have students copy the verse in their best handwriting. Have them add an illustration to go with the verse. Provide books on squirrels and other woods animals. Have students create a woods scene or mural for the classroom. Write the words "piece" and "peace" on the board. Discuss the different meanings of these words (homophones). Share the poem: "Squirrels" by Jack Prelutsky, Something Big Has Been Here

Page 31: Compound Words

CONCEPT: Compound words

TEACHER GOALS: To teach the children
To read and write compound words and give the meaning of each, and
To write compound words in sentences.

MATERIALS NEEDED: Worksheet 9

TEACHING PAGE 31:
Have the children read the title and sentence at the top of the page. Ask them to tell what a compound word is and to give some examples.

Have them read the directions and finish the page independently.

Have the children use the words in sentences orally first, then write them on a sheet of writing tablet paper. Collect the papers and correct the spelling, punctuation, capitalization, and grammar. Have the children recopy the sentences. Take class time for the children to read sentences aloud.

ACTIVITIES:
1.   Do Worksheet 9.
Have the children read the directions for each section, then do the exercises by themselves. Give help to the students who need it. Check by having the children read the compound words and the words. Write them on the board as they give them so they can check their own spelling. Have them correct any mistakes.

2.   Have the children make up a list of compound words that they know and use. Write the list on the board and let each contribute. These lists may be done at home with the parents helping if you wish.

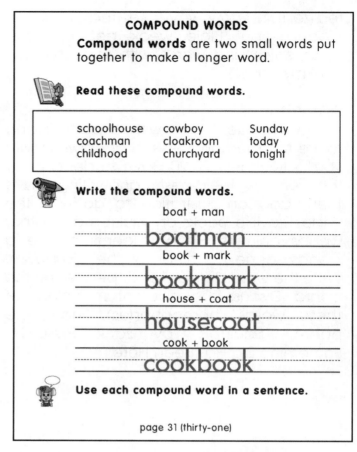

COMPOUND WORDS
Compound words are two small words put together to make a longer word.

Read these compound words.

schoolhouse	cowboy	Sunday
coachman	cloakroom	today
childhood	churchyard	tonight

Write the compound words.

boat + man
boatman
book + mark
bookmark
house + coat
housecoat
cook + book
cookbook

Use each compound word in a sentence.

page 31 (thirty-one)

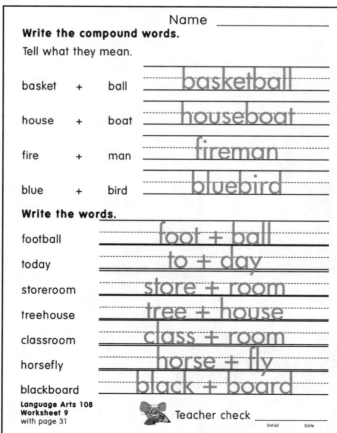

Name _____

Write the compound words.
Tell what they mean.

basket   +   ball   basketball

house   +   boat   houseboat

fire   +   man   fireman

blue   +   bird   bluebird

Write the words.

football   foot + ball

today   to + day

storeroom   store + room

treehouse   tree + house

classroom   class + room

horsefly   horse + fly

blackboard   black + board

Language Arts 108
Worksheet 9
with page 31

Teacher check _____
Initial   Date

Page 32: Activity Page

CONCEPTS: *sn, st,* long *o,* and long *e,* reading comprehension: following directions

TEACHER GOAL: To teach the children
To write words that contain *sn* or *st,*
To write words with the long */o/* and long */e/* sounds, to read to follow directions, and
To follow directions in the order in which they are given.

MATERIALS NEEDED: crayons, scissors, string, staples, paste or glue

TEACHING PAGE 32:
Have the children read the direction and sentence at the top of the page. Tell the children to read the part of the word that is there, then to write *sn* or *st* in the space to make a word. Do the first one together.
Check the first exercise by writing the correct words on the board. Have the children check their own papers and correct any mistakes. Have the children read all the word.
Discuss the picture. Ask the children if the animals are saying "No!" or "Go!"
Have the children read the directions. Then have the children read the words with the long */o/* sound.
Have them make sentences using the words.

ACTIVITY:
Dictate the following words and have the children write them on a sheet of writing tablet paper.

seen	seem	green
mean	team	bean
clean	steam	dream
cream		

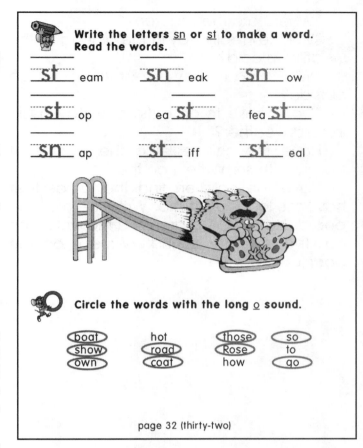

Write the letters <u>sn</u> or <u>st</u> to make a word. Read the words.

st eam   sn eak   sn ow
st op   ea st   fea st
sn ap   st iff   st eal

Circle the words with the long <u>o</u> sound.

boat   hot   those   so
show   road   Rose   to
own   coat   how   go

page 32 (thirty-two)

(Use each word in a sentence so the children will know which spelling to use for words that sound the same.)
Collect the papers and correct by drawing a line through the incorrect spelling and by writing the correct spelling behind it. Have the children write each misspelled word five times on the back of the paper.

TEACHING READING:
Read the story "Snow" in *Reader 4.*
Ask the children if they have ever seen snow. Have several children tell about their experiences with snow. Read the title aloud and then have them read the story silently.
Ask the children these questions:
"Where has the snow fallen?"
"Where have the birds gone?"
"When will they return?"
"What has formed on the lake?"
"What will happen to the ice?"
"Where are bears sleeping?"
"When will they come out?"

"Where are the children?"

"Will they really stay inside as long as the weather is cold?"

"What can they wear if they go outside?"

"Do you like to go outside or stay inside in cold weather?"

Have the children find the word that begins with *sn*. Write it on the board.

Have the children find the words that have the long /o/ sound. Write them on the board. Have the children find the word that has the long /e/ sound. Write it on the board.

SELF TEST 3

CONCEPTS: sentences, verb forms, rhyming words

TEACHER GOAL: To teach the children to check their own progress periodically.

TEACHING PAGE 33:

Have the children read all the directions on the page. Be sure they understand everything they are to do. Let them complete the page independently.

Correct the page as soon as possible. Go over it with the child so he can see what he did well, and where he needs more work. Have him correct any mistakes as you are going through the page.

ACTIVITIES:

1. Reteach concepts the child misses.
2. If several children miss the same things, reteach in a small group.

SPELLING WORDS:

fuel
cue
cruel
mew
pew
new
few
spew
view
you

Self Test 3

Match the parts of the sentences.

Snow has fallen — for the winter.
Children are inside — on the tops of the hills.
The birds have gone — drinking cocoa.

Write the right word.

Ice has _____ on the lake.
formed / forming

The weather _____ cold.
is / are

Write the compound word.

cook   book
cookbook

Match the rhyming words.

coast — weep
steep — stew
mew — toast

7/9   Teacher check _____
                        Initial   Date

page 33 (thirty-three)

LIFEPAC TEST AND ALTERNATE TEST 108

CONCEPTS: rhyming words, possessives, sequence, contractions, plurals, alphabetical order, listening comprehension, ordinal numbers, sentences, subject-verb agreement, sentence writing, punctuation, capitalization

TEACHER GOAL: To teach the children
To check their own progress periodically.

TEACHING the LIFEPAC TEST:

Administer the test to the class in a group. Ask the children to read the directions or read them to the class. In either case, be sure that the children clearly understand. Put examples on the board if it seems necessary. Give ample time for each activity to be completed before going on to the next.

Read the story. (Circle the sentence.)
Don and Bob are going to the park. They each take a lunch. When they get to the park, they will eat their lunches. Then they will play catch with the softball. When they grow tired, they will pick up their lunches and go home.

Circle the sentence that tells the first thing Don and Bob will do at the park.

Dictation Sentence-(Write the sentence.)
He will coach our team.

Correct the test immediately and discuss with the child.
Review any concepts that have been missed.
Give those children who do not achieve the 80% score additional copies of the worksheets and a list of vocabulary words to study. A parent or a classroom helper may help in the review.

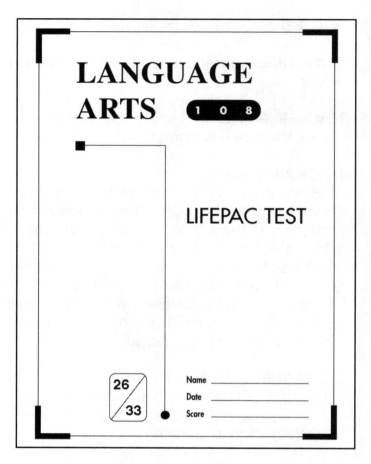

LANGUAGE ARTS **1 0 8**

LIFEPAC TEST

26/33

Name _____
Date _____
Score _____

When the child is ready, give the Alternate LIFEPAC Test. Use the same procedure as for the LIFEPAC Test.

Read the Alternate Story. (Circle the sentence.)
Cindy and Heather are going to the zoo. They will each take a lunch. When they get to the zoo they will eat their lunches. Then they will see the animals. When they grow tired, they will go home.

Circle the sentence that tells the first thing Cindy and Heather will do at the zoo.

Dictation Sentence-(Write the sentence.) *Mom will cook the pie.*

SPELLING WORDS:

LIFEPAC words	Alternate words
pie	tie
tie	die
buy	guy
road	load
good	hood
soon	moon
fuel	spoon
cue	cruel
mew	new
view	you

LANGUAGE ARTS 108: LIFEPAC TEST

Write a rhyming word.

bike _____   field _____

poach _____   chew _____

boat _____   cruel _____

Write the words.

This is _____ dog.
me / (my)

_____ car is white.
(Our) / Out

Put 1, 2, 3 for first, second, and third.

_3_ I found my cat.

_2_ I looked for my cat.

_1_ My cat was lost.

Match the contractions.

cannot — I'll
do not — can't
they are — they're
I will — don't

page 1 (one)

Write the plurals.

fox **foxes**   deer **deer**

man **men**   child **children**

Write the words.

Do you have two _____ ?
book / (books)

We can buy four _____ .
toy / (toys)

Circle the word that comes first in the alphabet.

dog   (ant)   cat

Listen to the story.

Circle the sentence.

1. Don and Bob will pack up their lunches.

2. Don and Bob will play catch.

3. (Don and Bob will eat their lunches.)

page 2 (two)

Match the parts of the sentences.

Joan wasn't — like her new school
She didn't — very happy.
She didn't know — any of the children.

Write the word.

I _____ a new bike.
has / (have)

We can _____ for a ride.
(go) / gone

Write the sentence.

_____

page 3 (three)

197

LANGUAGE ARTS 108

ALTERNATE LIFEPAC TEST

26 / 33

Name _____
Date _____
Score _____

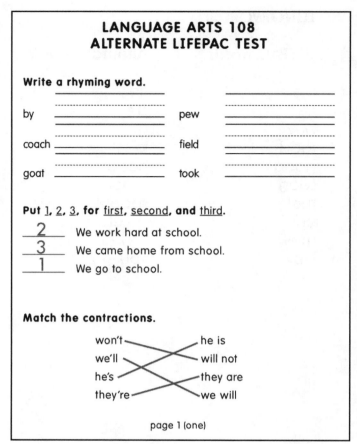

LANGUAGE ARTS 108 ALTERNATE LIFEPAC TEST

Write a rhyming word.

by _____   pew _____

coach _____   field _____

goat _____   took _____

Put 1, 2, 3, for first, second, and third.

2 We work hard at school.

3 We came home from school.

1 We go to school.

Match the contractions.

won't — he is
we'll — will not
he's — they are
they're — we will

page 1 (one)

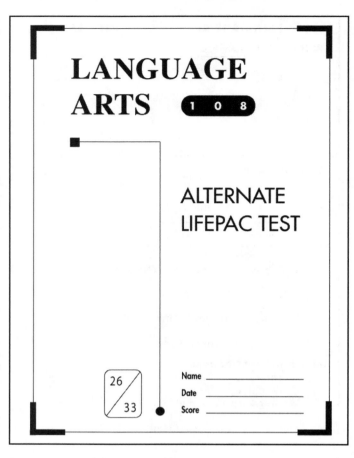

Write the words.

This is _____ hamster.
you / your

_____ hamster is tan.
Me / My

Write the plurals.

man men   fox foxes

child children   sheep sheep

Write the words.

Do you want four _____ ?
jar / jars

We can buy six _____ .
ball / balls

Circle the word that comes first in the alphabet.

jog   art   dip

page 2 (two)

Match the parts of the sentences.

Baby Zebra had — gave him a hanky.
Mother Zebra — a bad cold.
The hanky — went up, up, up.

Write the word.

We _____ going for a ride!
is / are

The bus _____ here!
is / are

Listen to the story.

Circle the sentence.

Cindy and Heather will eat their lunches.

They will see the animals.

They will go home.

Write the sentence.

_____
_____

page 3 (three)

Page 1: Self Awareness

CONCEPTS: self-awareness, membership

TEACHER GOALS: To teach each child
That he is a person created by God,
That no other person is exactly like him,
That he is a member of many groups (family, school, church, state, country),
That as a member of many groups he has both privileges and obligations,
That he can write his name and age and the names of his teacher, his school, and his church, and
That being a Christian is very important.

BIBLE REFERENCES: Genesis 2:7, Ephesians 6:1 through 4

TEACHING PAGE 1:

Ask the children to write their first, second, and last names, and their ages on the lines. Help only if necessary.

Read the rest of the page together, and have the children write in the names of the teacher, school, and church. Help those who need help with spelling.

Have the children tell what being a member of a group means to them. Talk about all the groups they belong to. Talk about the privileges and the obligations they have as part of a group.

Have them tell what they receive from their parents and what their parents expect from them. Have them tell what they do at home to help. Read the Bible verses and discuss them.

Talk about privileges and obligations for their school and church groups.

Have the children tell what it means to be a Christian. Have them tell how a Christian should act in his groups.

I am _____

I am _____ years old.

I go to _____ School.

My teacher is _____

My church is _____

page 1 (one)

ACTIVITY:

Have each child tell what his name is, how old he is, and what church he goes to. Have each one tell a little about his family.

Page 2: FUN WITH WORDS

CONCEPT: purpose of the LIFEPAC

TEACHER GOALS: To teach the children
To understand what they will learn in the LIFEPAC, and
To read the objectives.

BIBLE REFERENCE: Proverbs 22:6

TEACHING PAGE 2:
Have the children look at the pictures at the top of the page. Ask them to name each one and to give the vowel sound they hear (*cow, house, cloud*). Write the words on the board and have the children read them. Put the word *boot* on the board. Point out the difference in the *oo* sound in *book* and *boot*.

Have the children read the title and the top part of the page. Talk about the sentences so the children will know what they will be expected to learn in this LIFEPAC. Have the children close their LIFEPACs and ask them to name all the things they will be learning.

Have the children read the title and tell what objectives are. Have them read each objective and discuss it. Ask the children to tell why the objectives are there. Ask the children to tell how many accomplished the objectives for LIFEPAC 108. Ask them to tell how they will accomplish the objectives for LIFEPAC 109.

Have the children write the objectives in their writing tablets.

FUN WITH WORDS
Listening, reading,
and writing can be lots of fun.
In this LIFEPAC
You will learn about main ideas.
You will learn new sounds for letters.
You will learn to spell and
write new words.
You will learn to listen and
follow directions.
You will learn to write longer stories.

 Objectives

1. I can tell long and short vowel sounds.
2. I can write plurals.
3. I can write contractions.
4. I can write possessives.
5. I can write interesting stories.
6. I can put things in proper sequence.
7. I can tell how many syllables.

page 2 (two)

I. PART ONE

Page 3: ou and ow

CONCEPTS: sound of *ou* and *ow,* sound of long *o and* short *o*

TEACHER GOALS: To teach the children
To identify and read words with the sounds of *ou* as in *cloud* and as in *soup,*
To identify and to read the words with the sound of *ow* as in *clown* and as in *slow,*
To recognize that groups of letters do not always have the same sound, and
To try more than one sound when sounding out new words.

MATERIALS NEEDED: pictures of clowns

TEACHING PAGE 3:
Ask the children to read the letter groups at the top of the page. Have them name the pictures. Have them read the names under the pictures and tell which letters are in darker type. Ask the children to tell what sound these letters make. Point out that the sound is the same but the letters are different.
Have the children sound out and read the lists of words. Have them listen for the /ou/ow/ sound.
Ask the children to point to the first word *our* and listen. Write the word *sour* on the board. Say it and ask them to tell what is different about it. Finish reading the words at the top of the page together.
Write these words on the board and have the children read them:

coupon	routine
cougar	souvenir

Write the words *soul* and *touch* on the board and point out that these words also have different sounds for the letters *ou*.

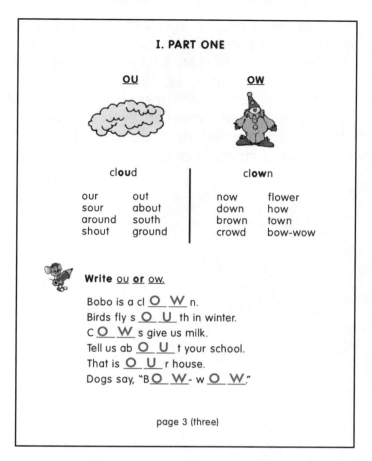

I. PART ONE

OU	OW
cloud	clown

our	out	now	flower
sour	about	down	how
around	south	brown	town
shout	ground	crowd	bow-wow

Write ou or ow.

Bobo is a cl **O W** n.
Birds fly s **O U** th in winter.
C **O W** s give us milk.
Tell us ab **O U** t your school.
That is **O U** r house.
Dogs say, "B **O W** - w **O W**."

page 3 (three)

Have the children read the direction in the middle of the page and do the exercise independently. Check by having the children read the sentences and give the letters they wrote on the blanks. They should correct any mistakes.

TEACHING READING:
Read the story "Bobo The Clown" in *Reader 5*.
Show the children several pictures of clowns or make a bulletin board display of these pictures. Ask what a clown is and where you would go to see one. Let the children share their experiences with clowns.
Present the words *Bobo, knows, laugh, goes,* and *clown* and have each one used in a sentence. Be sure the children know the meaning of each word.
Ask the children to look at the picture and tell what they see. Have them read the title.

Let the children read the story silently. Have them read each paragraph aloud.

Have the children find each word with the long /o/ sound. Have the children find and read words with the short /o/ sound and words that have an o that is neither long nor short. Tell the children that you will be talking about Bobo in the next lesson, also.

Page 4: Bobo, the Clown

CONCEPTS: long *o*, possessives, retelling a story

TEACHER GOALS: To teach the children
To identify and read words with the long /o/ sound,
To identify the possessive pronouns and tell what belongs to each, and
To retell the story in their own words, recalling details accurately.

TEACHING PAGE 4:
Read "Bobo, The Clown" again in *Reader 5.* Have the children tell the main idea of the story. Have the children review the words that have the long /o/ sound and write them on the lines.

Ask the children to find the possessives and possessive pronouns and tell what belongs to each. Point out the contraction *he's.*

Have the children tell whether or not they think this story could be true. Ask why they think so.

Have the children tell the story in their own words.

ACTIVITIES:
1. Have the children draw clowns on large sheets of paper. Cut them out and post them on the wall or in a hallway. Encourage each child to be creative and different.
2. This story could be used as the introduction to a unit on the circus. Some of the things they could do are:
    a. Draw circus pictures.
    b. Study wild animals that are in the circus.
    c. Learn about animal training.
    d. Read about the old circus trains and traveling circuses.
    e. Find out about the people in the circus.

BOBO, THE CLOWN

Write the words with the long <u>o</u> sound.

Bobo   knows   coat
yellow   old   goes
go   show

page 4 (four)

f. Read about the circuses in their winter quarters in Florida.
g. Work up their own circus acts and give a circus as a spring program or for a Mothers' Day program.
h. Make a large circus mural to be hung in the lunchroom or entry hall.
3. Read stories about the circus or circus animals or show films or filmstrips about circuses.

TEACHING READING:
Ask students to tell you what the five senses are: (sight, smell, taste, touch, hearing) Tell them to concentrate on the sense of smell and think of all their favorite smells. List them on the board. Tell them most animals have a better sense of smell than we do. Today's story is about Snoopers, a basset hound who has a good sense of smell.

Write these words on the board: basset hound, ground, droopy, eyesight, town, corner, younger, nibble, owner, alert, intruder, sniffer, critter. Have students read and learn the meanings of each word.

Read the story "Snoopers" together, then ask the following questions:

"Who does Snoopers belong to?" (Mr. Jordan)

"Where does Snoopers spend most of his time?" (at the feed store)

"What do we know about Snoopers?" (slow, poor eyesight and hearing, the best sniffer in town)

"How does he alert his owner when there is trouble?" (howls). Is Snoopers old or young? (old)

"Does he chase away the critters these days?" (probably not - he's even slower)

"What do the critters do to stay away from him?" (they use the back door)

Find words with oo: (Snoopers, droopy, good). Find words with ou/ow (as in cow): (ground, hound, out, town, mouse, loud, howl). Find words with ou/ow (as in slow): (low, slow, owner, slower, know). Find r-controlled words: (Jordan, or, sniffer, store, corner, first, younger, critters, other, farmers, alert, owner, intruder, slower, are, porch)

ACTIVITIES:

Use the list of phonetic words to: categorize the sounds, or write a sentence with several same sounding words (i.e. The hound was too loud so the mouse ran out of town.)

Provide a variety of items for students to smell (i.e. cinnamon & other spices, pickle juice) Identify and rate the aromas. Set up a center with 6-8 concealed containers (plastic film containers work great). Each container will have a different smelling object. Have students visit the center and guess by writing or drawing a picture of what they think the object or smell is.

Page 5: Activity Page

CONCEPTS: story: main idea and details, possessives

TEACHER GOALS: To teach the children
To express a main idea in a complete sentence,
To recall details, and
To write words showing possession.

VOCABULARY: about

TEACHING PAGE 5:
Have the children read the directions at the top of the page. Let them give the answer in a sentence. Remind them to write the answer in a complete sentence.

Have the children read the remaining directions on the page and complete the page independently. Remind them to circle two words for each sentence in the second exercise. Tell them to circle the word *first* and to write it on the line in the third exercise.

Check by having the children read the sentences with the correct answers.

Write about the story, "Bobo, the clown."

_____
_____
_____

Circle the right words.

Bobo's coat is (red) blue (long.)
Bobo's hat is (big) little (yellow.)
Bobo's car is new (little) (old.)

Write the words.

_____
_____ car goes fast.
Bobo / (Bobo's)

He has shoes on _____ feet.
(his) / him

_____
_____ car has balloons on it.
He / (His)

page 5 (five)

Page 6: Activity Page

CONCEPTS: syllables, *ou, oo,* and *ow,* writing stories

TEACHER GOALS: To teach the children
To review the meaning of syllables,
To find the number of syllables in words,
To write a story using good sentences and paragraphs with the correct punctuation, and
To read the story in front of the class.

MATERIALS NEEDED: drawing paper, crayons or paint

TEACHING PAGE 6:

Review the word *syllables* and ask what it means. Have children tell how many syllables they hear in the word *syllables* (three).

Have the children read the title and directions at the top of the page.

Do the first two words as a group, then let the children finish the exercise independently. Check by having the children read each word and tell how many syllables it has. Have them correct any mistakes. Have the children underline the *ow, ou,* or *oo* in each word and give its sound. Use the words in sentences.

The starred exercise is more difficult. Some children may need help.

Have the children read the next directions silently. Ask them to tell what the directions are telling them to do. Review what good sentences and paragraphs are and the rules for punctuation and capitalization, if necessary. Correct each child's story and return it to him for recopying.

Take time for each child to read his story and show his picture to the class. Before they begin, go over the rules for speaking to a group. (stand straight, look at audience, etc.). Have the children tell what a good audience is.

Syllables

Say these words.
Write how many parts are in each word.

clown __1__	flower __2__	school __1__
out __1__	shouting __2__	about __2__
house __1__	down __1__	ground __1__
bow __1__	mouse __1__	browner __2__
cows __1__	bow __1__	clouded __2__
proud __1__	now __1__	spouting __2__

H Can you tell how many syllables are in these words?

flowering __3__   underground __3__
outstanding __3__   cowcatcher __3__

Write a story about a funny clown in your LIFEPAC Tablet.
Write good sentences.
Write one or more paragraphs.
Draw a picture about your story.
Read your story and show your picture to the class.

page 6 (six)

TEACHING READING:

Show students a couple of beautifully wrapped packages. Ask them to guess what is in them. Record their answers and tell them you'll come
back to the packages after today's story.

Tell them today's story is titled: "My Gift". Ask students to share what they think this story might be about. Ask if they had a gift to give someone else, what would it be?

Read the story "My Gift" together, then ask the following questions:

"What event is going to happen?" (the big art show)

"Who is a good artist?" (Nathan)

"What about the speaker, is he/she a good artist?" (he doesn't think so)

"What does his teacher and parents say?" (do your best)

"What is it called when we can do something well?" (a gift)

"Who gives us those gifts?" (God)

"What gift might the speaker have?" (making people feel good)

"How does he/she do this?" (compliments, being happy for someone else's success,...)

"What did the speaker do for Nathan?" (tell him is a great artist, his drawing is awesome, should win first prize)

Find r-controlled words: (art, artist, sure, teacher, pastor, different, Lord). Find ow/ou words: (show, our, know, out, about). Find aw words: (draw, drawing, hawk, awesome)

ACTIVITIES:

Refer back to the packages. Ask students if they learned anything new about gifts. (gifts are from God – talents, abilities are gifts). Tell them the boxes represent gifts from God – see if they can give a new list of gifts (not things) i.e. artist, singer, dancer, writer, helper, listener, teacher, ... or ask them now to think of special things they can do well. List their answers on the board. Emphasis these things as gifts from God. Notice how many different gifts there are! Each one is different – making each of us different, unique and special. Discuss the story and the feelings the speaker had for Nathan. Was he jealous of Nathan's artwork? (no – he understood it was Nathan's gift). This may lead into more discussion about others and how to be happy for their special gifts. Refer to the Bible for these verses: James 1:17 "Every good gift and every perfect gift is from above, and comes down from the Father of lights..." 1 Timothy 4:14 "Do not neglect the gift that is in you..." 1 Cor. 7:7 "But each has his own gift from God, one in this manner and another in that." Have students make a thank you card to God for their special gifts.

Page 7: ou and ow

CONCEPTS: sound of *ou* and *ow,* reading comprehension

TEACHER GOALS: To teach the children
To identify and read words with the sounds of *ou* as in *cloud* and as in *soup,*
To identify and to read the words with the sound of *ow* as in *clown* and as in *slow,* and
To read for understanding.

TEACHING PAGE 7:
Have the children read the direction at the top of the page and the two groups of words in bold type. Tell the children to read the sentences very carefully, then to write in the blank space. Remind them to read the sentence again to be sure the word they have chosen makes sense. Tell them each word is to be used only once. Check by having the children read the sentences aloud.

Some children may need help with this page.

ACTIVITIES:
1. Write these words on the board and have children write a sentence for each one on a sheet of writing tablet paper:

around   down
crowd   found
ground

Let each child read one or two of his sentences aloud to the class or to his small group.
2. Write these words on the board and have the children read them:

grow   yellow
know   pillow

Have the children tell how these *ow* words are different.

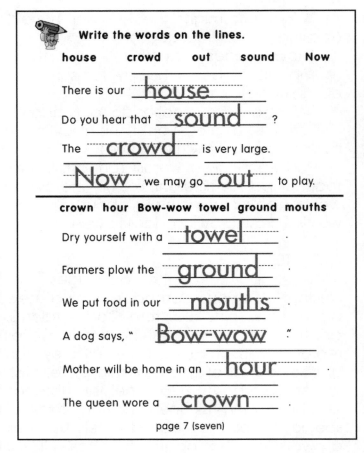

Write the words on the lines.

house   crowd   out   sound   Now

There is our **house** .
Do you hear that **sound** ?
The **crowd** is very large.
Now we may go **out** to play.

crown hour Bow-wow towel ground mouths

Dry yourself with a **towel** .
Farmers plow the **ground** .
We put food in our **mouths** .
A dog says, " **Bow-wow** "
Mother will be home in an **hour** .
The queen wore a **crown** .

page 7 (seven)

TEACHING READING:
Read the story "Thank You, God" in *Reader 5.*

Present the words *moon, flowers, butterflies, rainbow, clouds, every* on the board and pronounce each one. Have the children repeat them after you. Have the children read the list several times. Be sure they know the meaning of each word.

Point out the /oo/ sound in moon, the long /o/ sound of *ow* in rainbow, and the *ow* in flowers and the *ou* in clouds which have the same sound. Point out also that butterflies is a compound word in which the *y* was changed to an *i* before the *es* was added to make the plural. Ask what sound the *y* in *every* has (long e).

Have the children look at the picture on this page and tell what they see.

Have them read the title and tell what they think we are thanking God for. Have them read the poem silently.

Read the poem aloud. Ask the children to name the things the author was thankful for.

Ask them how this poem makes them feel (happy, sad, etc.).

Tell them you will be talking about "Thank You, God" in the next lesson.

Page 8: Thank You, God

CONCEPTS: creation, poetry, rhyming words

TEACHER GOALS: To teach the children

To thank and praise God for what He has done for us,

To tell how a poem is different from a story,

To identify the rhyming words in the story,

To retell the poem in their own words,

To identify the main idea of the poem, and

To write either an individual or a group poem.

BIBLE REFERENCES: Genesis 1 and 2

MATERIALS NEEDED: Bible

TEACHING PAGE 8:

Read "Thank You, God" again in *Reader 5*.

Ask the children if they noticed anything different about what they just read (words at the end of each two sentences rhymed, and each sentence began with a capital letter). Ask who can tell what this kind of writing is called (poem).

Ask who is saying this poem (child in the window). Ask the children to tell what the main idea of the poem is (thanking God for everything in the world He made for us to use and enjoy). Have the children name everything God made that we are thanking Him for in the poem.

Have the children read the title on Page 8. Tell them to list things they are thankful for. Some children may need help in spelling these words.

Have the poem read aloud, verse by verse. Have the children give the words that rhyme and other words that rhyme with them.

Tell the children that a poem is different from a story because every line must begin with a capital letter and because

Thank you, God

I am thankful for many things.

_____

I will say, "Thank you, God" for all of these things.

page 8 (eight)

sometimes words are left out to make the lines rhyme better.

Ask the children to think of other things they could see from their windows that could have been put into the poem. Write them on the board.

From the list on the board, let the children choose words that rhyme and make up a poem of their own (frogs, logs, dogs, pollywogs, lakes, snakes, drakes, flowers, showers, small things, tall things, etc.) on their writing tablets. Children who need help could work in a small group. Help with spelling as needed.

Correct the children's poems and have them recopy them neatly on the teaching paper. Have them write a title for their poem. Have them read their poems and show their pictures to the class. Put them up as a wall display, or put them together to make a class booklet.

ACTIVITIES:

1. Read Genesis 1 and 2 and talk about more things God made.

2. Have the children write poems about animals. Have them draw pictures to go with their poems. Let the children read them to another class or print them in the school newspaper. If your school has no school newspaper, type the poems and run them off so each child has a copy to take home to read to his parents.

3. Read prayers and songs that praise God, poems about things God has made, poems about animals, or poems written by older children in your school.

Page 9: Activity Page

CONCEPTS: reading comprehension, oral expression

TEACHER GOALS: To teach the children
To review subject-verb agreement, and
To learn to speak clearly and in complete sentences.

TEACHING PAGE 9:

Have the children read the direction at the top of the page. Tell the children to read each sentence carefully, to read both words that are under the line, to decide which word is best, and to draw a circle around it. Have the children read the sentence again using the word they circled to be sure it is the correct word before they copy it on the line.

Do the first sentence together. Have a child read it aloud.

Let the children finish the exercise by themselves. Check by having the children read the sentences using the words they wrote. Have children correct any mistakes.

Meet with small groups to discuss the material in the box. Choose a child to be the leader under your supervision. Help them keep the discussion centered on the subject. Encourage each child to contribute to the discussion. Have them tell what they think and why they think that way.

Bring out the idea that even though people make many kinds of things to use, God gave us our minds and the ability to think and plan and invent things.

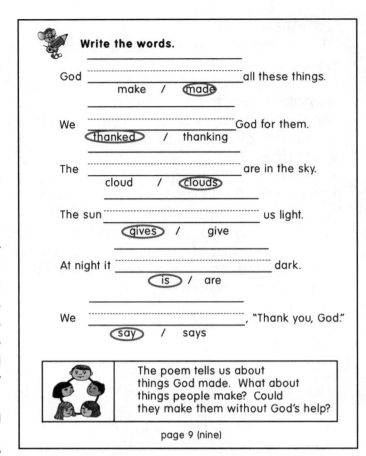

Write the words.

God _____ all these things.
make / (made)

We _____ God for them.
(thanked) / thanking

The _____ are in the sky.
cloud / (clouds)

The sun _____ us light.
(gives) / give

At night it _____ dark.
(is) / are

We _____, "Thank you, God."
(say) / says

The poem tells us about things God made. What about things people make? Could they make them without God's help?

page 9 (nine)

Page 10: Contractions

CONCEPT: contractions

TEACHER GOALS: To teach the children
To select words that are contractions, and
To write contractions in sentences.

MATERIALS NEEDED: Worksheet 1

TEACHING PAGE 10:

Have the children read the title at the top of the page.

Read the first sentence together. Have the children circle the answer. Then have them write it on the line. Have the children finish the page. Remind them to look at each word choice carefully.

ACTIVITY:

Do Worksheet 1.

Have the children read the direction at the top of this Worksheet. Have them read all the words on the page. Then have them write a short sentence using each word.

Remind the children to write neatly, to space the words well, to write complete sentences that tell something, to put a capital letter on the first word, and to use the right punctuation mark.

The teacher should collect the papers, correct them, and have the children recopy the corrected sentences on a sheet of writing tablet paper.

Let each child read two or three of his sentences to the class.

Contractions

I _____ go to town.
cant / (can't)

My finger _____ dirty.
isnt / (isn't)

_____ tell you how I fell.
Ill / (I'll)

I _____ fall down again.
wont / (won't)

_____ around my finger?
What / (What's)

I _____ safe.
(wasn't) / wasnt

page 10 (ten)

Name _____

Write a sentence for each word.

can't
_____
_____

paint
_____
_____

play
_____
_____

haven't
_____
_____

don't
_____
_____

Read your sentences.

**Language Arts 109
Worksheet 1
with page 10**

Teacher check _____
Initial   Date

SELF TEST 1

CONCEPTS: syllables, rhyming, possessives

TEACHER GOAL: To teach the children
To check their own progress periodically.

TEACHING PAGE 11:
Have the children read all the directions on the page. Be sure they understand exactly what they are to do.

Read the words. Have the children write the number of syllables they hear. (Write the number.) 1. *clowning,* 2. *town,* 3. *found*

Let them complete the page independently. Correct the page as soon as possible. Go over it with the child so he can see what he did well, and where he needs more work. Have him correct any mistakes as you are going through the page.

ACTIVITIES:
1. Reteach concepts the child has missed.
2. If several children miss the same things, work with them in a small group session.

SPELLING WORDS:

now
cow
how
crowd
clown
brown
our
out
shout
yellow

SELF TEST 1

Write the number.

1. _____ 2. _____ 3. _____

Write a word that rhymes.

out _____ town _____

Write the possessives.

We can be _____ children.
Gods / (God's)

I like to go to _____ church.
me / (my)

_____ mother gave her a rose.
(Rose's) / Roses

6/8   Teacher check _____
page 11 (eleven)   Initial   Date   My Score

II. PART TWO

Page 12: Building a Town

CONCEPTS: long *u*, sounds of *ou, ow, oy*, retelling a story

TEACHER GOALS: To teach the children
To identify and read words with the sound of long *u*,
To identify and read words with the sounds of *ow, ou,* and *oy*,
To recall details of a story,
To review possessives, contractions and verb endings, and
To retell the story in their own words.

TEACHING PAGE 12:

Present the words *Toby* and *Tony*. Be sure the children understand the meaning of each word. Have them tell why Toby and Tony have capital letters.

Have the children look at the picture and tell what is happening. Have them read the title.

Have the story read silently, then ask these questions:

"Who had the dump truck?" (Toby)

"Who had the road grader?" (Tony)

"What did the boys decide to do?" (build a town)

"What was in their town?" (houses, stores)

"What was around their town?" (roads)

"How did the boys use their toys?" (carry sand, grade roads)

"How do you think they made their houses?" (dishes or small pails)

Have the story read aloud a paragraph at a time. Have the children give the main idea of each paragraph in their own words.

Have the children find and circle words that have the long /u/ sound, the /ow/ sound, the /ou/ sound, and the /oy/ sound.

Have the children circle all the plurals in the story.

II. PART TWO

BUILDING A TOWN

Toby had a new dump truck.
Tony had a new road grader.
"Let's build a town," said Toby.
"We could use our toys to build houses and stores."
"Yes," said Tony, "we could build long roads all around our town."

The boys worked hard.
They used their toys
to build roads and buildings.
Toby and Tony played
with their town for a long time.
It was fun.

page 12 (twelve)

Have the children find and circle the contraction and the possessives.

Ask the children to find and circle a word with the *d* ending (*used*), the *ed* ending (*played*), and the *ing* ending (*building*).

Let several children retell the story in their own words. Help them recall details if necessary. Encourage them to tell the story in the same order as it is written.

Page 13: oi and oy

CONCEPTS: sounds of *oi* and *oy*, writing a report

TEACHER GOALS: To teach the children
To learn the sound of oi and oy, and
To write a report.

VOCABULARY: report

MATERIALS NEEDED: Bible, history book, pictures of Jesus as a child, construction paper

TEACHING PAGE 13:
Have the children reread "Building A Town" in Reader 5.

Have the children read the first direction and write a complete sentence in answer to the question. Let several children read their sentences.

Have the children read the next directions. Help them sound out the words and have them listen for the /oi-oy/ sound. Write *oi* and *oy* on the board and have the children read them several times. Have them circle the letters on the page. Have the children use each word in a sentence. These sentences may be written on a sheet of writing tablet paper if you wish.

Talk about reports and how to write one.

Explain what is meant by a report. The children should understand that a report must contain only true facts about the subject chosen. They should also learn that a good report is not written until after they have read about the subject in several different books.

Have books and stories available for the children to read or for you to read to them. Find pictures of Biblical cities in Sunday School materials or Bible history books.

Several of the Christian publishing houses have excellent films, filmstrips and videos for rent or sale that show cities and towns of Jesus' time.

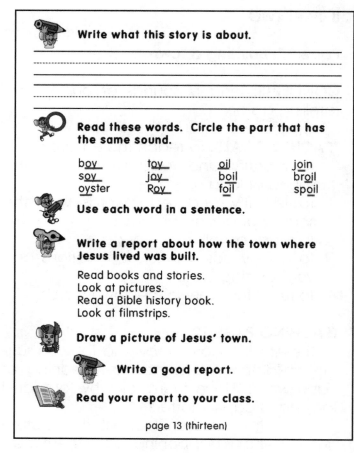

Write what this story is about.

Read these words. Circle the part that has the same sound.

boy   toy   oil   join
soy   joy   boil   broil
oyster   Roy   foil   spoil

Use each word in a sentence.

Write a report about how the town where Jesus lived was built.

Read books and stories.
Look at pictures.
Read a Bible history book.
Look at filmstrips.

Draw a picture of Jesus' town.

Write a good report.

Read your report to your class.

page 13 (thirteen)

This first report should be short, probably not more than a page long. When it is finished, correct the spelling, punctuation, capitalization, sentence structure, grammar, and content. Have the child recopy it. Have him draw a picture to go with it and mount both of them on a large sheet of construction paper to be displayed.

Have the children read their reports to the class.

ACTIVITIES:
Dictate the *oy-oi* words from Page 13 and have the children write them on writing tablet paper. Correct papers. Have the children write misspelled words five times on the back of their paper.

Page 14: Activity Page

CONCEPT: *oi* and *oy*

TEACHER GOALS: To teach the children
To write words using *oi* and *oy*,
To identify the sounds of long *o*, long *u*,
oi and *oy*, and
To learn to read and follow directions
independently.

TEACHING PAGE 14:

Have the children read the directions for each section. Name the pictures. (rose, cube, boy, oil, cucumber, toes, boil, pony, goat, toys, rock, pew, oyster, music, top, hoe) Be sure they understand what they are to do. Let them do the page independently. Check by having children read the words, tell which letters they wrote in the blanks, name the pictures, and tell which letter they circled.

TEACHING READING:

Provide 5 interesting objects. Tell students we're going to play "Lost and Found".
Tell them these objects have been FOUND that someone else LOST.
Relate the following information about each object.
Object #1: has someone's name on it, you don't like it
Object #2: has someone's name on it, but you like it
Object # 3: you think you know who it belongs to, but aren't sure, you like it
Object # 4: don't know who it belongs to, don't like it.
Object #5: don't know who it belongs to, you like it
Have students (no teacher input) discuss what to do with each item. Have them make a decision for each item and record them. Do not make any comments on their decisions at this time. Introduce today's story: The Gold Coin

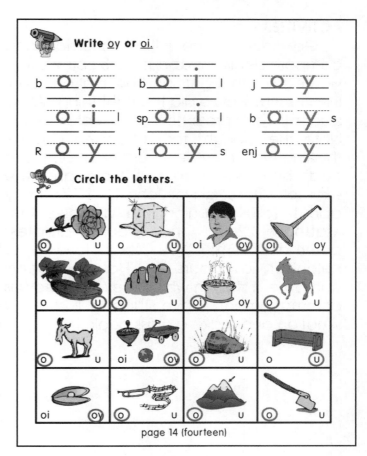

page 14 (fourteen)

Read the story "The Gold Coin" together, then ask the following questions:
"What did Howie find in the sandbox?" (a gold coin)
"Who was in the sandbox with him?" (Joy)
"What did Howie say he would do with the coin?" (put it in a jar and set it on his dresser)
"Did the other children agree with him?" (no)
"What did Joy suggest?" (make a sign to find the owner)
"Why did Howie change his mind about keeping the coin?" (he knew how he wanted to be treated)
"Where would Howie put the coin in the meantime?" (on his dresser in a jar)
Find ow/ou words: (Howie, hour, shouted, found, about, wow, house). Find oi/oy words: (Joy, coin)

ACTIVITIES:

Go back to the initial discussion and compare decisions about the 5 objects with Howie's first thoughts and his final decision. Discuss why Howie did the right thing. Allow students to express how they feel about it. Note the thought that changed Howie's thinking was "how he would want others to treat him." Refer to the Bible and the examples Jesus gave: John 13: 1-17 – Story about Jesus washing the disciples feet Matthew 22:39 the second greatest commandment: "You shall love your neighbor as yourself". Have students compose a story in which they followed this commandment. Have students illustrate a situation and make a class book.

Page 15: Activity Page

CONCEPTS: *oi* and *oy*, reading comprehension

TEACHER GOALS: To teach the children
    To identify the sound of *oi/oy*, and
    To be able to recall details after reading a story.

TEACHING PAGE 15:
    Talk about the pictures with the children. Have them listen for the /oi/ sound. Have them circle the pictures that have the /oi/ sound (flag, bed, soil, choice, toil).
    Read the next direction. Discuss each picture. Have them listen for the /oy/ sound. Have them circle each picture with the /oy/ sound (boy, fan, toy, sign, joy).

TEACHING READING:
    Read "The Pony Show" in *Reader 5*.
    Present the new word *could* and have the children use it in several sentences.
    Ask the children to look at the picture and tell what they see. Have a child read the title of the story.
    Have the children read the story silently.
    Ask questions such as these:
    "What was going to happen?"
    "What did Pam ask her mother?"
    "What was Pam's pony's name?"
    "When did they go to the show?"
    "Where did the children ride?"
    "How did they ride?"
    "Did JoJo win a prize?"
    "Was Pam upset because JoJo didn't win?"
    "What do you think will happen next?"
    "Do you think they will go to more pony shows?"

TEACHING READING:
    Ask students to raise their hand if they've ever visited the nurse at school. Ask what they think the nurse at school is supposed to

Circle pictures with the **oi** sound.

Circle pictures with the **oy** sound.

page 15 (fifteen)

do. List responses. Share experiences. Introduce today's story: Nurse Jane
    Tell students it's a rhyming story and will sound more like a poem.
    Read the story "Nurse Jane" together, then ask the following questions:
    Why does it say life on the playground can be tough? (bad things can happen, get hurt)
    "Were the children in this story having a good day or bad day?" (bad day)
    "What did Ted and Randy do?" (bumped into a tree)
    "What happened to Alice?" (scraped her knee)
    "What happened to Roger?" (he got stung by a bee)
    "Who ate mud pies?" (Ellen and Trisha)
    "Why did Sandy cry?" (she had blisters)
    "Who is going to help them?" (Nurse Jane)

"Why does it say you're lucky to have a nurse like Nurse Jane?" (kind, nice, understanding)

"How do you know?" (she doesn't scold or get mad, she understands feelings)

Find r-controlled words: (her, Roger, Orbin, for, Nurse, Charles, Sherman, started, blisters, dirt, shirts, sore, or, understands, hurts)

ACTIVITIES:

Talk about safety on the playground. Make up a list of safety rules for the class to follow. Invite the school nurse to your classroom for a special talk or lesson (health, teeth, cleanliness, eating). If a child's parent is a nurse, invite him/her as a guest speaker. Make cards or posters to express appreciation to the school nurse. Make up a rhyming story about another person at school (librarian, secretary, custodian, lunchroom workers)

Page 16: The Pony Show

CONCEPTS: long *o*, retelling a story, predicting outcomes

TEACHER GOALS: To teach the children
To read words with the sound of long *o*,
To retell the story in their own words with accurate recall of details and sequence of events, and
To use the information in the story to predict what might happen next.

TEACHING PAGE 16:
Read "The Pony Show" again from *Reader 5*.

Have the children read the story aloud. Let several children retell the story in their own words. Encourage them to put in all the details and to tell about the events in the order they happened.

Read the directions.

Have the children find all the words in the story that have the long /o/ sound and copy them. Have several children read their lists. Have the children point out the various combinations of letters that make the long /o/ sound (Pony, Show, Oh, Pam, going, JoJo, Pam's, So, ponies, rode).

TEACHING READING:
Provide nonfiction books on tornadoes. Share pictures and stories from the books. Ask if anyone has ever seen a tornado. If yes, ask them to describe it. Write descriptions on the board. Introduce today's story: Tornado. Tell students it is a nonfiction story which gives us factual information about tornadoes.

Write these words on the board: tornado, powerful. tunnel, thunderstorm, worst, force, destroys, buildings, rubble, damage, dangerous. Have students read and learn the meanings of the words.

Read the story "Tornado" together, then ask the following questions:

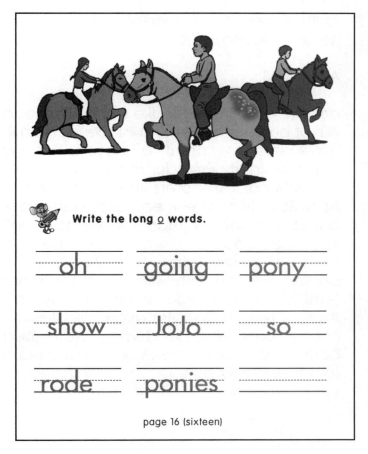

Write the long <u>o</u> words.

oh   going   pony

show   JoJo   so

rode   ponies

page 16 (sixteen)

"Where does a tornado begin?" (in the clouds of a strong thunderstorm)

"Where can a tornado occur?" (anywhere in the world)

"What is the most common area called?" (tornado alley). If the resources are available, show students the area on a map which makes up Tornado Alley.

"What are the worst months?" (April, May and June)

"What are tornadoes made of?" (air, dirt, grass, leaves, trash)

"How is a tornado described?" (black finger, fast moving train)

"Why do we call them twisters?" (they twist back and forth as they move)

"Why are tornadoes dangerous?" (they destroy everything in their path)

"What should you do if you see a tornado?" (get to a safe place)

Find r-controlled words: (tornado, powerful, thunderstorm, dirt, finger, turns, forth, twisters, force, short, dangerous, ever, never, direction)

ACTIVITIES:

Do further research on tornadoes to acquire more facts. Make a giant tornado out of butcher paper and list the facts on it. Have students paint a picture with a tornado in it. Provide maps and have students color the area known as Tornado Alley. Scientific experiment (exact directions can be found in many "easy science" resource books): Demonstrate how a tornado works using two 2-Liter soda bottles. Fill one with water, turn the other (empty) bottle upside down and securely tape or use an adapter available at some hobby stores. When you turn the water filled bottle upside down the water will whirl like a tornado. Kids love it!

Page 17: Activity Page

CONCEPTS: reading comprehension, *oa* and silent *e*, *ow*, oral expression

TEACHER GOALS: To teach the children
To understand the meaning of what they read,
To write words with *oa*, *ow*, and silent *e*,
To learn to speak clearly and in complete sentences, and
To write rhyming words.

VOCABULARY: answers, sheet

MATERIALS NEEDED: Worksheet 2

TEACHING PAGE 17:

Have the children read the direction at the top of the page. Have the children read each question and write a complete sentence in answer to it on a sheet of writing tablet paper. You may wish to read through the list of questions as a group to be sure they understand each one.

Collect the papers when the children have finished. Check for content, sentence structure, punctuation, capitalization, spelling, and neatness. Hand the papers back no later than the next day after the lesson was done.

Have each child read one or two of his answers after you reread the questions.

Have the children read the next direction and the word endings. Have them give several rhyming words for each ending. Have them finish their lists on a sheet of writing tablet paper. Write the endings on the board and write rhyming words as the children read them from their lists. Have the children add to and correct their lists.

The endings, *owed*, *oed*, and *own*, may be done as a group exercise or as an independent exercise. Check as above.

Present the word *should*. Have the children read the material in the box in their small groups and discuss it.

Write your answers on a sheet of LIFEPAC Tablet paper.

1. What is the story, "The Pony Show" about?
2. What did Pam ask her mother?
3. What did her mother say?
4. Did Pam's pony get a prize?
5. Was Pam happy? Why?

Write words that rhyme.

-oa	-ode		-one	-oan

Write more rhyming words on a sheet of LIFEPAC Tablet paper.

-owed   -oed   -own

How do you feel when you don't win or you aren't first? How should you feel? Should you stop trying?

page 17 (seventeen)

ACTIVITY:

1. Dictate the following words and have the children write them on a sheet of writing tablet paper. Correct the papers and have children write each misspelled word five times on the back of the paper.

road	bone
rode	toad
Joan	alone
stone	moan
*showed	*grown

2. Do Worksheet 2.

Have the children read the directions on the page. Be sure they understand what they are to do. Let them do the entire page by themselves. Check by writing the endings on the board and by having the children read words from their lists for you to write under each. Have the children read the lists several times and listen for the rhyming part.

Check the second exercise by having the children read the words they circled. Have the children correct any mistakes.

Name _____

Write two words for each ending.

-ake _____   _____
     _____   _____

-een _____   _____
     _____   _____

-ite _____   _____
     _____   _____

-ose _____   _____
     _____   _____

-y   _____   _____
     _____   _____

-ay _____   _____

Circle words with the long u sound.

you   bus   you'll   used

us   cute   but   pup

use   mew   cube   fuel

**Language Arts 109
Worksheet 2
with page 17**

Teacher check _____
                Initial   Date

Page 18: Activity Page

CONCEPTS: title, main idea

TEACHER GOALS: To teach the children
To find the main idea of a story, and
To choose a title for a story.

TEACHING PAGE 18:
Have the children read the title and the direction at the top of the page. Have them tell what they see in the pictures.

Have the children read the page silently and underline the best title for each story. Remind the children to read carefully and to read all the titles before they choose one. Ask them what a good title should do. (Tell the main idea.)

Check by having the stories and the title read. Have the children tell why that title is the best one. Ask the children to tell the main idea of each story.

ACTIVITY:
Read several titles from familiar books. Have the children tell what the book might be about. Emphasize the importance of titles.

page 18 (eighteen)

Page 19: Activity Page

CONCEPT: reading comprehension: what happens next

TEACHER GOAL: To teach the children
 To understand what they are reading so they can tell what happens next.

TEACHING PAGE 19:

Have the children read the direction at the top of the page. Have them read each story and decide which sentence tells what will happen next.

Remind the children to read carefully and to read both sentences before they draw a line under one. Check by having the children read the stories aloud with the sentence they underlined. Have the children correct any mistakes.

 Draw a line under what will happen next.

The animals are happy.
They are going on a picnic.
They go up the hill.

The animals will eat.
The animals will sleep.

The dog is running after the cat.
The dog is barking.
The cat runs and runs.

The cat will stop to eat.
The cat will run up a tree.

The farmer plants the wheat seeds.
The wheat grows tall.
Soon the wheat is ready to cut.

The farmer will cut the wheat.
The farmer will go away.

page 19 (nineteen)

Page 20: Activity Page

CONCEPT: subject-verb agreement

TEACHER GOAL: To teach the children
To select the verb that agrees with the subject.

TEACHING PAGE 20:
Have the children read the direction and the words in the boxes. Have them tell which ones should be used with a plural subject and which ones with a singular subject. Ask which should be used with the word *you*.

Let the children do the entire page by themselves. Check by having them read the sentences.

Have the children use the words in sentences they make up. They may give them orally or write them in their writing tablet.

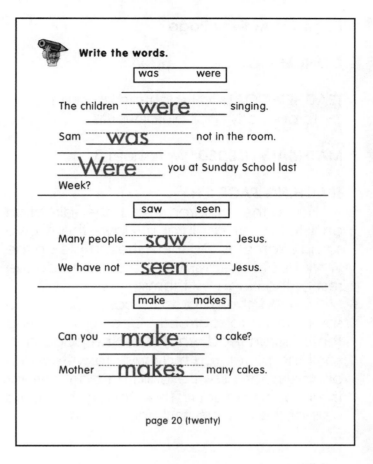

Write the words.

was	were

The children **were** singing.

Sam **was** not in the room.

Were you at Sunday School last Week?

saw	seen

Many people **saw** Jesus.

We have not **seen** Jesus.

make	makes

Can you **make** a cake?

Mother **makes** many cakes.

page 20 (twenty)

227

Page 21: Activity Page

CONCEPT: plurals

TEACHER GOAL: To teach the children
To correctly spell plural words.

MATERIALS NEEDED: Worksheet 3

TEACHING PAGE 21:

Have the children read the direction and tell what a plural is. Have them give some examples. Do the first example on the Worksheet together. Let the children do the rest of the page by themselves.

Remind them to read carefully and to spell the plural correctly. Check by having the children read what is on the page and spell the plural. You may wish to write them on the board so the children can correct their own papers. The teacher should collect the papers and check them over.

ACTIVITY:

Do Worksheet 3.

Have the children read the directions on the page. Be sure they understand what they are to do in each section. Let them complete the page by themselves.

Write the endings and words on the board one at a time and check by having the children read words from their lists for you to write under the endings.

Have the lists read several times. Have the children add to and correct their lists.

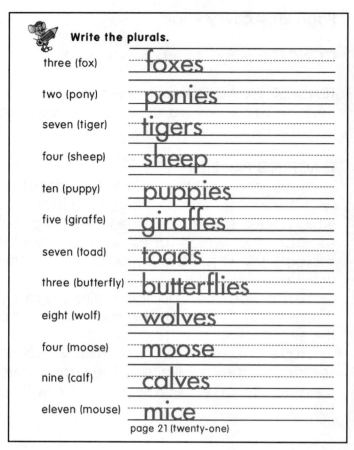

Write the plurals.

three (fox)	foxes
two (pony)	ponies
seven (tiger)	tigers
four (sheep)	sheep
ten (puppy)	puppies
five (giraffe)	giraffes
seven (toad)	toads
three (butterfly)	butterflies
eight (wolf)	wolves
four (moose)	moose
nine (calf)	calves
eleven (mouse)	mice

page 21 (twenty-one)

Name _____

Write two words for each ending.

-un _____ _____

-im _____ _____

-amp _____ _____

-ock _____ _____

-ell _____ _____

-ug _____ _____

-ank _____ _____

-ing _____ _____

Write rhyming words.

deck _____   think _____

thump _____   spend _____

batter _____   ditch _____

Language Arts 109
Worksheet 3
with page 21

Teacher check _____
Initial   Date

Page 22: Activity Page

CONCEPT: contractions

TEACHER GOALS: To teach the children
To write words as contractions, and
To write contractions as words.

TEACHING PAGE 22:

Have the children read the directions to both sections on the page. Tell them to read the words carefully and to write the contractions on the top part of the page. Tell them to write the words that the contractions stand for on the bottom half of the page.

Check by having the children read the words and contractions. Write them on the board so the children can check their spelling. The teacher should recheck the papers.

Have the children use the contractions in sentences. They may give them orally or write them in their writing tablets.

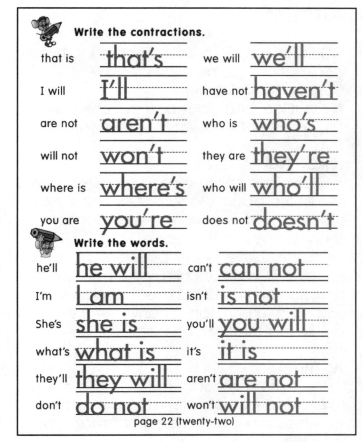

Write the contractions.

that is	that's	we will	we'll
I will	I'll	have not	haven't
are not	aren't	who is	who's
will not	won't	they are	they're
where is	where's	who will	who'll
you are	you're	does not	doesn't

Write the words.

he'll	he will	can't	can not
I'm	I am	isn't	is not
She's	she is	you'll	you will
what's	what is	it's	it is
they'll	they will	aren't	are not
don't	do not	won't	will not

page 22 (twenty-two)

SELF TEST 2

CONCEPTS: subject-verb agreement, rhyming, contractions, plurals

TEACHER GOAL: To teach the children
   To check their own progress periodically.

TEACHING PAGE 23:
   Have the children read the directions on the entire page. Be sure they know exactly what they are to do in each section. Let them complete the page.
   Correct the page as soon as possible. Go over it with the child so he can see what he did well, and where he needs more work. Have him correct any mistakes as you are going through the page.

ACTIVITIES:
   1. Reteach concepts the child missed.
   2. If several children miss the same kinds of things, work with them in a small group, if possible.

SPELLING WORDS:

   boy
   joy
   toy
   soy
   oyster
   oil
   boil
   foil
   spoil
   join

SELF TEST 2

Write the words.

Pam _____is_____ taking JoJo to the show.
          is / are

They _____are_____ going to ride in the show.
          is / are

Write rhyming words.

cow _____   toad _____

boy _____   boil _____

Write the contractions.

are not ___aren't___   she is ___she's___

cannnot ___can't___   that is ___that's___

Write the plurals.

show ___shows___   man ___men___

pony ___ponies___   deer ___deer___

11/14   Teacher check _____
                    Initial   Date

page 23 (twenty-three)

III. PART THREE

Page 24: Old, Old Goat

CONCEPTS: long *o*, real or make-believe, dramatizing story

TEACHER GOALS: To teach the children
To read words with the sound of long *o*,
To know the difference between real and make-believe situations, and
To dramatize stories.

TEACHING PAGE 24:
Read "Old, Old Goat" from *Reader 5*.
Have the children look at the picture and tell what is happening.
Have them read the title. Have them read the story silently.
Have the story read aloud by paragraphs. Have the children tell what was in each paragraph in their own words.
Ask the children to find and read the exclamations. Encourage them to read with expression. Ask the name of the punctuation mark at the end of each exclamation.
Read the first direction.
Have the children find and read the words that have the long /o/ sound. Have them write them.
Read the next direction. Have them find words with the short /o/ sound, the /ow/ sound, and the /oo/ sound. Have them write them.
Read the last direction.
Have the children find rhyming words (goat, coat, boat). Have them write them.
Ask the children to think about the story and tell whether or not it could really have happened. Do goats really chew on things like this? Do goats eat grass? Let the children share experiences about goats. Some children may have goats at home and want to tell about them.

III. PART THREE

OLD, OLD GOAT

Write the long *o* words.

old   coat   goat

Write words with the *o* sound.

Short o   ow   oo

stopped   down   looked

Write rhyming words.

goat   boat

coat

page 24 (twenty-four)

Let one child act the part of the goat. Have the rest of the class read the story while this child does what they are reading. Let several children have a turn. Encourage the class to read with expression. Ask the child playing the goat to keep his actions in time with the readers.

ACTIVITIES:
1. Read *The Three Billygoats Gruff* and let the children act it out.
2. Read other stories about goats.

Page 25: Activity Page

CONCEPTS: real and make-believe, long *o*

TEACHER GOALS: To teach the children
To tell the difference between real and make-believe, and
To write words with the sound of long *o*.

TEACHING PAGE 25:

Have the children read the question and direction at the top of the page. Let several give their reasons.

Have the children read the next direction. Tell them to read each sentence carefully and decide whether it is true or false. Have them write yes or no on the lines. Check by having the children read the sentences and tell which word they wrote. Have them give a reason for writing what they did .

Have the children read the next direction and the word endings. Have them give several rhyming words and write their lists. Check by putting the lists of rhyming words for each ending on the board. Have the children add to and correct their lists. Have them read the list several times.

ACTIVITIES:

1. Read stories that are obviously either real or make-believe.

2. Dictate these words and have the children write them on a sheet of writing tablet paper. Correct the papers and have the children write each misspelled word five times on the back of the paper.

old	goat
cold	told
coat	boat
vote	sold
hold	tote

Could "Old, Old, Goat" really happen?
Tell <u>why</u> **or** <u>why</u> <u>not.</u>

Write <u>yes</u> **or** <u>no.</u>

Goats use spoons. no

Coats are good to eat. no

Goats are animals. yes

Goats say, "Mew, Mew." no

God made goats. yes

We can make goats. no

Goats give milk. yes

Goats go to school. no

Write words that rhyme.

-old	-oat	-ote

Write more rhyming words on a sheet of LIFEPAC Tablet paper.

page 25 (twenty-five)

Page 26: Activity Page

CONCEPTS: reading comprehension, writing sentences

TEACHER GOALS: To teach the children
To understand what they are reading so they can tell what happens next, and
To write in complete sentences with the proper punctuation.

TEACHING PAGE 26:
Have the children read the direction at the top of the page. Tell them to read the short stories very carefully and to write a sentence that tells what they think will happen next. Remind them of the rules for writing good sentences.

Let several children read their ideas to the class. Talk about their ideas. Emphasize the importance of doing the right thing in each situation. Have the children tell why they should always do the right thing even though it is very hard sometimes.

Collect the papers and correct the sentences. Have the child recopy sentences with more than one mistake in them.

Write what you think will happen next.

A new family came to live next door to Jane. They did not go to church or Sunday School.

Tom and Andy found two dimes on the sidewalk. Down the street they saw a little boy crying because he had lost his dimes.

page 26 (twenty-six)

Page 27: Activity Page

CONCEPTS: reading comprehension: sequence of events, details

TEACHER GOALS: To teach the children
To read to understand the order of events, and
To recall details.

TEACHING PAGE 27:

Have the children read the direction. Remind them to read all the sentences carefully before they number them in the order they happened. Let the children do the entire page by themselves.

Check by having the children read the sentences in order. Have them correct any mistakes. Have the children tell how they know which sentence comes first, next, and last.

TEACHING READING:

Read "Animals" from *Reader 5*.

Have the children look at the picture and tell what they see. Have them read the title. Ask them to tell what they think the story will be about. Have the story read silently.

Ask questions such as these:
"Are all animals alike?"
"How are animals different?"
"Can you name some animals with four feet? two feet? no feet?"
"Can you name some animals with hair or fur?"
"Can you name some animals with scales? feathers?"
"Are birds animals?"
"How did the animals get on the earth?"

Write 1, 2, 3 for first, next, and last.

_3_	Jane sleeps all night.
_1_	Jane gets ready for bed.
_2_	Jane goes to bed.
_1_	Mother cooks the dinner.
_3_	Ann asks the blessing.
_2_	Don sets the table.
_2_	He reads his lesson.
_1_	Joe gets his reading book.
_3_	He puts his book away.
_2_	The bud is starting to open.
_3_	The flower is pink.
_1_	I see a bud on my plant.
_3_	Father takes us for a ride.
_2_	Father fixes our car.
_1_	Our car will not run.

page 27 (twenty-seven)

Page 28: Animals

CONCEPTS: recalling details, classifying

TEACHER GOALS: To teach the children
To recall details of what they have read, and
To classify animals into categories.

BIBLE REFERENCE: Genesis 1:19 through 31

MATERIALS NEEDED: animal books

TEACHING PAGE 28 :

Read the direction.

Have the children draw a line from the question to the answer.

Can you think of an animal that has two feet and can fly? (bird)

has four feet and a very tough skin with very little hair? (elephant or rhinoceros)

has six feet and flies? (many insects)

has four feet, hair, and a long neck? (giraffe)

Have the children think of some riddles like these and write one on the bottom line of the page.

Go through the story "Animals" and have the children give examples for each kind of animal described. Talk about hibernation and animals that work for people.

Ask the children what the main idea of the story is.

ACTIVITY:

Read stories about different kinds of animals.

TEACHING READING:

Provide a picture of a dolphin. Make a chart recording students' responses to what they know about dolphins.

Write these words on the board: dolphin, gentle, rubbery, Bottlenose, television, mammals, surface, breath, memories, thousands. Have students read and learn the meanings of the words. Introduce

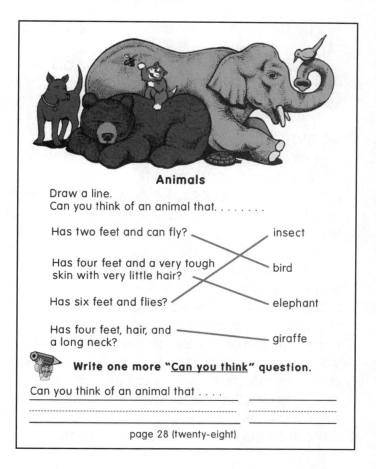

Animals

Draw a line.
Can you think of an animal that . . . .

Has two feet and can fly?   insect

Has four feet and a very tough skin with very little hair?   bird

Has six feet and flies?   elephant

Has four feet, hair, and a long neck?   giraffe

Write one more "Can you think" question.

Can you think of an animal that . . . . _____

_____

page 28 (twenty-eight)

today's story: Playmates of the Sea (nonfiction)

Read the story "Playmates of the Sea" together, then ask the following questions:

"What word describes a dolphin's skin?" (rubbery)

"What two words describe a dolphin's personality (how they act)?" (gentle, playful)

"What dolphin is the most common to us?" (Bottlenose)

"Why are we familiar with this dolphin?" (they're seen a sea parks and on TV shows)

"What kind of animal is a dolphin?" (small whale, mammal)

"How many different kinds of dolphins are there?" (over 39)

List some things we know about dolphins from this story: (smart, large brains, easy to train, good memories, do tricks, jump, twist, spin, do back flips, small ears, fantastic hearing, see with their ears, useful to man).

Add any new information to the previous chart.

Find the ph word: (dolphin) – Add other PH words : Phonics, Philip, photo, graph, Stephanie...

ACTIVITIES:

Provide nonfiction books on dolphins. Give students opportunities to look at the pictures in the books. Review the chart with information. Have students think of other information they'd like to know about dolphins. Record their questions and work as a class to obtain the answers. Give students clay and have them make a model dolphin. Display. Make ocean scene dioramas including at least one dolphin. Have students share stories if they have visited Sea World or another place where dolphins perform. Write an imaginary story about a dolphin (Daphne the Dolphin is late for the show...). Be an animal trainer and write how to train a dolphin to do tricks.

Page 29: Activity Page

CONCEPTS: classifying, main idea, plural, writing a report

TEACHER GOALS: To teach the children
    To understand classification,
    To tell the main idea of a story,
    To write the plural of words, and
    To write a report.

MATERIALS NEEDED: Worksheet 4

TEACHING PAGE 29:

Have the children read the directions on the page. Be sure they understand everything they are to do. Then let them complete the work on the page independently. Check by having the children read the animals and their matching descriptions, their sentences that tell the main idea, and the plural for each animal. Have them correct any mistakes.

Review how to write a report. Have the children choose animals to write their reports about. Have them read about the animals in books, encyclopedias, or textbooks. Have them write a two or three page report about the animal's appearance, habits, food, shelter, and uses. Correct the report and have the child recopy it. He may draw a picture of his animal if he likes or find a photograph of it.

Give each child a chance to read his report to the class. Remind the class of the rules for a good reader and a good audience.

Have the children make their report into a booklet to take home.

ACTIVITY:

1. Make covers for the report booklets. Have the children cut pictures from magazines or use the pictures they drew earlier in class.
2. Do Worksheet 4.
Have the children read the direction

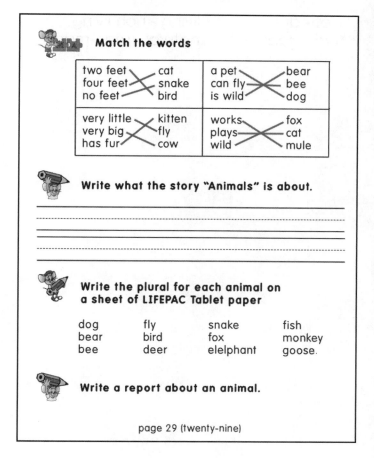

page 29 (twenty-nine)

and the headings in the boxes. Tell them to cut first along the line and then to cut the small boxes apart. Have them paste the small boxes that name things that are alive in the first large box and the ones that names things that are not alive in the second large box. Check by having the children read what they have pasted in each box. Have them correct any mistakes.

Have the children name other living and non-living things that could have been put in the boxes. You could make a third group of things that were once alive, but are no longer (lumber, cotton or wool clothing, wooden furniture, many kinds of food, etc.)

3. Write categories similar to these on the board and have the children write lists of things that belong in them. Have the lists read aloud.

hard - soft	long - short
large - small	tall - short
smooth - rough	round - square

Language Arts 109 Teacher Notes

wet - dry   living - non-living
furry - scaly   natural - man-made

Name _____

Cut and paste.

Things which are alive	Things which are not alive
animals trees men weeds flowers birds boys women grass girls	rocks cars hills moon houses boxes ground towns

rocks	flowers	women
trees	birds	grass
animals	boys	boxes
cars	hills	girls
men	moon	ground
weeds	houses	towns

**Language Arts 109
Worksheet 4**
with page 29

Teacher check _____
Initial   Date

Page 30: Building Rockets

CONCEPTS: sequence, retelling a story, predicting the outcome

TEACHER GOALS: To teach the children
To recall events in the sequence they happened,
To retell the story in their own words, and
To tell what might happen next in the story.

TEACHING READING:
Read "Building Rockets" in *Reader 5*.
Present the words *Joel's, building, together, Mr. Jones, launch, ready* and have the children give meanings for them. Have them use each word in a sentence.

Have the children read the title and sentences at the top of the page and discuss them.

Have the children look at the picture and tell what they see. Have a child read the title of the story.

Ask the children to read the story silently. Have several children tell the story in their own words. Help them recall details and sequence if necessary.

Have the story read aloud, a paragraph at a time, and talk about what is happening. Let all the children read the count-down together.

Ask the children why they think the children in the picture are standing so far back. Let the children share their experiences with building rockets, or with watching older brothers building them.

TEACHING PAGE :
Read the directions.
Have the children number the sentences in order.

ACTIVITIES:
1. If possible, get a rocket kit and put the rocket together. Let the children help with the reading of directions, finding parts,

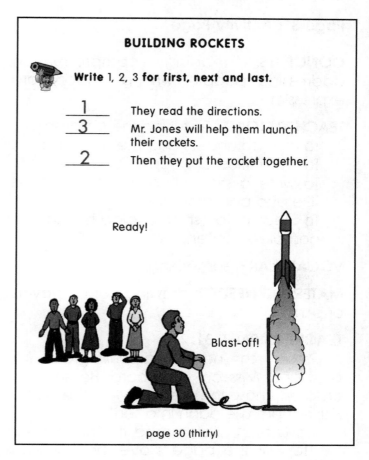

BUILDING ROCKETS

Write 1, 2, 3 **for first, next and last.**

<u>1</u>   They read the directions.
<u>3</u>   Mr. Jones will help them launch their rockets.
<u>2</u>   Then they put the rocket together.

Ready!

Blast-off!

page 30 (thirty)

putting parts together, and so on as they are able. Launch the rocket outside in a cleared area.

2. Make a bulletin board display of pictures of rockets that have been launched by our country for space exploration.

3. Read books about space and rockets, about astronauts, and about the planets.

Page 31: Activity Page

CONCEPTS: reading comprehension, addressing people, writing a story, oral expression

TEACHER GOALS: To teach the children
To read to understand the meaning,
To learn titles for people,
To write a story using good sentences, title and paragraphs, and
To learn to speak clearly and in complete sentences.

VOCABULARY: something

MATERIALS NEEDED: drawing paper, crayons or paints

TEACHING PAGE 31:

Present the new words *built, group, Mr., Mrs.,* and *Miss* on the board. Be sure the children know the meanings of the words. Have them use each in a sentence.

Have the children read the direction at the top of the page. Have the questions read aloud and answered in complete sentences. If you wish, you may have the children write the answers in complete sentences. Check by having the children read their answers.

Have the children read the next direction and the list of names. Be sure the children understand the meaning of each of the titles: *Mr.* for both older and younger men, *Mrs.* for married women, and *Miss* for unmarried women and young girls. You may also include *Master* for a very young boy if you wish, although it is not used as much now. Usually for a very young boy no title is used at all except for very formal occasions. Emphasize that it shows respect to use titles when talking to older people.

Have the children read the next direction and do the exercise. Write the correct titles on the board. Have the children correct any mistakes.

Have the children read the directions at the bottom of the page. Have them write

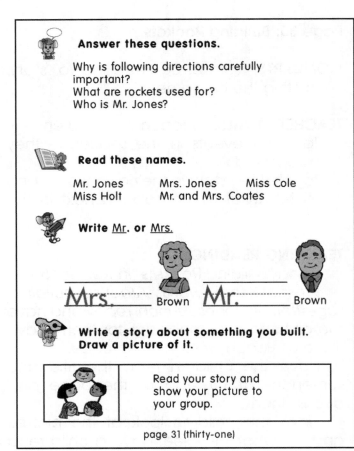

Answer these questions.

Why is following directions carefully important?
What are rockets used for?
Who is Mr. Jones?

Read these names.

Mr. Jones   Mrs. Jones   Miss Cole
Miss Holt   Mr. and Mrs. Coates

Write <u>Mr.</u> or <u>Mrs.</u>

Mrs. Brown   Mr. Brown

Write a story about something you built.
Draw a picture of it.

Read your story and show your picture to your group.

page 31 (thirty-one)

stories at least two or three pages long. Let the children read their stories and show their pictures in their small groups. All the groups may meet at the same time. Choose a child to be leader of each group. The teacher should go from group to group helping if necessary. This kind of small group session is easier to lead, so you may wish to choose children as leaders who are shy or timid.

ACTIVITIES:

1. Have the children write a sentence using each of the names in the second exercise.

2. Dictate these titles and have the children write them on a sheet of writing tablet paper.

Mr.

Mrs.

Miss

Have the children write a list of the people they know who have those titles in their names.

SELF TEST 3

CONCEPTS: long o, rhyming words, abbreviations/titles, sentences, main idea

TEACHER GOAL: To teach the children
To check their own progress periodically.

TEACHING PAGE 32:

Have the children read all the directions on the page. Be sure they understand everything they are to do.

Main Idea Sentences: (circle the main idea)
Old, old goat stopped.
There by the road was some green grass.
Old, old goat took a bite.
Oh, Oh! The grass was good.
Old, old goat began to eat.
Green grass is good to eat.

Correct the page as soon as possible. Go over it with the child so he can see what he did well, and where he needs more work. Have him correct any mistakes as you are going through the page.

ACTIVITIES:

1. Reteach concepts the child misses.
2. If several children miss the same kinds of things, reteach in a small group, if possible.

SPELLING WORDS:

house
sound
pound
hour
sour
loud
wow
crown
crow
grow

SELF TEST 3

Circle the words.

long o

go	bone	goat	not
got	oh	cow	boat
yellow	how	tote	soy
boy	toe	wow	hoe

Write a rhyming word.

how _____   road _____

toe _____   cold _____

Write Mr. or Mrs.

Mrs. _____   Mr. _____

Put an S by the sentence.
____ The black cow.
S The dog jumped.

Circle the main idea.
Old goat did not like boats.
Coats are not good to eat.
Old goat liked to eat green grass.

14/18

Teacher check _____
page 32 (thirty-two)

Page 33:

Take Home Activity Page

CONCEPT: following directions

TEACHER GOALS: To teach the children
To read to follow directions, and
To follow directions in the order in which
they are given.

VOCABULARY: activity

MATERIALS NEEDED: scissors, brass fasteners.
crayons

TEACHING PAGE 33:
Ask the children to tell what is in the picture. Ask them to tell what they will do with the parts.
Read the directions with the children and let them do the page by themselves and take it home.

TAKE HOME ACTIVITY
Bobo, the Clown

Color and cut out Bobo.
Put him together with
small brass fasteners.

page 33 (thirty-three)

LIFEPAC TEST AND ALTERNATE TEST 109

CONCEPTS: possessives, *oi* sound, *oy* sound, contractions, plurals, rhyming words, and syllables, subject verb agreement, complete sentences, main Idea

TEACHER GOAL: To teach the children
To check their own progress periodically.

TEACHING the LIFEPAC TEST:

Administer the test to the class as a group. Ask to have directions read or read them to the class. In either case, be sure that the children clearly understand. Put examples on the board if it seems necessary. Give ample time for each activity to be completed before going to the next.

Syllable Words-(Write the number of syllables.) *rocking, cow, clowning, town*

Main Idea Sentences-(Circle the main idea.)

The teacher should read the following sentences and then have the students circle the correct main idea sentence.

The children at Joel's school are building rockets. They have kits with all the rocket parts in them. Mr. Jones will help them launch their rockets.

Correct immediately and discuss with the child.

Review any concepts that have been missed.

Give those children who do not achieve the 80% score additional copies of the worksheets and a list of vocabulary words to study. A parent or a classroom helper may help in the review.

When the child is ready, give the Alternate LIFEPAC Test. Use the same procedure as for the LIFEPAC Test.

Syllable Words-(Write the number of syllables.) *talking, sow, winter, clown*

Main Idea Sentences-(Circle the main idea.)

LANGUAGE ARTS 1 0 9

LIFEPAC TEST

28/35

Name _____
Date _____
Score _____

The teacher should read the following sentences and then have the students circle the correct main idea sentence.

There are many kinds of animals.
Some animals are very little.
Some are very big.
Many animals have hair or fur.

SPELLING WORDS:

LIFEPAC WORDS Alternate words

LIFEPAC WORDS	Alternate words
now	how
crowd	clown
out	our
shout	boil
boy	foil
oyster	join
oil	pound
sound	loud
hour	wow
grow	crow

LANGUAGE ARTS 109: LIFEPAC TEST

Match the words and possessives.

a car that belongs to Father — Father's car

a coat that belongs to me — my coat

a cat that belongs to Jo — Jo's cat

a cake that belongs to Mother — Mother's cake

children who belong to God — God's children

the church we go to — our church

Circle the words with the long oi or oy sound.

(boil)   (soy)   (boy)
try   (soil)   buy
(toy)   (toil)   (choice)

1 (one)

Write the contractions.

is not   isn't   they will   they'll

you will   you'll   are not   aren't

she is   she's   who is   who's

Write the plurals.

pony   ponies   tiger   tigers

Write a word that rhymes.

cold   coat

out   boil

soy   cow

page 2 (two)

Write the number of syllables.

1. [2]   2. [1]   3. [2]   4. [1]

Write the words.

Toby and Tony __are__ playing.
           is are

They __are__ building a town.
     is are

Put an s by the complete sentence.

__S__ They jumped on the tire.

____ To the school.

Circle the main idea.

The rocket store is not open.

Real rockets cost a lot of money.

(Mr. Jones and the children will build and launch rockets.)

3 (three)

LANGUAGE ARTS 109

ALTERNATE LIFEPAC TEST

26/33

Name _____

Date _____

Score _____

LANGUAGE ARTS 109
ALTERNATE LIFEPAC TEST

Circle the words with the <u>oi</u> or <u>oy</u> sound.

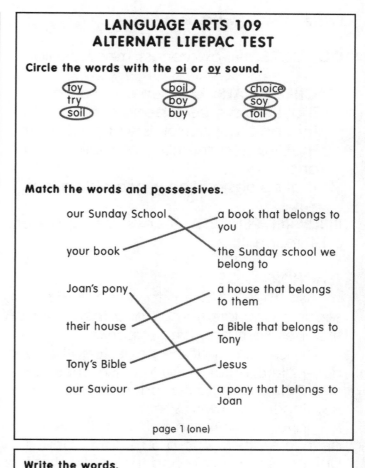

(toy)   (boil)   (choice)
try   (boy)   (soy)
(soil)   buy   (toil)

Match the words and possessives.

our Sunday School   a book that belongs to you

your book   the Sunday school we belong to

Joan's pony   a house that belongs to them

their house   a Bible that belongs to Tony

Tony's Bible   Jesus

our Saviour   a pony that belongs to Joan

page 1 (one)

Write the plurals.

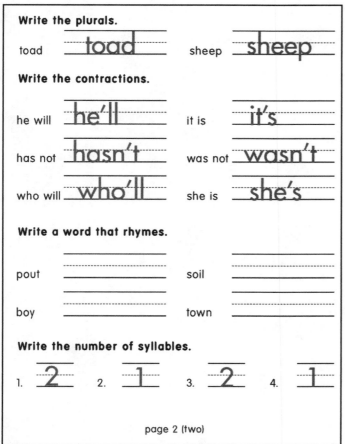

toad   toad   sheep   sheep

Write the contractions.

he will   he'll   it is   it's

has not   hasn't   was not   wasn't

who will   who'll   she is   she's

Write a word that rhymes.

pout _____   soil _____

boy _____   town _____

Write the number of syllables.

1. 2   2. 1   3. 2   4. 1

page 2 (two)

Write the words.

The children _____ is /(are) _____ building rockets.

They _____ is /(are) _____ having fun.

Put an <u>S</u> by the complete sentence.

_____ in the car.

__S__ The boys walked to school.

Circle the main idea.

Animals are nice to have for pets.

Animals are our friends.

(There are many kinds of animals.)

page 3 (three)

Page 1: Self-Awareness

CONCEPTS: self-awareness, membership

TEACHER GOALS: To teach each child
That he is a special person,
That no other person is exactly like him,
That he is a member of many groups, and
That he has privileges and obligations.

BIBLE REFERENCES: Genesis 2:7; Ephesians 6:1 through 4

TEACHING PAGE 1:

Ask the children to write their first, second, and last names, and their ages on the lines. Help only if necessary.

Read the rest of the page together and have the children write in the names of the teacher, school, and church. Help those who need help with spelling.

Have the children tell what it means to be a member of a group. Talk about the privileges they have and their obligations to the group.

Have them tell what they receive from their parents and what their parents expect from them.

Do the same with the school group and the church group.

Talk about what being a Christian means. How do they feel and act? How do they know they are a Christian?

ACTIVITY:

Have each child tell what his name is, how old he is, what church he goes to, and something about his family.

I am _____

_____

_____

_____

I am _____ years old.

I go to _____ School.

My teacher is _____

_____

My church is _____

_____

page 1 (one)

Page 2: FUN WITH WORDS

CONCEPT: purpose of the LIFEPAC

TEACHER GOALS: To teach the children
To understand what they will learn in the LIFEPAC, and
To read the objectives.

BIBLE REFERENCE: Proverbs 22:6

TEACHING PAGE 2:

Have the children read the title at the top of the page. Have them read each sentence and talk about it. Ask them to tell what is in the picture and to identify the punctuation marks.

Have the children read the list of objectives and talk about each one. Have them tell why it is helpful to have objectives. Ask them to tell how many of the objectives for Language Arts LIFEPAC 109 they accomplished. Have them tell if some still need extra work.

FUN WITH WORDS

In this LIFEPAC you will think about all the things you have learned in the other LIFEPACs.

You will think about long and short vowels.

You will think about writing good sentences and stories.

You will think about many other things, too.

 Objectives

1. I can tell all the letters and sounds.
2. I can listen and follow directions.
3. I can write contractions, possessives, and plurals.
4. I can write sentences and stories.
5. I can tell what will happen next.
6. I can put things in proper sequence.

page 2 (two)

I. PART ONE

Page 3: Letter Review

CONCEPTS: vowels, capital and small letters

TEACHER GOALS: To teach the children
To identify and write the vowels, and
To identify each small letter and its capital.

MATERIALS NEEDED: Worksheet 1

TEACHING PAGE 3:
Have the children read the titles and sentences at the top of the page and talk about what they mean. Discuss the meaning of letters, vowels, and consonants.

Have the children read the directions on the page and do the work independently. Check by having the children read the vowels or write them on the board. The children may write each small letter and its capital on the board. Have the children correct any mistakes.

ACTIVITIES:
1. Do Worksheet 1.
Have the children read the directions on the page. Be sure they understand what they are to do in each section. Let them complete the page.

Correct the page. Have the children write any incorrectly made letter until they can make it correctly. Have them practice any of their names with which they may still be having trouble.

2. For the children who have made mistakes, work with the letter charts and alphabet cards individually or in small groups. Children who know their letters well may help those who still need help.

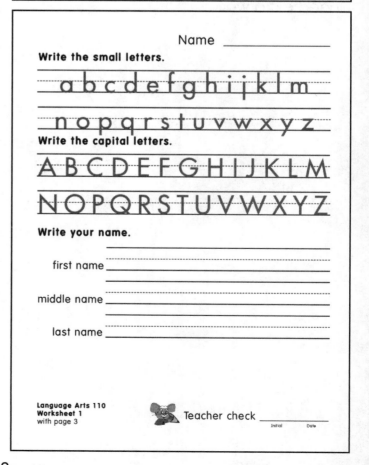

Page 4: Short Vowels

CONCEPT: short vowel sounds

TEACHER GOAL: To teach the children
To identify short vowel sounds.

TEACHING PAGE 4:
Have the children name the letters at the top of the page and give the short sound and the long sound for each.

Have them read the sentences and the direction and do the page independently.

Check by having the children read the vowels they circled.

ACTIVITIES:
1. For the children who are not sure of the vowel sounds, work with the drillcards individually or in small groups.
2. Give a long vowel word and a short vowel word and have the child tell which is the short vowel word.
3. Give the short vowel sound and have the child give a word with the sound in it.

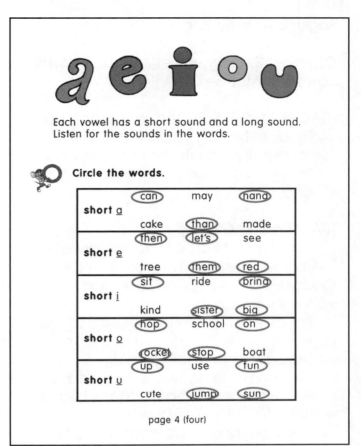

Each vowel has a short sound and a long sound. Listen for the sounds in the words.

Circle the words.

short a	can	may	hand
	cake	than	made
short e	then	let's	see
	tree	them	red
short i	sit	ride	bring
	kind	sister	big
short o	hop	school	on
	rocket	stop	boat
short u	up	use	fun
	cute	jump	sun

page 4 (four)

Page 5: Activity Page

CONCEPTS: long vowel sounds, r-controlled vowels, sentences

TEACHER GOALS: To teach the children
To identify long vowel sounds,
To identify *r*-controlled vowels, and
To write sentences using good grammar and punctuation.

TEACHING PAGE 5:

Have the children read the directions on the page, then do the work independently. Check by having the children read the words they circled.

For children who are not sure of the long vowel sounds, work with the drillcards individually or in small groups.

Give a long vowel word and a short vowel word and have the children tell which is the long vowel word.

Give the long vowel sound and have the children give a word with the sound in it.

ACTIVITIES:

Have the children write sentences using the *r*-controlled words on a sheet of writing tablet paper. Correct the sentences for good grammar, correct use of the word, correct punctuation, and capitalization. Have the children read several of their sentences aloud.

TEACHING READING:

Write the word "disaster" on the board. Have a discussion with students about disasters. If possible, share a current event involving some kind of disaster locally or worldwide. Allow the discussion to include how people help each other during these times.

Show students a rock. Tell them in the Bible God tells us He is our Rock. Ask them to explain what they think God means by that. Discuss their responses. Introduce today's story: God is Our Rock

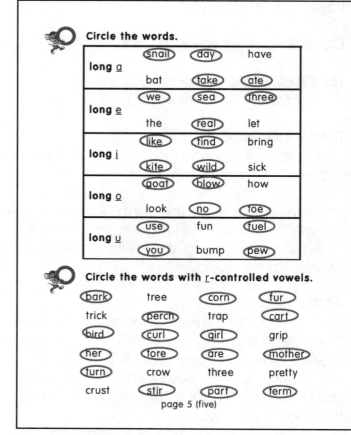

Write these words on the board: knelt, tornado, knocked, taught, strength, kitchen, answered. Have students read the words and learning their meanings.

Read the story "God is Our Rock" together, then ask the following questions:

"What kind of disaster is this story talking about?" (tornado)

"Is it a natural disaster or man-made?" (natural)

"Why did Larson look at the rock he found in Trevor's yard?" (it reminded him of the Bible verse)

"How was Larson feeling about Trevor's situation?" (bad, sad, helpless)

"What did he do first?" (prayed)

"What did the children decide to do to help the Mortons?" (clean up trash, have a car wash)

"What did Larson want Trevor to know more than anything?" (God is great, He is our Rock)

"How did Larson tell Trevor this?" (He gave him a rock saying: God is our Rock)

"How do you think Trevor feels about what his classmates are doing?" (good)

"What would you do if you were Trevor?" Larson? (answers will vary)

Find r-controlled words: (Larson, Trevor, Morton, yard, tornado, whirled, remembered, verse, teacher, Lord, hard, mother, later, car, together, sure). Find words with wh: (whirled, everywhere, awhile, when)

ACTIVITIES:

Have students bring in a rock (no bigger than their fist). With a permanent marker, write "God is Our Rock" on each student's rock. Have students write a story about a time when they needed to remember God will help us and be strong for us. Have students bring in stories from the newspaper that tell about tragedies or disasters. Gather students in a group to pray for these situations – including God's strength for those involved. Find a local cause in which the class may be able to do something to help others (i.e. adopt a family for Christmas, canned food drive, cards to nursing home). Have students make a card with the words "God is Our Rock" to give to someone who might need it.

Page 6: Activity Page

CONCEPTS: vowels, *r*-controlled vowels, color words, rhyming words

TEACHER GOALS: To teach the children
To fill in the missing vowel in words,
To fill in the *r*-controlled vowel in words,
To write rhyming words, and
To identify color words.

MATERIALS NEEDED: Worksheet 2

TEACHING PAGE 6:
Have the children read the direction at the top of the page. Have them read the letters and tell what they are (vowels).
Write these words on the board and have the children fill in the missing vowels. Point out that several vowels may be used with the same consonants to get different words.

b_d	h_t	w_ll
bad	hat	wall
bed	hit	well
bid	hot	will
bud	hut	

Do the same with the *r*-controlled exercise using these words. Let the children complete both exercises independently.

c_d	t_n
card	torn
cord	turn
curd	

Have the children read the direction and circle the color words.
Check the exercises by having the children read the words they wrote and spell each one. Have them read the color words.

ACTIVITIES:
1. Do Worksheet 2.

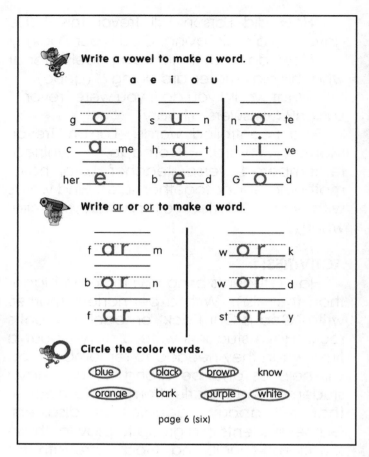

page 6 (six)

Have the children read the first direction. Remind them that *er* and *ir* sound the same. Write the words on the board as the children decide on the spelling. Have the children fill in the missing letters.
Have the children read the next direction. Have them do this section by themselves.
Have the children read the last direction.
When you are sure they understand what they are to do, have them finish the page by themselves.
2. Write these words with missing vowels on the board and have the children put in vowels to form words. These may be done on the board or on a sheet of writing tablet paper.

b_g (bag, beg, big, bog, bug)
p_ck (pack, peck, pick, pock, puck)
m_ss (mass, mess, miss, moss, muss)

st_ck (stack, stick, stock, stuck)

m_le (male, mile, mole, mule)

b_ll (ball, bell, bill, boll, bull)

w_re (ware, were, wire, wore)

f_r (far, fir, for, fur)

p_rk (park, perk, pork)

TEACHING READING:

Give each student a red barn shape and piece of paper. Have them glue the barn anywhere on the paper they choose. Then instruct them to add details to create the rest of the picture.

Write these words on the board: built, themselves, remembered, building, gallons, tomato, rowdy, freeway, boards, folks. Have students read the words and learning their meanings. Introduce today's story: The Old Red Barn

Read the story "The Old Red Barn" together, then ask the following questions:

"How long ago was the red barn built?" (50 years)

"Who built it?" (Farmer Anders and his wife)

"What was the last thing they did?" (paint it)

"How many gallons of red paint did it take?" (22)

"Who lived in the red barn?" (Sally Sue, Smooze, Betsy Boo, chickens and turkeys)

"What was the problem?" (the freeway was going to go through their property; they had to move)

"How did they feel about moving?" (sad)

"What did they do with the animals?" (found them homes)

"Where did the Anders move?" (small house in town)

"How were they feeling then?" (sad still, they missed their red barn)

"How did their friends help?" (they built them a porch from the wood of the old red barn)

"How did they feel now?" (content, happy)

Name _____

Write er or ir.

h er | st ir | b ir d

sh ir t | p er ch | moth er

j er k | f ir st | aft er

Write or or ar.

h or n | st ar | or ange

b ar k | c ar | or der

m ar k | st ar t | f or k

Read the sentences. Draw a line under each word with an r-controlled vowel.

Father is starting the car.

Mother wore her new dress.

Are you going to church?

Carl got some corn at the store.

The bird is on a perch.

My burned finger hurts.

Is that horn for you or for me?

Language Arts 110
Worksheet 2
with page 6

Teacher check _____
Initial   Date

Find r-controlled words: (barn, farmer, hardest, part, ladder, her, Anders, horse, turkeys, yard, stories, together, porch, farm)

ACTIVITIES:

Give students another paper to draw the same picture they did with the red barn, only this time, no red barn. Have them add the freeway that went through where they put the red barn in their first picture. Some details may be the same and others will change. Discuss changes they've noticed around where they live (new buildings, new roads, remodeling). Have students write a story as if they were neighbors living near the old red

barn. Have students write a cheer up letter to Farmer Anders and his wife. As a class come up with imaginative thoughts or comments the animals might have. Have students draw and cut out pictures of each animal (to put on a bulletin board) and put thought or dialogue bubbles near them.

Page 7: Activity Page

CONCEPTS: *wh*, writing a story

TEACHER GOALS: To teach the children
To identify the sound of *wh*, and
To write a story using a title and good sentences.

MATERIALS NEEDED: drawing paper, crayons

TEACHING PAGE 7:
Have the children read the direction at the top of the page. Have them give the correct sound for *wh*. Have them read each sentence pronouncing the *wh* words correctly. Have them circle the *wh* words and read them aloud.

Ask the children to tell what is happening in the picture. Ask them to give reasons why the kitten might be crying. Have them read the story and think about what might happen next.

Have the children read the directions at the bottom of the page. Talk about them. Tell the children to copy the first part of the story on their paper and to write at least two pages to complete the story. They may write as many more pages as they like.

Correct the children's stories as they finish. Have them recopy them as corrected.

Take class time for each child to read his story and show his picture to the class. Review what a good reader should do (stand straight, read clearly and loudly, look at the class from time to time, etc.).

Ask the children to tell what a good audience should do also (sit quietly and listen attentively).

TEACHING READING:
Read the story "Joseph's Dream" in *Reader 5*.

Have the children read the title of the story. Have a child tell the story or have

wh
Listen and circle the words with the <u>wh</u> sound.

White whales are very large.
Where is my whistle?
Which wheel is behind you?
What did she whisper to you?
When did the baby start to whimper?
Why is the white kitten crying?

Little Kitten was lost.
She wanted her mother.
She began to cry.

 Write a story that tells what will happen next.
Write good sentences.
Write a good title.
Draw a picture about your story.
Read your story to the class.

page 7 (seven)

several tell parts of the story of Joseph (Genesis 37:5-10). Have the children talk about the dreams Joseph had and what they meant.

Have the children read the story silently.

Ask questions similar to these:
"What did Joseph see in his dream?"
"What bowed down to Joseph?"
"Who sent his dream?"
"How does God speak to us today?"
Have the children find the word with *wh*.

Have them find words with vowel digraphs.

Have them find *ow* words.

Page 8: *Th* Words

CONCEPTS: *th* sound, reading comprehension: recalling details, retelling a story

TEACHER GOALS: To teach the children
To identify and read words with the two sounds of *th*,
To recall accurately details of what they have read, and
To retell the story in their own words.

TEACHING PAGE 8:
Have the children look at the picture and tell what is happening. Have them read the title. Ask the children to give both sounds for *th* and give words with each sound.
Have the children read the story silently.
Ask these questions:
"How many boys were playing?" (three)
"How many more boys came?" (one)
"How many were there then?" (four)
"Who said, 'This is fun?'" (Joel)
"What do you call the words someone says?" (direct quotation)
"Why did the boys like some toys better than others?" (more fun)
"Do you have some toys you like better than others?"
"What are they?"
"Who do you think the fourth boy was?" (another brother or a friend)
"Where did the boys get the toys?" (from parents)
Have the story read aloud. Have the children count the *th* words and write the number in the blank.
Write on the board:
    th   *th*
    with   the
Have the children tell which of the *th* words in the story should go under each heading. Write them on the board. Have the children read each list several times, listening for the *th* sound. You may want to tell the children that the *th* in *with* is called a soft *th* and that the *th* in *the* is called a hard *th*. Have them practice both sounds.

TH WORDS

Three boys were playing by their house.
Then another boy came to play with them.
They were playing with many things.

Joel said, "This is fun, but I like these toys better than those.
I think they're more fun.
Is that what you think?"

The other boys said, "Yes, that's what we think, too."

Joel said, "I must thank my mother and father for the toys.
They gave them to me."

 How many <u>th</u> words can you find?

I found ___27___ th words.

page 8 (eight)

(*th* as in *with* - three, with, things, think, thank)
(*th* as in *the* - their, then, another, them, they, these, than, those, they're, that, the, other, that's, mother, father)
Ask the children to tell the meaning of these words and what kind of word each is.

their (possessive)
they're (contraction)
that's (contraction)
these (something close by)
those (something farther away)

Have the children tell what the word *they* stands for each time it is used (first paragraph - the boys, second paragraph (they're) - the toys, last paragraph - mother and father).
Have the children tell what the word *them* stands for each time it is used (first paragraph - the boys, last paragraph - mother and father).

Have the children read the first sentence in the second paragraph. Tell the children that this sentence is comparing things. Tell them that whenever they hear the word *than* in a sentence, someone is comparing one thing to another to see which is better or taller or longer or heavier or bigger.

Have the children give some examples:

John is *taller* than Mary.

The red book is *bigger* than the blue book.

If you have time, let each child give an example.

Have several children retell the story in their own words. Encourage them to remember the details accurately and to put the events in sequence.

Have the children read the direct quotations and tell who is speaking.

ACTIVITY:

Write the words *boy* and *boys* on the board. Have the children write them at the top of a sheet of writing tablet paper and write rhyming words for each. Collect the papers and correct, or write the words on the board and have the children correct their own lists. Remind the children that the rhyming words may not be spelled the same even though they sound alike.

TEACHING READING:

Have students complete the sentences in their best penmanship: If I could have a pet, it would be a _____ because _____. It would have (describe) _____. I would take care of it by _____. Have students draw a picture to go with the sentences. Make a book or display on a bulletin board. Introduce today's story: Cory's Kitten

Read the story "Cory's Kitten" together, then ask the following questions:

Where did Cory ask Mother to go? (the corner market)

How many times has she gone there? (everyday this week)

Why did Cory want to go? (to see the kittens)

How did she get there? (rode her bike)

How many kittens were there? (seven) Describe them: (all were gray except one girl was black, two boys, four girls)

Which one was Cory's favorite? (the black one)

How long did Cory visit the kittens? (five weeks)

What happened at the end of that time? (they needed homes of their own)

Why was Cory surprised when Dad said let's go look at the kittens? (she hadn't asked if she could have one)

Why did Cory's parents surprise her with a kitten? (Mrs. Thurston told them how well she had been caring for them)

Find r-controlled words: (Cory, corner, market, mother, parked, door, toward, Darby, were, girls, favorite, owner, for, her, Thurston, ever)

ACTIVITIES:

Have a "Cats on Parade" day (or week). Invite students who have a cat (stuffed or real) to bring it school for sharing. Have students bring pictures of their cat or others they find in magazines and make picture board cat collage. Invite a veterinarian to talk to the class about caring for cats. Make a list of things to do to care for a pet. Compare cats and dogs. Make a chart showing the pros and cons. Make a list of words that rhyme with cat (at, bat, brat, chat, fat, flat, gnat, hat, mat, pat, rat, sat, splat, that). Write a story or poem using the words. Share these popular clichés and what they mean: i.e. "Who let the cat out of the bag?", "That's the cat's meow", "It's raining cats and dogs!" Have students draw literal pictures of each saying. Make a book or display.

Read some fun fiction books about cats: i.e. *Socks* (chapter book) by Beverly Cleary, *Six-Dinner Sid* by Inga Moore, *The Kids' Cat Book* by Tomie dePaola, *Hi Cat* by Keats. Make CAT hats (headbands with pointed ears) and eat goldfish crackers for a snack.

Page 9: Activity Page

CONCEPTS: there, their, than, then

TEACHER GOALS: To teach the children
To understand the correct use of *their* and *there, than* and *then.*

TEACHING PAGE 9:
Write the words *than, then, their, there,* on the board. Have the children give their meanings and use them in sentences.

Have the children read the directions on the page. Have them do the page independently. Check by having the children read the sentences and spell the words they wrote in the blanks.

ACTIVITY:
Have the children use than, then, their, and there in sentences. Have each child read one or two sentences aloud to the class. Have them give the spelling of the words after reading their sentences.

TEACHING READING:
Tell students they'll be reading another story about Cory and her Kitten. Have students get together in groups of 3-4. Tell them Cory's kitten needs a name. Ask students to tell you what they remember about the kitten from the last story (black, blue eyes, girl). Write these things on the board. Tell the groups you will give them 2-3 minutes to think of a name for Cory's kitten. At the end of the time write each group's name idea on the board. Introduce the story: The Kitten Gets a Name

Read the story "The Kitten Gets a Name" together, then ask the following questions:

"Who did Cory show the kitten to first?" (the Mortons- her neighbors)

"Who did she call?" (best friends - Julie and Clark)

"What was Cory's problem?" (she couldn't decide on a name)

Write there or their.

That is ____ their ____ house.

____ There ____ they go.

Put the toys over ____ there ____ .

____ Their ____ car is red.

Write than or then.

What will you do ____ then ____ ?

I like cats better ____ than ____ dogs.

____ Then ____ we will go home.

Do you like candy better ____ than ____ cake?

page 9 (nine)

"What did Julie suggest?" (Blackie) Why? (the kitten is black)

"How did Cory feel about that name?" (it was boring)

"What did Dad suggest?" (to watch the kitten to see if she does something that will help)

"What did Cory find out?" (the kitten follows her everywhere)

"What was Dad's idea after Cory told him?" (to help her figure it out by seeing her shadow)

"Where did Cory find the kitten when she called her?" (right behind her, of course!)

"Why is Shadow a perfect name for the kitten?" (it's black and it follows her)

Find r-controlled words: (Cory, her, over, Morton, darling, Clark, boring, closer, perfect)

ACTIVITIES:

Have students do a homework assignment to find out how they got their name. Were they named after a family member, a friend or someone famous? Does their name have an ancestral heritage? Do they like their name? Why or why not? If they could pick another name, what would it be and why? Make up a word search with all the students names in the class. Give to students for a fun time of finding their classmates' names. Take students outside to find their shadows. Turn off the lights in the classroom. Using a lamp, show students the fun of making shadow pictures with their hands. Trace each child's silhouette. Cut out on black, mat on white and give as a gift to Mom and Dad. Write a story: My Shadow Gets in the Way, The Day I Got a Kitten, or another related story starter.

Page 10: Where Does It Go?

CONCEPTS: sequence, alphabet, number words

TEACHER GOALS: To teach the children
To put letters, numbers, and sentences in order,
To write the missing letters in the alphabet, and
To write the missing number words.

MATERIALS NEEDED: number and alphabet charts

TEACHING PAGE 10:

Have the children read the title and the directions on the page. Let the children do the page independently. Check by having the children read the alphabet and the number words. Have alphabet and number charts available so the children can see them to check their own letter formation and spelling of number words. Have the sentences read in correct sequence. Have the children correct any mistakes.

ACTIVITY:

Review the alphabet and number words with those children who still need help.

TEACHING READING:

Read the poem "Clouds" in *Reader 5*.
Have the children look at the picture of the clouds. Have them tell you what they think the clouds look like. Have several children tell about interesting clouds they have seen.
Have the children read the poem.
Ask the children these questions:
"What does the poem say clouds are like?"
"Where do the clouds sail?"
"What would the author like to do one day?"
"Would you like to sail away with the clouds?"

"Where would you like them to go?"
"Could you really sail away with the clouds?"
"Could you really visit far-away places?"
Have the children find the rhyming words. Write them on the board. Have the children find the lines that are repeated in the poem. Have them find the *ay* and *ai* words.

ACTIVITY:

Have the children draw clouds on paper. Tell them they can picture other ways to travel with the clouds. Give them these examples: cars, boats, airplanes, submarines, helicopters.

Page 11 : Activity Page

CONCEPT: alphabetical order

TEACHER GOAL: To teach the children
To put words and letters in alphabetical order.

MATERIALS NEEDED: alphabet charts

TEACHING PAGE 11:

Have the children read the title and directions on the page. Be sure they understand what they are to do. Have the children do the page independently. Check by having the children give the order of the letters and the word that comes first.

ACTIVITY:

Give a letter and have the children tell whether it comes in the first part, middle part, or last part of the alphabet. You may wish to write the alphabet on the board. Divide it into thirds (a b c d e f g h i), (j k l m n o p q r), and (s t u v w x y z). Do this any time you have a few extra minutes to get children ready for dictionary work. If the children can tell from which part of the alphabet a letter comes, they will not have to waste time paging through the entire dictionary looking for the letter they need.

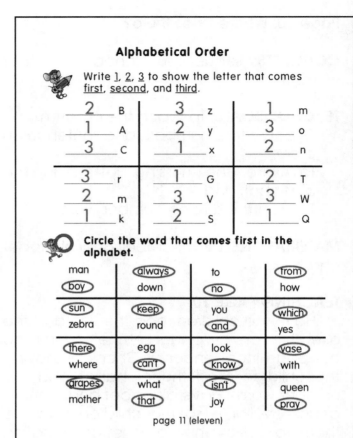

Alphabetical Order

Write 1, 2, 3 to show the letter that comes first, second, and third.

2	B	3	z	1	m
1	A	2	y	3	o
3	C	1	x	2	n

3	r	1	G	2	T
2	m	3	V	3	W
1	k	2	S	1	Q

Circle the word that comes first in the alphabet.

man	always	to	from
boy	down	no	how
sun	keep	you	which
zebra	round	and	yes
there	egg	look	vase
where	can't	know	with
grapes	what	isn't	queen
mother	that	joy	pray

page 11 (eleven)

Page 12: Activity Page

CONCEPTS: reading comprehension: sequence of events, main idea, title

TEACHER GOALS: To teach the children
To read to understand the order of events, and
To identify the main idea and title of a story

TEACHING PAGE 12:
Have the children read the directions at the top of the page. Have them read the parts of the story silently and number them in order. Have them read the direction at the bottom of the page and write a title for the story. Review what a title is. Ask them to tell which words should be capitalized in a title.

Check by having the children read aloud the parts of the story in order and the titles they wrote. Have them tell which words they capitalized.

Have several children tell the story in their own words.

Have the children give the main idea of the story. Ask if their titles told the main idea of the story. Have the children rewrite any that did not.

Encourage them to recall all the details and to put events into proper sequence.

ACTIVITY:
Have the children dramatize the story. Have them make up things for Yellow Bird to say.

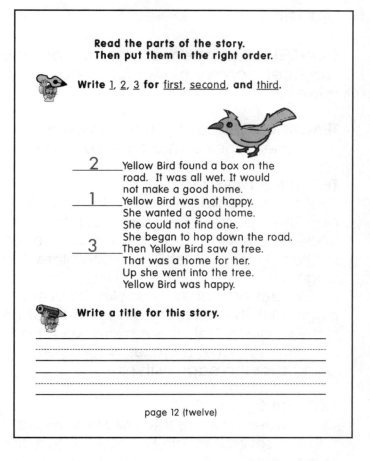

Read the parts of the story.
Then put them in the right order.

Write 1, 2, 3 for first, second, and third.

2 ___ Yellow Bird found a box on the road. It was all wet. It would not make a good home.

1 ___ Yellow Bird was not happy. She wanted a good home. She could not find one. She began to hop down the road.

3 ___ Then Yellow Bird saw a tree. That was a home for her. Up she went into the tree. Yellow Bird was happy.

Write a title for this story.

page 12 (twelve)

SELF TEST 1

CONCEPTS: sequence, letters of the alphabet, consonant digraphs, r-controlled vowels

TEACHER GOAL: To teach the children
　　To check their own progress periodically.

TEACHING PAGE 13:
　　Have the children read all the directions on the page. Be sure each child understands what is to be done in each section. Have the children complete the page.
　　Correct as soon as possible. Go over the page with the child, showing him what he did well and what needs more work. Have him correct any mistakes while you are going over the page with him.

ACTIVITIES:
　　1.　Reteach items the child has missed.
　　2.　If several children have missed the same kinds of things, reteach in a small group.

SPELLING WORDS:

　　blue
　　black
　　orange
　　purple
　　green
　　yellow
　　red
　　cry
　　why
　　by

II. PART TWO

Page 14: Listen and Do

CONCEPTS: listening, following directions

TEACHER GOALS: To teach the children
That listening or reading and following directions are very important for learning, and
To check their work over and correct any mistakes before handing it in.

MATERIALS NEEDED: chart paper, Worksheet 3

TEACHING PAGE 14:

Have the children read the page. Talk about each rule so that each child understands what it means. Have them tell why each rule is important.

Put the rules on a large sheet of tagboard and keep in the classroom. Review the rules frequently.

ACTIVITY:

Do Worksheet 3.

Have the children turn their Worksheets face down on their desks. Have pencils ready but not in hand. Tell the children that you will read them a story and that they must listen very carefully because you will only read the story once. Then tell them they must answer some questions about the story.

Read this story only once at a normal rate of speed. Do not emphasize any words.

Long ago there were no cars or trucks. There were no trains or airplanes. When people wanted to go somewhere, they walked, rode horses, or rode in wagons.

Some of the wagons were pulled by horses. Some were pulled by mules or oxen. The wagons were used to carry things the people needed. Covered wagons were used by people who were going to find a new home in the west.

II. PART TWO

LISTEN AND DO
Learning to listen and follow directions carefully is very important.
It will make your work much easier to do.
Here are some rules to remember:

1. **Listen** to what your teacher says.
2. **Read** the story carefully.
3. Read **all** the directions slowly.
4. If you do not understand what to do, **ask** your teacher.
5. Read **all** the questions before you answer any of them.
6. When you finish your work, **read** it over again.
7. **Check** all your answers.

If you do all these things, you will be a good worker.

page 14 (fourteen)

Wagons are still used on farms today, but now they are pulled by tractors. Children have wagons, too. They fill them with toys and blocks or ride in them.

Have the children turn their Worksheets over and read the direction at the top. Have them answer the questions. Remind them to read carefully. Tell them to finish reading the page when they finish the questions.

Remind them that there may be more than one answer for some questions. Check the answers by having the children read the questions and answers aloud. The teacher should check each child's paper. If several made more than one mistake, have them do the entire exercise over again several days later. Go over the answers with them.

Have the children read the rest of the page and follow the directions. Give the children an opportunity to show their pictures to the group.

Name _____

Answer the questions.

This story is about _____ .
horses   (wagons)   food

Long ago there were no _____ .
(cars)   trees   (trucks)

Wagons were used for carrying _____ .
clouds   (food)   (water)

Now farm wagons are pulled by _____ .
ponies   (tractors)   cars

Do children have wagons?
(yes)   no

Are wagons still used today?
(yes)   no

Draw a picture about this story on the back of this paper.

Write a good title for this story at the top of your picture.

**Language Arts 110
Worksheet 3
with page 14**

Teacher check _____
             Initial   Date

Page 15 : Activity Page

CONCEPTS: following directions, oral expression

TEACHER GOALS: To teach the children
To learn to follow written directions,
To follow directions in the order in which they are given, and
To speak clearly and in complete sentences.

TEACHING PAGE l5:

Have the children read the direction at the top of the page and number the sentences in order according to the rules given on Page 14. Check by having the sentences read in order.

Have the children read the sentences, questions, and the material in the box. Have them discuss the rules in their small groups. Have each child in the group tell if he thinks he is or is not a good worker. Choose a child to be the leader.

ACTIVITY:

Give each child a chance to be the leader of the small group. The groups may meet for book reports, program or activity planning, art project planning, or similar activities. Help the child lead by giving suggestions and by helping him guide the discussion.

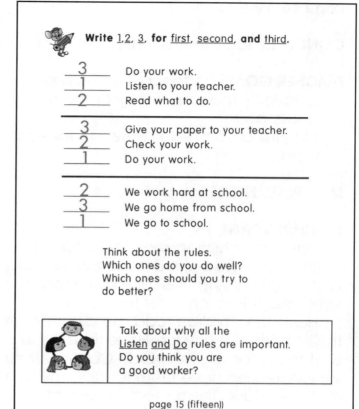

Write 1, 2, 3, **for** first, second, **and** third.

3	Do your work.
1	Listen to your teacher.
2	Read what to do.

3	Give your paper to your teacher.
2	Check your work.
1	Do your work.

2	We work hard at school.
3	We go home from school.
1	We go to school.

Think about the rules.
Which ones do you do well?
Which ones should you try to do better?

Talk about why all the
Listen and Do rules are important.
Do you think you are
a good worker?

page 15 (fifteen)

Page 16: Yy (i,e)

CONCEPTS: sounds of *y*, sentences

TEACHER GOALS: To teach the children
To identify the sounds of *y* at the end of words, and
To write a complete sentence for each word.

MATERIALS NEEDED: Worksheet 4

TEACHING PAGE 16:

Have the children read the information at the top of the page and do the exercise. Check by having the children read the word and tell which letter they circled.

Have the children read the direction at the bottom of the page. Have them write a sentence for each word. Correct their sentences and have them recopy any with mistakes. Have them read several of their sentences aloud.

ACTIVITY:

Do Worksheet 4.

Have the children read the directions at the top of the page and do the first two examples together. Let them finish the entire page by themselves. The starred exercise is more difficult. You may wish to work through it with some of the children or do not require it of them.

Check the page by having the children read the word and give the letter they wrote on the line. Have them correct any mistakes. If the children make too many mistakes, have them do the exercise again after you have reviewed the sounds of *y* at the end of the word.

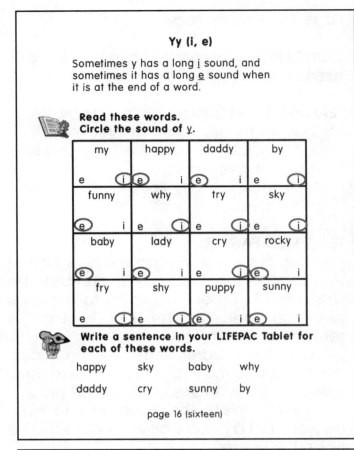

Yy (i, e)

Sometimes y has a long i sound, and sometimes it has a long e sound when it is at the end of a word.

**Read these words.
Circle the sound of y.**

my	happy	daddy	by
e ⓘ e	i ⓔ	e ⓘ	i e ⓘ
funny	why	try	sky
ⓔ i	e ⓘ	e ⓘ e	e ⓘ
baby	lady	cry	rocky
ⓔ i	ⓔ i	e ⓘ	ⓔ i
fry	shy	puppy	sunny
e ⓘ	e ⓘ	ⓔ i	ⓔ i

Write a sentence in your LIFEPAC Tablet for each of these words.

happy	sky	baby	why
daddy	cry	sunny	by

page 16 (sixteen)

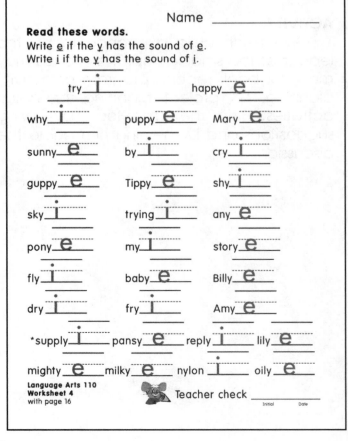

Name _____

Read these words.
Write e if the y has the sound of e.
Write i if the y has the sound of i.

try___i___   happy___e___

why___i___   puppy___e___   Mary___e___

sunny___e___   by___i___   cry___i___

guppy___e___   Tippy___e___   shy___i___

sky___i___   trying___i___   any___e___

pony___e___   my___i___   story___e___

fly___i___   baby___e___   Billy___e___

dry___i___   fry___i___   Amy___e___

*supply___i___ pansy___e___ reply___i___ lily___e___

mighty___e___ milky___e___ nylon___i___ oily___e___

**Language Arts 110
Worksheet 4
with page 16**   Teacher check _____
                                        Initial   Date

Page 17: Activity Page

CONCEPTS: silent consonants, *ph* and *gh* as the sound of *f*

TEACHER GOALS: To teach the children
To find silent consonants in words, and
To read words in which the *ph* and *gh* have the sound of *f*.

VOCABULARY: silent

MATERIALS NEEDED: magazines or newspapers

TEACHING PAGE 17:

Have the children read the direction and question at the top of the page. Read each word and have the children repeat it after you. Have them tell which letter is silent. Be sure the children understand that the letters must be put in when they write the words, even though they do not hear them.

Have the children tell the meaning of each word or use it in a sentence.

Have the next set of directions read by the children. Read each word and have the children listen for the sound of *f*. Have them tell which letters make the sound.

This page is only an introduction. Do not expect the children to master the spelling or pronunciation of all these words.

ACTIVITY:

Have the children find words with silent letters or with the sound of *f* in newspapers or magazines.

TEACHING READING:

Read the story "Dolphin" in *Reader 5*. Ask the children to look at the end of the second line in the first stanza. The three dots are called an ellipsis. The dots mean to stop and think about what was written. Ask the children if they can find another ellipsis.

Have the children tell what they see in the picture. Have several children tell what they know about dolphins. Have the children read the story silently.

page 17 (seventeen)

Ask questions similar to these:
"Who is talking to the dolphin?"
"What does the author want to do?"
"Could a dolphin live on land?"
"Could the author live in the sea?"
"If he could live on the land, what could the dolphin do?"
"If he could live in the sea, where would the author sleep?"
"Do you think it would be fun to trade places with a dolphin?"

Have the children find the word which has *ph* as the sound of *f*.

Have the children find the rhyming words in the story. Write them on the board.

ACTIVITY:

Have the children draw a picture.

Tell them they may draw the dolphin on land or a person in the sea. Tell them they may draw themselves doing something they would do if they could be a dolphin.

Page 18: Pronouns

CONCEPT: pronouns

TEACHER GOAL: To teach the children
To use pronouns in place of nouns.

TEACHER PAGE 18:
Review the word pronoun and ask the children to tell the meaning. Ask them to give examples of pronouns.

Have the children read "My Father and Mother" in *Reader 5*.

Ask these questions:

"How do the mother and father help?"

"What does the girl like about mealtime?"

"Does the girl always get what she wants?"

"What is the difference between wants and needs?"

"Does the girl appreciate the things her mother and father do?"

"How does she show her love to her mom and dad?

"What are some ways you could show your family that you appreciate the things they do for you?"

Have the children read the direction and the first sentence. Have them look at the next sentence. Ask the children how it is like the first sentence. Have them write a pronoun in the second sentence to replace the word *mother*.

Read the next sentence.

Have the children write one pronoun to replace the words *Dad, Sis,* and *Jack.*

Write the pronouns.

Mother baked a cake for supper.

_____She_____ baked a cake for supper.

Dad, Sis, and Jack will eat the cake.

_____They_____ will eat the cake.

page 18 (eighteen)

Page 19: Activity Page

CONCEPT: categories

TEACHER GOALS: To teach the children
To understand the meaning of words, and
To be able to put them in categories.

VOCABULARY: people

TEACHING PAGE 19:

Have the children read the directions on the page. Be sure they understand what they are to do. Let them complete the page independently. Give help only if necessary. Check by having the children read the three that are alike in each group and tell why they are alike. Have them tell why the fourth word is different. Check the second exercise by having the children tell where they wrote *G* and where they wrote *P* and why.

Read the story of the Creation from the Bible. Talk about it. Bring out the fact that everything was created by God, but that people take the materials and make things out of them to use. Use the word created but do not expect the children to really understand it. The meaning they should get is that only God can create and that people can only use His creations.

ACTIVITY:

Write categories similar to these on the board and have the children write lists of things that belong in them. Have the lists read aloud.

hard - soft	long - short
large - small	tall - short
smooth - rough	round - square
wet - dry	living - non-living
furry - scaly	natural - man-made

Circle the three that are alike.

all	some	why	many
should	what	could	would
cow	duck	hen	bird
boys	children	her	girls
last	first	next	lost
fire	four	three	five
like	ride	sit	night
when	then	where	what
boys	cats	rabbits	girl

Write G for things God has made.
Write P for things people have made.

G	our world	p	streets and roads
G	people	G	day and night
p	houses	G	sunshine
G	animals	G	
p	trucks	p	dinner
G	rain and snow	G	rocks
p	schools	p	clothing
G	hills and trees	p	paper
		G	water

page 19 (nineteen)

Page 20: Plurals

CONCEPTS: plurals, writing sentences

TEACHER GOALS: To teach the children
To identify and write plurals, and
To write a complete sentence for each plural.

TEACHING PAGE 20:

Have the children read the direction. Tell them to read each word carefully. Have them write its plural on the lines. Write the list on the board and let the children correct their spelling .

ACTIVITY:

Have the children write sentences using each of the plural words.

Collect the papers and check for correct use of the plural, spelling, sentence structure, capitalization, and punctuation. Give them back to the children for correction. Let each child read two or three sentences aloud.

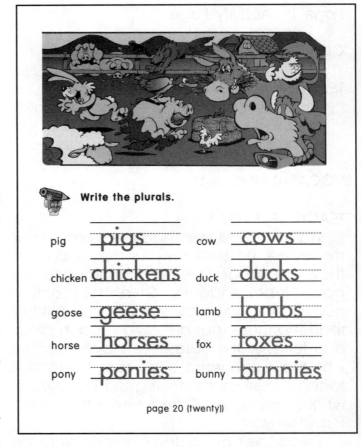

Write the plurals.

pig	pigs	cow	cows
chicken	chickens	duck	ducks
goose	geese	lamb	lambs
horse	horses	fox	foxes
pony	ponies	bunny	bunnies

page 20 (twenty))

Page 21: Activity Page

CONCEPTS: reading comprehension: main idea

TEACHER GOALS: To teach the children
To read to understand the meaning of sentences, and
To be able to group sentences that have the same main idea.

VOCABULARY: together

MATERIALS NEEDED: Worksheet 5

TEACHING PAGE 21:

Have the children read the direction at the top of the page. Ask the children to tell what a main idea is (what the sentence is about).

Tell them to read all three sentences carefully and to put an *X* in front of the two that have the same main idea or are about the same thing. Give help only if necessary. Some children may need more guidance than others. Check by having the children read the two sentences with the same main idea and tell why the other sentence does not go with the other two.

Have the children write a third sentence that will have the same main idea as the other two sentences. Point out to the children that some of the sentences will be very general. In *group one* almost anything about an animal would be all right, in others the main idea is more specific. In *group two* the main idea is God's creation of things in our world. Give help if necessary.

Collect the papers and correct for sentence structure, spelling, capitalization, and punctuation. Have the children recopy and read aloud.

ACTIVITIES:

1. Do Worksheet 5.
Have the children read the direction at the top of the page. Have them read the groups of sentences and choose the two that have the same main idea. Check by

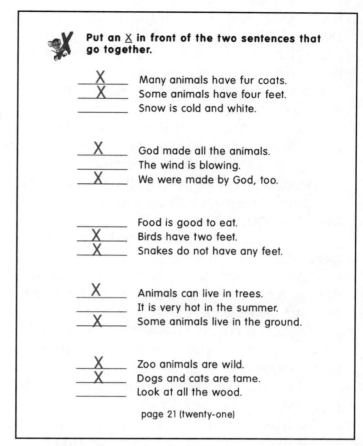

Put an X in front of the two sentences that go together.

X Many animals have fur coats.
X Some animals have four feet.
_____ Snow is cold and white.

X God made all the animals.
_____ The wind is blowing.
X We were made by God, too.

_____ Food is good to eat.
X Birds have two feet.
X Snakes do not have any feet.

X Animals can live in trees.
_____ It is very hot in the summer.
X Some animals live in the ground.

X Zoo animals are wild.
X Dogs and cats are tame.
_____ Look at all the wood.

page 21 (twenty-one)

having the children read the two sentences that go together. Have them tell why the third sentence does not belong with the others. Ask them to tell the main idea of each group. Talk about the sentences.

Have the children write or give another sentence orally with the same main idea as the two they chose.

2. Ask the children to give the main idea of a sentence, paragraph, or story frequently when they are reading or when you are reading to them.

3. Ask the children to give an appropriate title for each of the groups of sentences on page 21.

TEACHING READING:

Gather students in a circle. Tell them you are the gardener and they are plants in your garden. Have them squat down to become seeds, then take them through slow-movements as sprouting plants. Have them offer ideas to demonstrate growing plants. If you have music, do it to music. After they have practiced the movements, read them today's story, "Little Garden". Have them listen to the questions, then act out the growing part.

Read through the story a second time, one verse at a time. Have students repeat the words and do the movements.

Have students return to their seats. Read the story one more time together. Ask the following questions:

"Who is the gardener talking to?" (her garden)

"What does she do for her garden?" (loosens the soil, plants the seeds, waters the ground, gives shade)

"What does she see first?" (the sprouts)

"What does she see next?" (the stems and leaves)

"Why do the plants reach for the sky?" (plants grow toward light)

"What is most important to the gardener?" (she cares for the plants)

Find ow/ou words: (grow, rows, ground, sprouts, know, how). Find the oo word: (loosen). Find the oi word: (soil). Find r-controlled words: (garden, perfect, water, summer, tender)

ACTIVITIES:

Give students a paper cut-out of a plant pot and scrap paper. Have them be creative by designing a plant which grew in the garden. Plant seeds! Select a variety of seeds and plant them in soil individually or in groups. Provide a calendar with boxes to draw a picture to record each day's progress. Have students do a sequence activity page showing the steps from seed to mature plant. They can either draw them or you can find resource books on plants. Soak lima beans overnight in wet paper towels. Give students a bean the next day to observe the little sprout that should be "popping out". (Do extras, not all will sprout). Learn the song: "The Garden Song" – A

Name _____

Put an X in front of the two sentences that go together.

__X__ Birds can sing.
_____ Milk is good for you.
__X__ I like to sing songs.

__X__ We love Jesus.
_____ Sunday School is on Sunday.
__X__ Jesus saved us from our sins.

_____ We play with our friends.
__X__ We go to church.
__X__ We go to Sunday School.

__X__ We should listen to our teachers.
__X__ We should listen to our parents.
_____ We should eat a good dinner.

__X__ The Bible is God's word.
_____ Books have stories in them.
__X__ We read our Bibles every day.

**Language Arts 110
Worksheet 5**
with page 21

Teacher check _____
Initial   Date

Child's Celebration of Song   (They love this song!)

Page 22: Contents Page

CONCEPTS: contents page, sentences, small group discussion

TEACHER GOALS: To teach the children
To use the Contents Page of the LIFEPAC and other books,
To write a complete sentence with good grammar, correct punctuation and capitalization, and an interesting thought, and
To participate in, and take their turn leading, small group discussions.

TEACHING PAGE 22:

Have the children read the material at the top of the page. Have them tell what a Contents Page is used for.

Have them read the directions. Have them turn to the Contents Page of this LIFEPAC and read it through. This may be done silently or aloud. (Only parts of the Contents Page are on the worksheet.)

Have the children find and fill in the titles and page numbers. Check by having them read aloud.

Have the children read the directions at the bottom of the page. Ask them to tell what a good sentence is. Give them class time to write the sentences or do this later in the day for the next day's assignment. When they are finished, correct the sentences and have them recopy any in which mistakes were made.

Choose a child as leader of each small group. Have the children read their sentences to the group. The group should decide whether each is a complete sentence. The groups may meet at the same time. Move from group to group helping as necessary.

ACTIVITY:

Have the children find and use the Contents Page in all their LIFEPACs and in any other textbooks they may have.

CONTENTS PAGE

The contents page tells you what you will find in a book.

Find the contents page of this LIFEPAC. Write the words and numbers.

I. **PART ONE** . . . . <u>3</u>
   Vowels

   <u>Consonant</u> digraphs

   A - B - C Order

III. <u>Part Three</u> **24**

   <u>Punctuation of Sentences</u>

Write <u>six</u> good sentences on a sheet of LIFEPAC Tablet paper. Read your sentences to your group.

page 22 (twenty-two)

SELF TEST 2

CONCEPTS: *y* sound, *ph* and *gh* as the *f* sound, pronouns, plurals, silent letters

TEACHER GOALS: To teach the children
To check their own progress periodically.

TEACHING PAGE 23:
Have the children read all the directions on the page. Be sure they understand what is to be done in each section. Let the children complete the page.

Correct the page as soon as possible. Go over the page with the child, showing him what he did well and where he needs to work harder. Have him correct any mistakes while you are going over the page with him.

ACTIVITIES:
1. Reteach items the child misses.
2. If several children miss the same kinds of things, reteach in a small group.

SPELLING WORDS:

I'll
I'm
haven't
I'd
it's
isn't
who'll
can't
won't
didn't

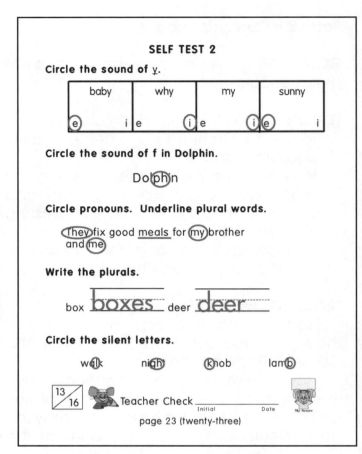

SELF TEST 2

Circle the sound of y.

baby	why	my	sunny
e i	e i	i e	i e i

Circle the sound of f in Dolphin.

Dolphin

Circle pronouns. Underline plural words.

They fix good meals for my brother and me

Write the plurals.

box **boxes**   deer **deer**

Circle the silent letters.

walk   night   knob   lamb

13/16   Teacher Check _____
Initial   Date
page 23 (twenty-three)

III. PART THREE

Page 24: Good Sentences

CONCEPTS: sentences, punctuation marks

TEACHER GOALS: To teach the children
To identify the three kinds of sentences, and
To identify and write a period, a question mark, and an exclamation point.

TEACHING PAGE 24:
Review the meaning of statement, question, and exclamation with the children. Have the children read the material at the top of the page. Have them name the three kinds of sentences, then read the title and material in the middle of the page. Have the children give examples for each kind of sentence.

Have the direction read at the bottom of the page and let the children do the exercise. Check by having the children read the sentences and tell which punctuation mark they put at the end.

TEACHING READING:
Read the story "The Wait" in *Reader 5*.
Have the children talk about the picture. How do the toys look?
Do you think this will be a real story or a make-believe story?
Have the children read the story silently.
Ask questions similar to these:
"What are the toys doing?"
"Who do they think will come?"
"What will the boy and his sis do when they arrive?"
"What does the boy always choose to do?"
"Does the boy come every day?"
"Is this story real or make-believe?"

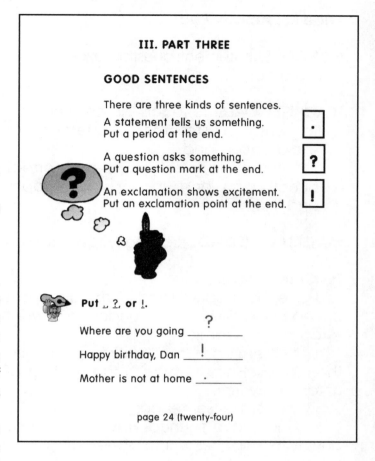

III. PART THREE

GOOD SENTENCES

There are three kinds of sentences.

A statement tells us something. Put a period at the end. **.**

A question asks something. Put a question mark at the end. **?**

An exclamation shows excitement. Put an exclamation point at the end. **!**

Put ., ?, or !.

Where are you going _____?_____

Happy birthday, Dan ____!____

Mother is not at home ___.___

page 24 (twenty-four)

Page 25: Activity Page

CONCEPTS: statement, question, exclamation, writing a story

TEACHER GOALS: To teach the children
To write a statement, question, or exclamation, and
To write a story using correct punctuation and spelling, paragraphs and title.

MATERIALS NEEDED: drawing paper, crayons

TEACHING PAGE 25:

Have the children read all the directions on the page. Be sure they understand what to do in each section.

Let them do the entire page by themselves. Help them with the spelling of unfamiliar words.

Correct the sentences in the LIFEPAC when they have finished. Have them copy any with mistakes on a sheet of writing tablet paper.

Have the children review how to write a good story before they begin. Tell them to write two, three, or more pages. Require more from more capable children. Review what a good title is.

As each child finishes his story, correct the spelling, sentence structure, grammar, capitalization, and punctuation. Have the child recopy the story as corrected. Remind him to be neat and space his words well.

Have each child draw a picture to go with his story.

Take class time for each child to read his story and show his picture. The stories may be put in booklet form, or mounted on the wall with their pictures for all to read. The title of the story also should be written on the picture.

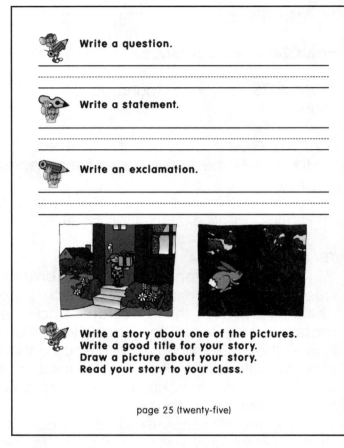

Page 26: Activity Page

CONCEPTS: sentence punctuation, subject-verb agreement

TEACHER GOALS: To teach the children
To select the correct ending punctuation for sentences, and
To write sentences in which the subject and verb agree.

TEACHING PAGE 26:

Have the children read the directions on the page. Be sure they understand what they are to do. Have them complete the page independently.

Check the first section by having the children read each sentence, tell whether it is a statement, question, or exclamation, and tell which punctuation mark they wrote at the end .

Check the second exercise by having the children read the sentences. Point out the plural subjects and the correct verbs. Be sure the children understand that the word *you* may mean one person or many. Remind the children that you should always have the plural form of the verb. Have them give more examples.

ACTIVITY:

Have the children write five sentences using the word *you* with the proper verb form. Correct the sentences and have the children recopy any with mistakes. Have the children read their sentences aloud.

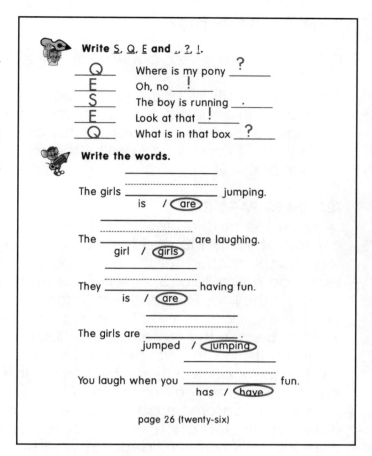

Write S, Q, E and ., ?, !.

Q   Where is my pony __?__
E   Oh, no __!__
S   The boy is running __.__
E   Look at that __!__
Q   What is in that box __?__

Write the words.

The girls _____ jumping.
is / are

The _____ are laughing.
girl / girls

They _____ having fun.
is / are

The girls are _____.
jumped / jumping

You laugh when you _____ fun.
has / have

page 26 (twenty-six)

Page 27: Activity Page

CONCEPT: subject-verb agreement

TEACHER GOALS: To teach the children
That singular or plural subjects must be followed by singular or plural verbs, and
That *you* is always followed by the plural form of the verb.

TEACHING PAGE 27:

Have the children read the direction at the top of the page and the words at the top of each section. Tell them to read each sentence carefully and to write one of the words on the lines. Remind them to read the sentence over after they have written the word to be sure the sentence makes sense. Tell them that in the first section, one word will be used twice. Check by having the children read the sentences aloud.

After the children read the sentences in each section, talk about what they say. Let the children give their ideas and tell how they feel about Jesus.

ACTIVITY:

Read stories about Jesus' love for us and the first commandment.

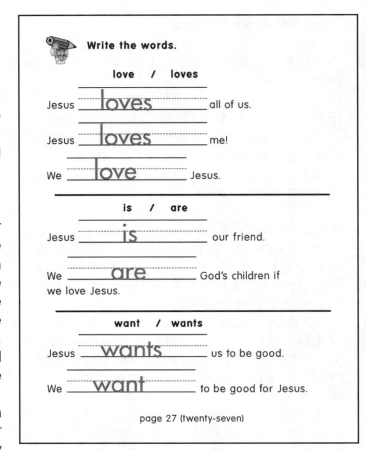

Write the words.

love / loves

Jesus ___loves___ all of us.

Jesus ___loves___ me!

We ___love___ Jesus.

is / are

Jesus ___is___ our friend.

We ___are___ God's children if we love Jesus.

want / wants

Jesus ___wants___ us to be good.

We ___want___ to be good for Jesus.

page 27 (twenty-seven)

Page 28: Verbs

CONCEPTS: subject-verb agreement, verb tense

TEACHER GOALS: To teach the children
To select singular or plural subjects or verbs, and
To select verbs in the present, past, or future tense.

TEACHING PAGE 28:

Have the children read the direction and do the entire page by themselves. Remind them to read carefully and to choose the word that makes the sentence sound right.

Check by having the children read the sentences. Have them correct any mistakes. Be sure the children understand why the correction was made.

Ask the children which sentences have plural subjects and which have singular subjects. Ask them to tell which verbs tell when something is happening now, has already happened, and has not happened yet.

ACTIVITIES:

1. Write these verb forms on the board. Discuss them before having the children write a sentence for each one. Correct the sentences and have the children recopy any with mistakes.

is	are	
was	were	
go	went	
has	have	had
stop	stopped	stopping
throw	threw	thrown

2. Do Worksheet 6.
Have the children write the correct verbs in the boxes after each noun.

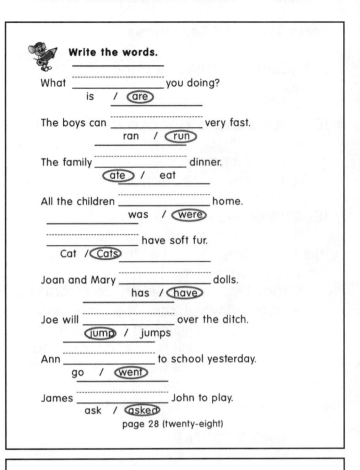

Write the words.

What _____ you doing?
is / (are)

The boys can _____ very fast.
ran / (run)

The family _____ dinner.
(ate) / eat

All the children _____ home.
was / (were)

_____ have soft fur.
Cat / (Cats)

Joan and Mary _____ dolls.
has / (have)

Joe will _____ over the ditch.
(jump) / jumps

Ann _____ to school yesterday.
go / (went)

James _____ John to play.
ask / (asked)

page 28 (twenty-eight)

Write the word.

	is - are	was - were
we	are	were
they	are	were
John	is	was
you	are	were
mother	is	was
Ben	is	was
she	is	was
those	are	were
he	is	was
Bob and Bill	are	were
all of us	are	were

Language Arts 110
Worksheet 6
with page 28

Teacher check _____
Initial   Date

279

Page 29: Good Sentences

CONCEPTS: sentences, punctuation marks

TEACHER GOALS: To teach the children
To identify a statement or question, or exclamation, and
To use the correct ending punctuation.

TEACHING PAGE 29:
Have the children read the directions at the top of the page. Let them do the entire page by themselves.

Check by having the children read each sentence, tell what kind of sentence it is, tell what letter they wrote on the line in front of the sentence, and tell what punctuation mark they wrote on the line behind the sentence. Encourage the children to read the sentences with expression.

TEACHING READING:
Have students form groups of 3-4. Tell them their task is to think of as many TALL things as they can in 4-5 minutes (teacher choice on time). Tell them they will get a point for everything they think of that is not mentioned by another group. (Work fast, but quietly). Assign someone in the group to be the recorder. Once the time is up draw point boxes on the board for each group. Give a point for each original idea (it has to be tall, too). List all the tall ideas on the board while assigning points. Introduce today's story: What is Tall?

Read the story "What is Tall?" together. Optional: Obtain books or other source to show pictures of tall buildings, giraffes, basketball players as you read the first three lines. Ask the following questions:

"What is the tallest living thing in the world?" (the Redwood tree)

"Where does it grow?" (northern California and southern Oregon)

"Why does it grow there? (perfect sunshine and water)

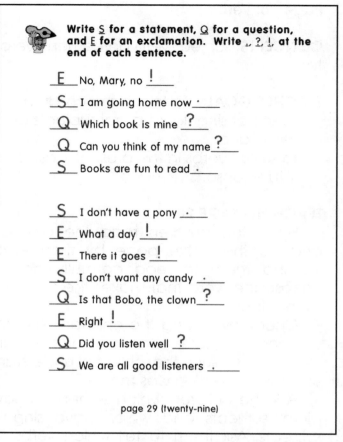

Write S for a statement, Q for a question, and E for an exclamation. Write ., ?, ! at the end of each sentence.

E   No, Mary, no !

S   I am going home now .

Q   Which book is mine ?

Q   Can you think of my name ?

S   Books are fun to read .

S   I don't have a pony .

E   What a day !

E   There it goes !

S   I don't want any candy .

Q   Is that Bobo, the clown ?

E   Right !

Q   Did you listen well ?

S   We are all good listeners .

page 29 (twenty-nine)

"How tall can the Redwood grow? (200-300 feet) (Emphasize the comparison to a football field)

"How long do these giant trees live? (one-two thousand years)

"Why can they live so long? (thick bark protects them)

Find r-controlled words: (giraffes, towers, York, forests, northern, California, southern, Oregon, perfect, water, over, bark, measures, other, hazards, sure, forever, after, player). Find words with oo : (Redwood, football, foot). Find words with ou/ow as in out/cow/low: (towers, grow, amount, found, thousand, about)

ACTIVITIES:
Have students get back in groups of three and compare their heights. Write Tall, Taller, Tallest on the board. Have students whose name from their group goes under each heading. Measure students heights and make a chart to show how tall each

one is. If you also did this at the beginning of the year, now would be a chance to see how much each child has grown. Provide books on Redwood trees. Share pictures and other information. Have students do paintings of the giant trees. Ask those who like basketball to find out how tall their favorite players are and report to the class. Have others research to find the height of tall buildings: (Eiffel Tower, Sears Tower, Empire State Building). Write stories: If I Were Tall..., I Wouldn't Want to Be Tall.... Make a list of rhyming words with TALL: (all, ball, call, crawl, fall, hall, mall, stall, wall). Write poems, songs or stories using the rhyming words. Read folktales about BIGGER THAN LIFE characters: Paul Bunyan, John Henry.

Page 30: Activity Page

CONCEPT: contractions

TEACHER GOALS: To teach the children
　　To match words and contractions, and
　　To write contractions from words.

TEACHING PAGE 30:

　　Have the children read the directions on the page. Let them do the entire page by themselves. Check by having the children read the words and the contractions and the sentences containing the contractions. Have them spell the contractions.

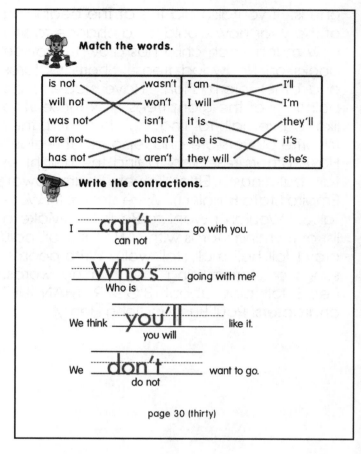

Match the words.

is not	wasn't	I am	I'll
will not	won't	I will	I'm
was not	isn't	it is	they'll
are not	hasn't	she is	it's
has not	aren't	they will	she's

Write the contractions.

I _**can't**_ go with you.
　　can not

**Who's** going with me?
Who is

We think _**you'll**_ like it.
　　you will

We _**don't**_ want to go.
　　do not

page 30 (thirty)

Page 31: Activity Page

CONCEPTS: possessives, subject-verb agreement

TEACHER GOALS: To teach the children
   To write words as possessives, and
   To select the correct form of the verb in present and past tense.

MATERIALS NEEDED: Worksheet 7

TEACHING PAGE 31:
   Have the children read the direction. Let them complete the page by themselves. Check by having the children read the sentences.

ACTIVITY:
   Do Worksheet 7.
   Have the children read the direction at the top of the page. Tell them to read the sentences carefully, to circle the correct possessive or possessive pronoun, and to write it in the blank. Check by having the children read the sentences. Have them tell what it is that belongs to the person or thing.
   Have the children use the possessives in sentences of their own.

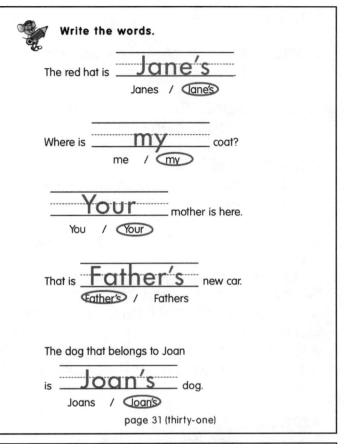

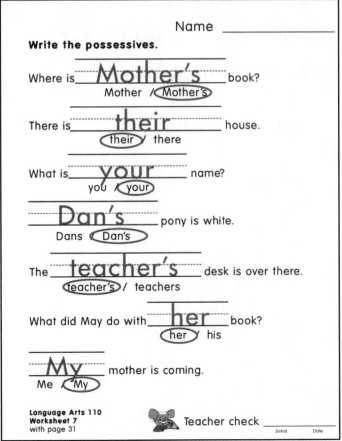

SELF TEST 3

CONCEPTS: kinds of sentences, possessives, verb forms

TEACHER GOAL: To teach the children
To check their own progress periodically.

TEACHING PAGE 32:

Have the children read all the directions on the page. Be sure they understand what they are to do in each section. Let the children complete the entire page by themselves.

Correct the page as soon as possible. Go over the page with the child. Show him what he did well and where he still needs to work. Have him correct any mistakes while you are going over the page with him. Have him reread any sentences in which he made errors.

ACTIVITIES:

1. Reteach items the child missed.
2. If several miss the same things, reteach in a small group, if possible.

SPELLING WORDS:

Ann's
Bob's
Don's
Jan's
Pam's
hers
his
ours
theirs
mine

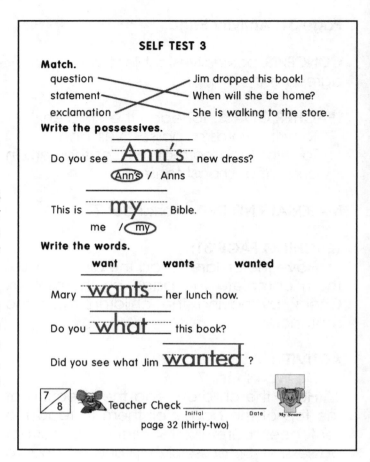

Page 33: Take Home Activity Page

CONCEPT: following directions

TEACHER GOALS: To teach the children
To read to understand directions, and
To follow directions in the order in which
they are given.

MATERIALS NEEDED: crayons, scissors,
drawing paper

TEACHING PAGE 33:
Have the children read the directions
aloud. Have them do what the directions
say to assemble the dog's head.
Have them trace the tongue several
more times. Put any or all of these kinds of
words on the tongues.

     wh words
     qu words
     ordinal numbers
     number words
     plurals
     contractions
     possessives
     possessive pronouns
     r-controlled words
     silent letter words
     short or long vowel words

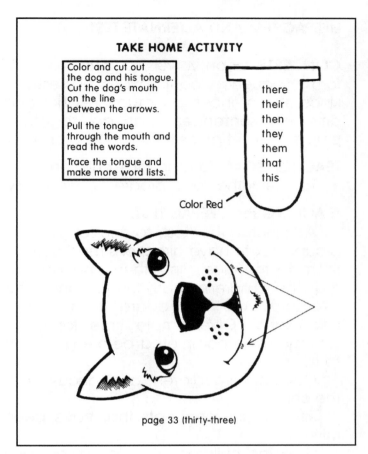

TAKE HOME ACTIVITY

Color and cut out
the dog and his tongue.
Cut the dog's mouth
on the line
between the arrows.

Pull the tongue
through the mouth and
read the words.

Trace the tongue and
make more word lists.

there
their
then
they
them
that
this

Color Red

page 33 (thirty-three)

LIFEPAC TEST AND ALTERNATE TEST 110

CONCEPTS: short vowels, long vowels, verb forms, sequence, contractions, possessives, kinds of sentences, punctuation, alike and different, sentences that go together, plurals, *ph* and *gh* as the *f* sound, pronouns

TEACHER GOAL: To teach the children
    To check their own progress periodically.

TEACHING the LIFEPAC TEST:
    Administer the test to the class as a group. Ask to have directions read or read them to the class. In either case, be sure that the children clearly understand. Put examples on the board if it seems necessary. Give ample time for each activity to be completed before going on to the next.
    Correct immediately and discuss with the child.
    Review any concepts that have been missed.
    Give the children who do not achieve the 80% score additional copies of the worksheets and a list of vocabulary words to study. A parent or a classroom helper may help in the review.

    When the child is ready, give the Alternate LIFEPAC Test. Use the same procedure as for the LIFEPAC Test.

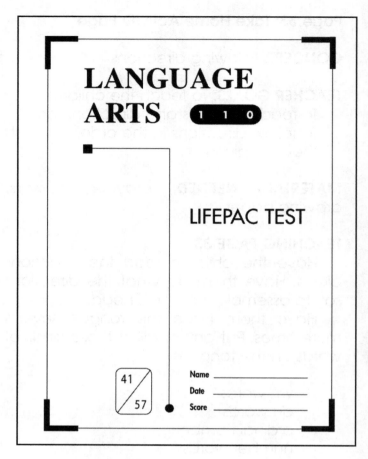

LANGUAGE ARTS 1 1 0

LIFEPAC TEST

41 / 57

Name _____
Date _____
Score _____

SPELLING WORDS:

LIFEPAC words	Alternate words
blue	purple
black	green
orange	red
cry	why
I'll	I'll
can't	isn't
who'll	won't
Don's	Ann's
Pam's	Jan's
ours	theirs

LANGUAGE ARTS 110: LIFEPAC TEST

Circle the words with short vowels.

(can)   (this)   know   (us)

so   (went)   (got)   why

(stop)   she   (thing)   (then)

we   (sat)   (sun)   (but)

Circle the words with long vowels.

(use)   can   (time)   (make)

(like)   (cake)   get   (mew)

(she)   (road)   (show)   yes

dad   (I'm)   how   (try)

Circle the words.

The children _____ playing.

   was (were)

I saw the dog _____ fast.

   ran (run)

Did you _____ Mother?

  (ask) asked

Who _____ my toys?

  (has) have

page 1 (one)

Write 1, 2, 3, for <u>first</u>, <u>second</u>, **and** <u>third</u>.

 _3_ I put my hat on.

 _1_ Where's my hat?

 _2_ Here's my hat.

Write the words.

I am __I'm__ is not __isn't__

The house that belongs to father is

__father's__ house.

Write Q, E, S, and ? ! ..

 _Q_ Who is that ___?___

 _S_ I want to go with you ___.___

Circle the three in each row that are alike.

(with)	(the)	go	(three)
this	(where)	(when)	(why)

page 2 (two)

Put an <u>X</u> **in front of the two sentences that go together.**

 _X_ Jesus wants us to be good.

 _X_ We want to be good for Jesus.

 _____ We like to read.

Write the plurals.

man men

puppy puppies

box boxes

Circle the letters that make the <u>f</u> **sound.**

tele(ph)one ele(ph)ant

Circle the pronouns.

Will (you) go with (me)?

(I) will ride with (them)

(She) is (my) friend.

3 (three)

LANGUAGE
ARTS 1 1 0

ALTERNATE
LIFEPAC TEST

41/51

Name _____

Date _____

Score _____

LANGUAGE ARTS 110
ALTERNATE LIFEPAC TEST

Circle words with short vowels.

(ask)   (it)   (sun)   pony
more   (fox)   how   (leg)
(fun)   are   (have)   (still)
(yes)   (got)   (up)   sound

Circle words with long vowels.

(baby)   off   (gave)   (tree)
run   (know)   (coat)   brown
(sleep)   catch   jump   (light)
(bike)   (you)   (maybe)   (use)

Circle the words.

He (was) were at school.

The cat go (went) up the tree.

Dan (is are) looking for you.

That boy (has have) your hat.

Write 1, 2, 3.

__2__ Ann went with Jo.

__1__ Jo asked Ann to go with her.

__3__ Then Ann went home.

page 1 (one)

Write the words.

I will __I'll__   do not __don't__

The coat that belongs to Mother is

__Mother's__ coat.

Write Q, E, S, and ?, !, .

__E__ Run, run __!__

__Q__ Which one is yours __?__

Circle the three that are alike.

(black)	(orange)	two	(green)
(four)	yellow	(five)	(three)

Put an X, in front of the two sentences which go together.

__X__ We listen to God's word.

____ We have lots of friends.

__X__ We read the Bible.

page 2 (two)

Write the plurals.

fox   __foxes__

baby   __babies__

goose __geese__

Circle the letters that make the f sound.

dol(ph)in   ele(ph)ant

Circle the pronouns.

(You) can ride with (us)

(We) will go with (him)

(They) cannot go with (us)

page 3 (three)

288

LIFEPAC

WORKSHEETS

Reproducible Worksheets
for use with the Language Arts
100 Teacher Handbook

Write <u>ar</u>. **Read the words.**

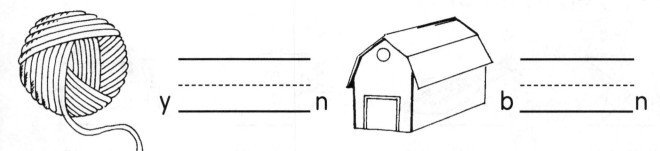

y _____ n   b _____ n

Write <u>or</u>.

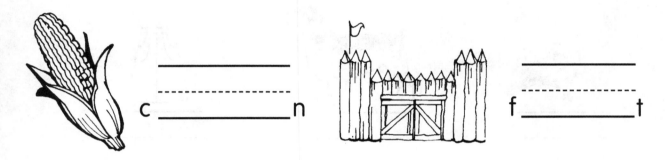

c _____ n   f _____ t

Circle the pictures with the <u>er</u>, <u>ir</u>, **or** <u>ur</u> **sound.**

Teacher check _____

Initial   Date

Name _____

Circle the pictures with r-controlled vowels.
Write <u>ar</u>, <u>er</u>, <u>ir</u>, <u>or</u>, **or** <u>ur</u>.

_____

_____

_____

_____

_____

_____

_____

_____

_____

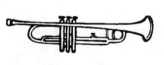

_____

_____

_____

_____

_____

Language Arts 106
Worksheet 2
with page 9

 Teacher check _____

Initial   Date

292

Name _____

Circle the three that are alike.

   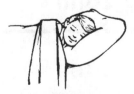

Language Arts 106
Worshceet 3
with page 17

 Teacher check _____

Initial   Date

293

Name _____

Circle the three that are alike.

cup	glass	dog	dish
be	will	he	me
one	boys	girls	cars
six	seven	eight	blue
purple	ten	green	brown
boxes	glasses	cats	wishes
isn't	can't	won't	the
girls	baby	penny	story
feet	moose	sheet	street
John's	Ann's	see	Tom's
can	fish	moose	deer

Language Arts 106
Worksheet 4
with page 17

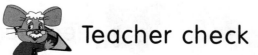

Teacher check _____
Initial   Date

294

Name _____

Write 1, 2, 3 **for** first, second, **and** third.

_____   I ran and ran.

_____   The bee came after me.

_____   I saw a bee.

_____   They take their fish home.

_____   They eat their fish.

_____   The boys are fishing.

_____   I ride my pony fast.

_____   I have a pony.

_____   His name is Blackie.

Language Arts 106
Worksheet 5
with page 19

Teacher check _____
Initial   Date

295

Name _____

Write rhyming words.

_____ eed   _____ ead   _____ eek   _____ eak

_____   _____   _____   _____

_____   _____   _____   _____

_____   _____   _____   _____

_____   _____   _____   _____

Write more rhyming words in your writing tablet.

Write the words.

feet	bee	beak	read

_____

I can _____ .

_____

A _____ can sting.

_____

A bird has a _____ .

_____

I have two _____ .

Language Arts 107
Worksheet 1
with page 5

Teacher check _____

Initial   Date

297

Name _____

Write <u>yes</u> or <u>no</u>. Is this a sentence?

I think I will go to

_____

I think I will go, too

_____

Did you see the

_____

Where is my big

_____

That is mine

_____

Write <u>S</u> by the statements, <u>E</u> by the exclamations, and <u>Q</u> by the questions.

_____ Do you mind if I go, too?

_____ Oh, my!

_____ Look, look!

_____ I am tired.

_____ Did you wind the clock?

_____ The lion is in the zoo.

Language Arts 107
Worksheet 2
with page 7

Teacher check _____

Initial   Date

298

Name _____

Write the words.

_____

Sy _____ his pie.

        eat / ate

_____

Father _____ Bob the kite.

        hand / handed

_____

The _____ were playing ball.

    boy / boys

_____

Mother _____ me a bike.

       gave / give

_____

_____ are fun to ride.

   Bike / Bikes

_____

The boy _____ home fast.

      ran / run

_____

Tom _____ first in line.

   was / were

Language Arts 107
Worksheet 3
with page 9

Teacher check _____

              Initial   Date

Name _____

Write 1 if you hear one part.
Write 2 if you hear two parts.

mind_____   the_____   running_____

wanted_____   singing_____   mile_____

dial_____   birthday_____   Sunday_____

fireman_____   Bible_____   slide_____

Read these words. How many parts do you hear?

minister_____   contraction_____

nursery_____   banana_____

dictionary_____   apostrophe_____

How many parts in these words?

sentences_____   animal_____

together_____   another_____

butterfly_____   invitation_____

Language Arts 107
Worksheet 4
with page 11

Teacher check _____
                         Initial   Date

300

Name _____

Write <u>S</u> by the statements, <u>E</u> by the exclamations, and <u>Q</u> by the questions. Put <u>.</u> , <u>?</u> , or <u>!</u> at the end.

_____ _____

_____ Babies like milk _____

_____ _____

_____ Did you see my knife_____

_____ _____

_____ No, I didn't see it _____

_____ _____

_____ Happy birthday, Lila _____

_____ _____

_____ Are you eight or nine_____

Write <u>yes</u> or <u>no</u>. Is this a sentence?

_____

The apples are ripe _____

_____

Find the big yellow _____

_____

Bananas are yellow _____

Language Arts 107
Worksheet 5
with page 12

Teacher check _____

Initial   Date

301

Write words that rhyme.

-ice   -ife

_____   _____

-                    -

_____   _____

_____   _____

-                    -

_____   _____

Write more rhyming words on a sheet of writing tablet paper.

Write these words.

mice   life   knife   spice

_____

- -

Pepper is a _____ .

_____

- -

Jesus gave his _____ for us.

_____

- -

You cut with a _____ .

_____

- -

The _____ like to eat.

_____

- -

I give my _____ to Jesus.

Language Arts 107
Worksheet 6
with page 14

Teacher check _____

Initial   Date

302

Name _____

Write 1, 2, 3 for first, second, and third.

_____ I ate all my ice cream.

_____ I buy some ice cream.

_____ I begin to eat my ice cream.

_____ Mother bird sits on her eggs.

_____ There are four baby birds.

_____ Mother bird lays four eggs.

_____ The mice look for food.

_____ The mice eat and eat.

_____ The mice find some cheese.

_____ Ann turns the light off.

_____ It is light in the room.

_____ Ann turns the light on.

_____ Tom has a new toy truck.

_____ He puts his new truck away.

_____ He plays with his new truck.

Language Arts 107
Worksheet 7
with page 15

Teacher check _____
Initial   Date

Name _____

Write the correct word endings.

cry   cried   crying

                                    _____   _____

fry   fr _____   fr_____

spy   sp_____   sp _____

hurry   hurried   hurrying

                                    _____   _____

worry   wor _____   wor _____

dry   dr _____   dry _____

try   tr _____   try _____

                                                            _____

study   studied   stud _____

Language Arts 107
Worksheet 8
with page 16

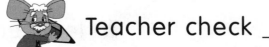 Teacher check _____

                                                    Initial   Date

304

Draw a line under what happens next.

It is getting light.
The sun is coming up.

We will get up.
We will go to bed.

_____

The sun is going down.
It is getting dark.

We will get up.
We will go to bed.

_____

Write what will happen next.

The house is on fire.
The firemen come.
They put water on the fire.

_____
- -
_____

Language Arts 107
Worksheet 9
with page 17

Teacher check _____
Initial   Date

305

Name _____

Cut and paste.

God made these.		People made these.	

trees	paper	plants
books	sky	people
rocks	stars	cars
lakes	sun	houses
streets	desks	bikes
glasses	sinks	airplanes
hills	moon	animals
bridges	pencils	rain

Language Arts 107
Worksheet 10
with page 20

 Teacher check _____

Initial   Date

306

Name _____

Draw a line under the best title.

Tom found a box.
He looked in the box.
Guess what he saw.
Nothing!
Nothing at all!

The Yellow Box
Tom Guesses
What Tom Saw

Little Rabbit was lost.
He ran here and there.
He looked for his mother.
He looked and looked.
Where is Mother?

The Lost Rabbit
The Last Rabbit
Mother Rabbit

See my kite.
It is flying.
It goes up.
It comes down.
I hold on to my kite.

My Kite
I Can Fly
My Car

Cows are animals.
They are very big.
They live on a farm.
Cows eat grass.
They give us milk.

Farms
Grass
Cows

Language Arts 107
Worksheet 11
with page 21

Teacher check _____

Initial   Date

Name _____

Write a title.

God is our Father
in heaven.

He loved us so much
that He sent Jesus
to save us.

He knows everything
we do or say. He hears
all our prayers.

_____

- -

_____

Ice is cold. When
we freeze water it
turns to ice.

We use ice in
iced tea or lemonade
to make it cold.

We skate on ice
in the wintertime.

_____

- -

_____

God made two
lights for us.

The sun gives us
light in the daytime.
At night we have
moonlight.

When it gets dark
we turn on lights
in our houses.

_____

- -

_____

We have many kinds
of plants. There are
water plants and
land plants.

Trees are very tall
plants. Flowers and
weeds are plants.

Vines are long
creeping plants.

_____

- -

_____

Language Arts 107
Worksheet 12
with page 21

 Teacher check _____
Initial   Date

308

Homonyms

tale ⟷ **tail**

plane - plain
tail - tale
right - write
sail - sale

to - two - too
die - dye
see - sea
be - bee

ate - eight
meet - meat
tied - tide
mane - main

sale ⟷ **sail**

ate ⟷ **eight**

Can you think of any more?

Language Arts 107
Worksheet 13
with page 30

Teacher check _____
Initial   Date

309

Name _____

Syllables

Say these words.
Write how many parts are in each word.

light _____   letter _____   schoolbook _____
showing _____   used _____   winter _____
bright _____   mewing _____   Jesus _____
wonderful _____   God _____   night _____
good _____   Sunday _____   yesterday _____

Find a word to fit in the blanks.

God   **Jesus**   **Saviour**
you   **Sunday**   **children**

_____

We are all _____ (2) of God.

_____

We go to church on _____ (2).

_____

Jesus is always with _____ (1) if you love
him.

_____

Jesus is the son of _____ (1).

_____   _____

_____ (2) is our _____ (2).

Language Arts 108
Worksheet 1
with page 3

 Teacher check _____
                                    Initial   Date

311

Write the possessives.

his	her	your	my

I have _____ Bible.

Joy has _____ Bible, too.

Do you have _____ Bible?

Tony will let you share _____ Bible.

our	their	children's	classes'

This is our Sunday School _____ room.

All the children have _____ books.

We all have _____ lessons done.

Soon the _____ mother will come.

Write a sentence for each of these possessives in your writing tablet.

| God's | my | mother's |
| Jesus' | our | their |

Language Arts 108
Worksheet 2
with page 4

Teacher check _____
Initial   Date

312

oo

1.

boots

2.

cook

Put a 1 if the <u>oo</u> sound is like <u>boots</u>. Put a 2 if the <u>oo</u> sound is like <u>cook</u>.

_____	soon	_____	moon	_____	hoot
_____	look	_____	book	_____	noon
_____	shook	_____	wool	_____	good
_____	school	_____	took	_____	broom
_____	pool	_____	spoon	_____	wood

Write the words.

Language Arts 108
Worksheet 3
with page 6

Teacher check _____

Initial   Date

313

Name _____

Number the words in the order they come in the alphabet.

1	**a**pple	3	**g**irl	1	**b**ird
2	**b**oy	1	**e**gg	3	**z**oo
3	**c**ow	2	**f**arm	2	**h**elp

____	doe	____	stone	____	look
____	hoot	____	moon	____	foot
____	cone	____	joy	____	pool

____	you	____	queen	____	other
____	wood	____	toe	____	end
____	zoom	____	note	____	ill

____	out	____	how	____	use
____	kick	____	vow	____	mule
____	root	____	now	____	ask

★____	back	____	clock	____	tube
____	big	____	crow	____	table
____	bed	____	can	____	took

Language Arts 108
Worksheet 4
with page 12

Teacher check _____

Initial   Date

314

Match the words.

I will	can't	who'll	there is
that is	I'll	there's	did not
cannot	that's	didn't	he is
let us	I've	he's	who will
I am	let's	who's	will not
I have	I'm	won't	who is

Write the contractions.

it is _____   I will _____

it will _____   let us _____

There will _____

Write the words.

hasn't _____   he'll _____

that'll _____   it's _____

Language Arts 108
Worksheet 5
with page 15

 Teacher check _____
Initial   Date

315

Name _____

Write what the story is about.

Little Rabbit ran this way and that way. He found something to eat. Then he went home and went to sleep.

Tony's dog was lost. Tony was looking for him, but he could not find him. Where could Tony's dog be?

Jim had a new coat. It was red. Mother and Father gave Jim his new coat. Jim liked his coat.

Language Arts 108
Worksheet 6
with page 17

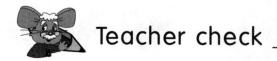

Teacher check _____
Initial   Date

316

Name _____

Write the plurals of these words.

kitten _____   puppy _____

_____   _____

mouse _____   woman _____

_____   _____

mule _____   box _____

_____   _____

baby _____   quail _____

Write the plurals in the puzzle.

Across
1. car
3. puppy
6. house
8. goose
9. shoe

Down
1. cup
2. kite
4. pet
5. spout
7. egg

Language Arts 108
Worksheet 7
with page 23

Teacher check _____

Initial   Date

317

TAKE HOME ACTIVITY
A KITE

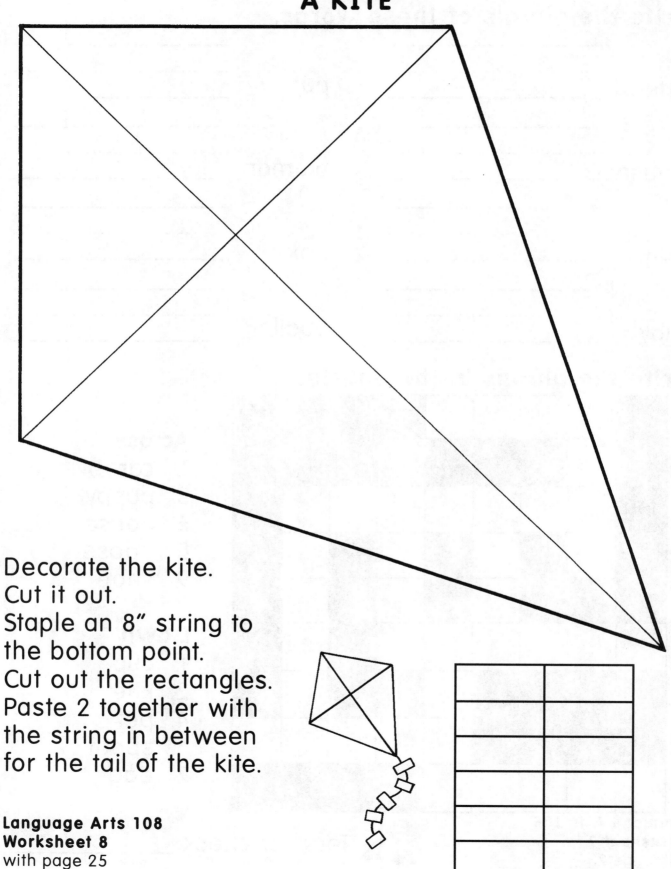

Decorate the kite.
Cut it out.
Staple an 8" string to
the bottom point.
Cut out the rectangles.
Paste 2 together with
the string in between
for the tail of the kite.

Language Arts 108
Worksheet 8
with page 25

318

Name _____

Write the compound words.

Tell what they mean.

_____
- -
basket   +   ball   _____

_____
- -
house   +   boat   _____

_____
- -
fire   +   man   _____

_____
- -
blue   +   bird   _____

Write the words.

_____
- -
football   _____

- -
today   _____

- -
storeroom   _____

- -
treehouse   _____

- -
classroom   _____

- -
horsefly   _____

- -
blackboard   _____

Language Arts 108
Worksheet 9
with page 31

Teacher check _____

Initial   Date

319

Write a sentence for each word.

can't

_____
- -
_____

paint

_____
- -
_____

play

_____
- -
_____

haven't

_____
- -
_____

don't

_____
- -
_____

Read your sentences.

Language Arts 109
Worksheet 1
with page 10

Teacher check _____
Initial   Date

321

Name _____

Write two words for each ending.

-ake _____   _____

-een _____   _____

-ite _____   _____

-ose _____   _____

-y _____   _____

-ay _____   _____

Circle words with the long u sound.

you   bus   you'll   used

us   cute   but   pup

use   mew   cube   fuel

Language Arts 109
Worksheet 2
with page 17

Teacher check _____

Initial   Date

322

Write two words for each ending.

_____   _____

-un
   _____   _____

-im
   _____   _____

-amp
   _____   _____

-ock
   _____   _____

-ell
   _____   _____

-ug
   _____   _____

-ank
   _____   _____

-ing

Write rhyming words.

_____   _____

deck _____   think _____

thump _____   spend _____

batter _____   ditch _____

Language Arts 109
Worksheet 3
with page 21

Teacher check _____

Initial   Date

323

Name _____

Cut and paste.

Things which are alive	Things which are not alive

rocks	flowers	women
trees	birds	grass
animals	boys	boxes
cars	hills	girls
men	moon	ground
weeds	houses	towns

Language Arts 109
Worksheet 4
with page 29

 Teacher check _____

Initial   Date

324

Name _____

Write the small letters.

_____
- -
_____

_____
- -
_____

Write the capital letters.

_____
- -
_____

_____
- -
_____

Write your name.

_____
first name _____

_____
middle name _____

_____
last name _____

Language Arts 110
Worksheet 1
with page 3

Teacher check _____
                    Initial   Date

325

Write er or ir.

h _____   st _____   b _____ d

sh _____ t   p _____ ch   moth _____

j _____ k   f _____ st   aft _____

Write or or ar.

h _____ n   st _____   _____ ange

b _____ k   c _____   _____ der

m _____ k   st _____ t   f _____ k

Read the sentences. Draw a line under each word with an r-controlled vowel.

Father is starting the car.

Mother wore her new dress.

Are you going to church?

Carl got some corn at the store.

The bird is on a perch.

My burned finger hurts.

Is that horn for you or for me?

Language Arts 110
Worksheet 2
with page 6

Teacher check _____

Initial   Date

326

Name _____

Answer the questions.

This story is about _____ .

horses   wagons   food

Long ago there were no _____ .

cars   trees   trucks

Wagons were used for carrying _____ .

clouds   food   water

Now farm wagons are pulled by _____ .

ponies   tractors   cars

Do children have wagons?

yes   no

Are wagons still used today?

yes   no

Draw a picture about this story on the back of this paper.

Write a good title for this story at the top of your picture.

Language Arts 110
Worksheet 3
with page 14

Teacher check _____

Initial   Date

327

Name _____

Read these words.

Write <u>e</u> if the <u>y</u> has the sound of <u>e</u>.
Write <u>i</u> if the <u>y</u> has the sound of <u>i</u>.

try __**i**__   happy __**e**__

why _____   puppy _____   Mary _____

sunny _____   by _____   cry _____

guppy _____   Tippy _____   shy _____

sky _____   trying _____   any _____

pony _____   my _____   story _____

fly _____   baby _____   Billy _____

dry _____   fry _____   Amy _____

*supply _____ pansy _____ reply _____ lily _____

mighty _____ milky _____ nylon _____ oily _____

Language Arts 110
Worksheet 4
with page 16

 Teacher check _____

Initial   Date

328

Put an X in front of the two sentences that go together.

_____ Birds can sing.
_____ Milk is good for you.
_____ I like to sing songs.

_____ We love Jesus.
_____ Sunday School is on Sunday.
_____ Jesus saved us from our sins.

_____ We play with our friends.
_____ We go to church.
_____ We go to Sunday School.

_____ We should listen to our teachers.
_____ We should listen to our parents.
_____ We should eat a good dinner.

_____ The Bible is God's word.
_____ Books have stories in them.
_____ We read our Bibles every day.

Language Arts 110
Worksheet 5
with page 21

 Teacher check _____
Initial   Date

329

Write the word.

	is - are	was - were
we		
they		
John		
you		
mother		
Ben		
she		
those		
he		
Bob and Bill		
all of us		

Language Arts 110
Worksheet 6
with page 28

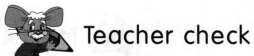 Teacher check _____

Initial   Date

Write the possessives.

_____

Where is _____ book?

Mother / Mother's

_____

There is _____ house.

their / there

_____

What is _____ name?

you / your

_____

_____ pony is white.

Dans / Dan's

_____

The _____ desk is over there.

teacher's / teachers

_____

What did May do with _____ book?

her / his

_____

_____ mother is coming.

Me / My

Language Arts 110
Worksheet 7
with page 31

Teacher check _____

Initial   Date

331

TESTS

Reproducible Tests
for use with the Language Arts
100 Teacher Handbook

LANGUAGE ARTS

ARTS 106

ALTERNATE LIFEPAC TEST

30 / 38

Name _____

Date _____

Score _____

LANGUAGE ARTS 106
ALTERNATE LIFEPAC TEST

Circle the pictures with the <u>er</u>, <u>ir</u>, <u>ur</u> sound.

Circle the words with the <u>ar</u> or <u>or</u> sound.

car	worn	tar
horn	jar	mop
job	gab	corn

Match the words.

he's	was not	can't	she is
I'm	he is	I'll	cannot
wasn't	I am	she's	I will
they'll	it is	won't	that is
it's	they will	that's	will not

Draw a line under what will happen next.

Jane is playing with her dolls.
Jane's mother is calling her for dinner.
Jane will play with her dolls.
Jane will go to mother.

Write the plurals.

puppy

_____

_____

story

_____

_____

Write the plurals.

baby

leaf

sheep

deer

Write the words.

_____ house is yellow.
Mays   May's

Is that _____ dog?
you   your

page 2 (two)

Match the rhyming words.

pick   sin

rat   nick

thank   mat

bin   sank

Write the sentence.

_____

- -

_____

- -

_____

LANGUAGE ARTS

1 0 7

ALTERNATE LIFEPAC TEST

33 / 41

Name _____

Date _____

Score _____

LANGUAGE ARTS 107
ALTERNATE LIFEPAC TEST

Circle the long <u>a</u> words.

sail	bait	wait
has	bad	quail
wail	got	hide

Put <u>1</u>, <u>2</u>, <u>3</u> for <u>first</u>, <u>second</u>, and <u>third</u>.

_____ We work hard at school.

_____ We come home from school.

_____ We go to school.

_____ I asked Mike to go with me.

_____ Mike and I go for a ride.

_____ Mike said he would go with me.

page 1 (one)

Match the rhyming words.

mail	week
teach	preach
wait	bait
seek	wail

Draw a line under what will happen next.

It is dinnertime.
Mother makes something to eat.
She calls the children.

The children will go away.

The children will eat.

How many parts in each word? Write 1 or 2.

summer _____   singing _____   laugh _____

walking _____   mad _____   jump _____

Write the words.

| sing | sang | singing |

They will _____ in the morning.

We _____ at lunch on Monday.

Write S by the statements, E by the exclamations, and Q by the questions. Put ., ?, or ! at the end.

_____ Look, Mother, look _____

_____ Give me that book _____

_____ Where is my hat _____

_____ Run, run _____

_____ Yes, he is _____

Circle the vowel digraphs.

speak   bet   read

wait   see   beat

meat   bait   cat

LANGUAGE ARTS

1 0 8

ALTERNATE
LIFEPAC TEST

26/33

Name _____

Date _____

Score _____

LANGUAGE ARTS 108
ALTERNATE LIFEPAC TEST

Write a rhyming word.

by _____   pew _____

coach _____   field _____

goat _____   took _____

Put 1, 2, 3 for first, second, and third.

_____ We work hard at school.

_____ We came home from school.

_____ We go to school.

Match the contractions.

won't   he is

we'll   will not

he's   they are

they're   we will

Write the words.

This is _____ hamster.
            you / your

_____ hamster is tan.
        Me / My

Write the plurals.

man _____   fox _____

child _____   sheep _____

Write the words.

Do you want four _____?
                      jar / jars

We can buy six _____.
                    ball / balls

Circle the word that comes first in the alphabet.

| jog | art | dip |

Match the parts of the sentences.

Baby Zebra had   gave him a hanky.

Mother Zebra   a bad cold.

The hanky   went up, up, up.

Write the word. _____

We _____ going for a ride!
is / are

The bus _____ here!
is / are

Listen to the story.

Circle the sentence.

Cindy and Heather will eat their lunches.

They will see the animals.

They will go home.

Write the sentence.

_____

- -

_____

LANGUAGE ARTS

109

ALTERNATE
LIFEPAC TEST

26 / 33

Name _____

Date _____

Score _____

LANGUAGE ARTS 109
ALTERNATE LIFEPAC TEST

Circle the words with the <u>oi</u> or <u>oy</u> sound.

toy	boil	choice
try	boy	soy
soil	buy	toil

Match the words and possessives.

our Sunday School   a book that belongs to you

your book   the Sunday school we belong to

Joan's pony   a house that belongs to them

their house   a Bible that belongs to Tony

Tony's Bible   Jesus

our Savio r   a pony that belongs to Joan

Write the plurals.

toad _____   sheep _____

Write the contractions.

he will _____   it is _____

has not _____   was not _____

who will _____   she is _____

Write a word that rhymes.

pout _____   soil _____

boy _____   town _____

Write the number of syllables.

1. _____   2. _____   3. _____   4. _____

Write the words.

The children _____ building rockets.
is / are

They _____ having fun.
is / are

Put an <u>S</u> by the complete sentence.

_____ in the car.

_____ The boys walked to school.

Circle the main idea.

Animals are nice to have for pets.

Animals are our friends.

There are many kinds of animals.

LANGUAGE ARTS

110

ALTERNATE LIFEPAC TEST

41 / 51

Name _____

Date _____

Score _____

LANGUAGE ARTS 110
ALTERNATE LIFEPAC TEST

Circle words with short vowels.

ask	it	sun	pony
more	fox	how	leg
fun	are	have	still
yes	got	up	sound

Circle words with long vowels.

baby	off	gave	tree
run	know	coat	brown
sleep	catch	jump	light
bike	you	maybe	use

Circle the words.

He **was were** at school.

The cat **go went** up the tree.

Dan **is are** looking for you.

That boy **has have** your hat.

Write 1, 2, or 3.

_____ Ann went with Jo.

_____ Jo asked Ann to go with her.

_____ Then Ann went home.

Write the words.

_____   _____
- - - - - - - - - - - - -   - - - - - - - - - - - - - -
I will _____   do not _____

The coat that belongs to Mother is

_____
- -
_____ coat.

Write Q, E, S, and ?, !, .

_____ Run, run _____

_____ Which one is yours _____

Circle the three that are alike.

black	orange	two	green
four	yellow	five	three

Put an X in front of the two sentences which go together.

_____ We listen to God's word.

_____ We have lots of friends.

_____ We read the Bible.

Write the plurals.

fox _____

baby _____

goose _____

Circle the letters that make the f͟ sound.

dolphin   elephant

Circle the pronouns.

You can ride with us.

We will go with him.

They cannot go with us.